D1041669

FABLES OF IDENTITY
Studies in Poetic Mythology

NORTHROP FRYE

Fables of Identity

Studies in Poetic Mythology

A Harvest/HBJ Book
Harcourt Brace Jovanovich, Publishers
San Diego   New York   London

ACKNOWLEDGMENTS

"The Archetypes of Literature" from *The Kenyon Review*, XIII, 1951. Copyright 1951 by Kenyon College. Reprinted by permission. "Myth, Fiction, and Displacement" from *Daedalus*, Summer 1961. Reprinted by permission of *Daedalus, Journal of the American Academy of Arts and Sciences.* "Nature and Homer" from *The Texas Quarterly*, 1958. Reprinted by permission. "New Directions from Old" from *Myth and Mythmaking*, Henry A. Murray, ed. Reprinted by permission of George Braziller, Inc., © 1960. "The Structure of Imagery in *The Faerie Queene*" from the *University of Toronto Quarterly*, XXX, January 1961. Reprinted by permission. "How True a Twain" from *The Riddle of Shakespeare's Sonnets*, © 1962 by Basic Books Publishing Co., Inc. Reprinted by permission of the publisher. "Recognition in *The Winter's Tale*" from *Essays on Shakespeare and Elizabethan Drama: In Honor of Hardin Craig*, University of Missouri Press, © 1962 by The Curators of the University of Missouri. Reprinted by permission of the University of Missouri Press. "Literature as Context: Milton's *Lycidas*" from *The Proceedings of the Second Congress of the International Literature Association*, W. P. Friederich, ed., University of North Carolina Studies in Comparative Literature, XXIII, 1959. Reprinted by permission of the International Comparative Literature Association. "Towards Defining an Age of Sensibility" from *ELH, A Journal of English Literary History*, Vol. 23, No. 2, June 1956. Reprinted by permission of The Johns Hopkins Press. "Blake After Two Centuries" from the *University of Toronto Quarterly*, XXVII, October 1957. Reprinted by permission. "The Imaginative and the Imaginary" from *The American Journal of Psychiatry*, Vol. 119, No. 4, October 1962. Reprinted by permission. "Lord Byron" from *Major British Writers*, Revised Edition, © 1959 by Harcourt, Brace & World, Inc. Reprinted by permission of the publisher. "Emily Dickinson" from *Major Writers of America*, © 1962 by Harcourt, Brace & World, Inc. Reprinted by permission of the publisher. "Yeats and the Language of Symbolism" from the *University of Toronto Quarterly*, XVII, October 1947. Reprinted by permission. "The Realistic Oriole: A Study of Wallace Stevens" from *The Hudson Review*, Vol. X, No. 3, Autumn 1957, © 1957 by *The Hudson Review*. Reprinted by permission of Northrop Frye, copyright assignee. "Quest and Cycle in *Finnegans Wake*" from *The James Joyce Review*, Vol. 1, No. 1, February 1957. Reprinted by permission of G. P. Putnam's Sons.

ISBN 0-15-629730-2

N O P Q R S T

Contents

for E. J. PRATT

⩔ Introduction

THIS BOOK IS A SELECTION OF MY CRITICAL ESSAYS, ALL BUT TWO of which were written after the completion of the *Anatomy of Criticism* (1957). That very theoretical book stated in its preface that a work of practical criticism was needed to complement it, and though this book is hardly the sequel that I then had in mind, there is a good deal of more specific criticism in it. The first four essays outline the theoretical assumptions on which the others are based. The first, "The Archetypes of Literature," was one of a series published in the *Kenyon Review* by various critics under the general title of "My Credo." I do not associate criticism with belief in quite the way that such a title implies, but the article is earlier than the *Anatomy of Criticism,* and is to some extent a summarized statement of the critical program worked out in that book. The next three papers are later than the *Anatomy,* are consistent with it, but can be read independently of it, and do not employ its elaborate apparatus. "Myth, Fiction, and Displacement" states my central principle about "myth criticism": that myth is a structural element in literature because literature as a whole is a "displaced" mythology. "Nature and Homer" explains how revolutions in the history of literature are invariably revolutions in literary form, and therefore a reshaping of literary conventions. "New Directions from Old" introduces the conception of the history of imagery, and the general outline of the medieval and Renaissance world-picture. This world-picture was elaborated by the Ptolemaic universe and the chain of being, but for literary criticism it is essentially a framework for images, and I expound it as such.

The rest of the book discusses various works and authors in the central tradition of English mythopoeic poetry, as outlined in the essay on Blake: a tradition in which the major and prevailing tendencies are Romantic, revolutionary, and Protestant., For the most part the critical method is the one indicated in the title of the Spenser paper which begins the series: an attempt to domesticate oneself in a poetic world by presenting its imagery as a structure, as the consistent and coherent environment, or imaginative home,

1

that we enter as we begin to read. It is the method followed by Yeats in his early essay on "The Philosophy of Shelley's Poetry," though I call imagery what he there calls philosophy.

The courteous reader is requested to keep in mind the fact that most of the essays in this book were originally papers read to specific audiences on specific occasions, and that the occasion sometimes forms part of the argument of the paper. The variations in their length usually go back to a chairman's allowance of twenty, thirty, or forty minutes. "Literature as Context" was given at the second congress of the International Comparative Literature Association at North Carolina in 1958, and so assumes an audience interested in the theory of comparative literature. "Towards Defining an Age of Sensibility" was read at an MLA conference in a group organized by Professor Earl Wasserman of Johns Hopkins, with the object of considering, as he put it in a note attached to the paper when it was printed in *ELH*, "the question of whether the literature of the later eighteenth century is merely transitional or whether it justifies and calls for a distinct kind of esthetic analysis." "Blake After Two Centuries," as the title implies, was written for the bicentenary year of Blake's birth, 1957. "The Imaginative and the Imaginary" was the "Fellowship Lecture" delivered at the meeting of the American Association of Psychiatrists in Toronto in 1962, as the second sentence indicates, and the interests of this audience have conditioned both the direction of the argument and the choice of quotations. The essays on Byron and Emily Dickinson were introductions to selections from these poets prepared for the anthologies *Major British Writers* (1959) and *Major Writers of America* (1962), published by Harcourt, Brace & World. As general introductions aimed mainly at undergraduate readers, they include biographical sketches which can claim no originality or first-hand research.

The earliest essay in the book is the Yeats paper, which was written immediately after *Fearful Symmetry* was published in 1947. It was thus written before most of the major scholarly interpretations of Yeats had appeared, and though I repudiate nothing in it, I should write it very differently now. The essay on the Shakespeare sonnets was contributed to a book which also printed the sonnets, to the great relief of the conscientious reader: I am sorry that it is hardly practicable to reprint here all the sonnets I refer to by number. Similarly, the Stevens essay is so close to the text of the *Collected Poems* and *The Necessary Angel* (not the *Opus Posthumous*, which appeared later than the essay) that it is hardly independent of them, though I think it should be a rewarding essay if read as it is intended to be read.

I am pleased to find that, in spite of the variety of occasions and audiences, the present collection makes a unified book that can be read through from beginning to end, if the reader so desires. There is some repetition, but most of it connects the theoretical and the practical parts of the book, so is too functional to be removed. The hinge of the total argument, I suppose, is my conception of Romanticism. The Romantic movement in English literature seems to me now to be a small part of one of the most decisive changes in the history of culture, so decisive as to make everything that has been written since post-Romantic, including, of course, everything that is regarded by its producers as anti-Romantic. One feature of this change that particularly interests me is the way in which the forms of human civilization come to be regarded as man-made rather than as God-made. Some comments on this may be found in the "Imaginative and the Imaginary" paper, which I place where it is because its center of gravity falls in the Romantic period. This aspect of the change gives a peculiar significance to two poets of that period, Blake and Byron. Blake raises most insistently the question of the reality of the poetic vision, a reality which is neither subjective nor objective, but is brought into being through creation itself. Byron raises most insistently the tragic situation of the artist that results when he moves into the center of civilization, the center being always the most isolated place. Of the four modern authors dealt with here, two, Stevens and Emily Dickinson, represent particularly the Blakean preoccupation with the reality of what is created. The other two, Joyce and Yeats, are more in the Byronic tradition, more concerned with the problem of the *poète maudit* and with what *Finnegans Wake* might well have called, and doubtless does call somewhere, the curse of ham. I deal with both largely in connection with Blake, but the difference in their more rhetorical center of gravity is clear enough even so.

Finally, the book is dedicated to E. J. Pratt, not merely for a great number of personal reasons, but as a contemporary poet who belongs centrally to the tradition dealt with here, and whose poetry helps, in a peculiarly vivid and immediate way, to make it more intelligible. My title comes from two phrases in his poem *Towards the Last Spike*.

N. F.

VICTORIA COLLEGE

❧I❧

⤜ The Archetypes of Literature

E VERY ORGANIZED BODY OF KNOWLEDGE CAN BE LEARNED PRO-
gressively; and experience shows that there is also something
progressive about the learning of literature. Our opening sentence
has already got us into a semantic difficulty. Physics is an organized
body of knowledge about nature, and a student of it says that he is
learning physics, not that he is learning nature. Art, like nature, is
the subject of a systematic study, and has to be distinguished from
the study itself, which is criticism. It is therefore impossible to
"learn literature": one learns about it in a certain way, but what
one learns, transitively, is the criticism of literature. Similarly, the
difficulty often felt in "teaching literature" arises from the fact that
it cannot be done: the criticism of literature is all that can be di-
rectly taught. So while no one expects literature itself to behave like
a science, there is surely no reason why criticism, as a systematic
and organized study, should not be, at least partly, a science. Not a
"pure" or "exact" science, perhaps, but these phrases form part of
a 19th century cosmology which is no longer with us. Criticism
deals with the arts and may well be something of an art itself, but
it does not follow that it must be unsystematic. If it is to be related
to the sciences too, it does not follow that it must be deprived of
the graces of culture.

Certainly criticism as we find it in learned journals and scholarly
monographs has every characteristic of a science. Evidence is ex-
amined scientifically; previous authorities are used scientifically;
fields are investigated scientifically; texts are edited scientifically.
Prosody is scientific in structure; so is phonetics; so is philology.
And yet in studying this kind of critical science the student be-
comes aware of a centrifugal movement carrying him away from
literature. He finds that literature is the central division of the
"humanities," flanked on one side by history and on the other by
philosophy. Criticism so far ranks only as a subdivision of liter-
ature; and hence, for the systematic mental organization of the sub-
ject, the student has to turn to the conceptual framework of the
historian for events, and to that of the philosopher for ideas. Even
the more centrally placed critical sciences, such as textual editing,

seem to be part of a "background" that recedes into history or some other non-literary field. The thought suggests itself that the ancillary critical disciplines may be related to a central expanding pattern of systematic comprehension which has not yet been established, but which, if it were established, would prevent them from being centrifugal. If such a pattern exists, then criticism would be to art what philosophy is to wisdom and history to action.

Most of the central area of criticism is at present, and doubtless always will be, the area of commentary. But the commentators have little sense, unlike the researchers, of being contained within some sort of scientific discipline: they are chiefly engaged, in the words of the gospel hymn, in brightening the corner where they are. If we attempt to get a more comprehensive idea of what criticism is about, we find ourselves wandering over quaking bogs of generalities, judicious pronouncements of value, reflective comments, perorations to works of research, and other consequences of taking the large view. But this part of the critical field is so full of pseudo-propositions, sonorous nonsense that contains no truth and no falsehood, that it obviously exists only because criticism, like nature, prefers a waste space to an empty one.

The term "pseudo-proposition" may imply some sort of logical positivist attitude on my own part. But I would not confuse the significant proposition with the factual one; nor should I consider it advisable to muddle the study of literature with a schizophrenic dichotomy between subjective-emotional and objective-descriptive aspects of meaning, considering that in order to produce any literary meaning at all one has to ignore this dichotomy. I say only that the principles by which one can distinguish a significant from a meaningless statement in criticism are not clearly defined. Our first step, therefore, is to recognize and get rid of meaningless criticism: that is, talking about literature in a way that cannot help to build up a systematic structure of knowledge. Casual value-judgments belong not to criticism but to the history of taste, and reflect, at best, only the social and psychological compulsions which prompted their utterance. All judgments in which the values are not based on literary experience but are sentimental or derived from religious or political prejudice may be regarded as casual. Sentimental judgments are usually based either on non-existent categories or antitheses ("Shakespeare studied life, Milton books") or on a visceral reaction to the writer's personality. The literary chit-chat which makes the reputations of poets boom and crash in an imaginary stock exchange is pseudo-criticism. That wealthy investor Mr. Eliot, after dumping Milton on the market, is now buying him again; Donne has probably reached his peak and will begin to taper off; Tennyson may be in for a slight flutter but the Shelley stocks are still bearish. This sort of thing cannot be part of any systematic study, for a systematic study can only progress: whatever dithers or vacillates or reacts is merely leisure-class conversation.

We next meet a more serious group of critics who say: the foreground of criticism is the impact of literature on the reader. Let us, then, keep the study of literature centripetal, and base the learning process on a structural analysis of the literary work itself. The texture of any great work of art is complex and ambiguous, and in unravelling the complexities we may take in as much history and philosophy as we please, if the subject of our study remains at the center. If it does not, we may find that in our anxiety to write about literature we have forgotten how to read it.

The only weakness in this approach is that it is conceived primarily as the antithesis of centrifugal or "background" criticism, and so lands us in a somewhat unreal dilemma, like the conflict of internal and external relations in philosophy. Antitheses are usually resolved, not by picking one side and refuting the other, or by making eclectic choices between them, but by trying to get past the antithetical way of stating the problem. It is right that the first effort of critical apprehension should take the form of a rhetorical or structural analysis of a work of art. But a purely structural approach has the same limitation in criticism that it has in biology. In itself it is simply a discrete series of analyses based on the mere existence of the literary structure, without developing any explanation of how the structure came to be what it was and what its nearest relatives are. Structural analysis brings rhetoric back to criticism, but we need a new poetics as well, and the attempt to construct a new poetics out of rhetoric alone can hardly avoid a mere complication of rhetorical terms into a sterile jargon. I suggest that what is at present missing from literary criticism is a coordinating principle, a central hypothesis which, like the theory of evolution in biology, will see the phenomena it deals with as parts of a whole. Such a principle, though it would retain the centripetal perspective of structural analysis, would try to give the same perspective to other kinds of criticism too.

The first postulate of this hypothesis is the same as that of any science: the assumption of total coherence. The assumption refers to the science, not to what it deals with. A belief in an order of nature is an inference from the intelligibility of the natural sciences; and if the natural sciences ever completely demonstrated the order of nature they would presumably exhaust their subject. Criticism, as a science, is totally intelligible; literature, as the subject of a science, is, so far as we know, an inexhaustible source of new critical discoveries, and would be even if new works of literature ceased to be written. If so, then the search for a limiting principle in literature in order to discourage the development of criticism is mistaken. The assertion that the critic should not look for more in a poem than the poet may safely be assumed to have been conscious of putting there is a common form of what may be called the fallacy of premature teleology. It corresponds to the assertion that a natural phenomenon is as it is because Providence in its inscrutable wisdom made it so.

Simple as the assumption appears, it takes a long time for a science to discover that it is in fact a totally intelligible body of knowledge. Until it makes this discovery it has not been born as an individual science, but remains an embryo within the body of some other subject. The birth of physics from "natural philosophy" and of sociology from "moral philosophy" will illustrate the process. It is also very approximately true that the modern sciences have developed in the order of their closeness to mathematics. Thus physics and astronomy assumed their modern form in the Renaissance, chemistry in the 18th century, biology in the 19th and the social sciences in the 20th. If systematic criticism, then, is developing only in our day, the fact is at least not an anachronism.

We are now looking for classifying principles lying in an area between two points that we have fixed. The first of these is the preliminary effort of criticism, the structural analysis of the work of art. The second is the assumption that there is such a subject as criticism, and that it makes, or could make, complete sense. We may next proceed inductively from structural analysis, associating the data we collect and trying to see larger patterns in them. Or we may proceed deductively, with the consequences that follow from postulating the unity of criticism. It is clear, of course, that neither procedure will work indefinitely without correction from the other. Pure induction will get us lost in haphazard guessing; pure deduction will lead to inflexible and over-simplified pigeonholing. Let us now attempt a few tentative steps in each direction, beginning with the inductive one.

II

The unity of a work of art, the basis of structural analysis, has not been produced solely by the unconditioned will of the artist, for the artist is only its efficient cause: it has form, and consequently a formal cause. The fact that revision is possible, that the poet makes changes not because he likes them better but because they are better, means that poems, like poets, are born and not made. The poet's task is to deliver the poem in as uninjured a state as possible, and if the poem is alive, it is equally anxious to be rid of him, and screams to be cut loose from his private memories and associations, his desire for self-expression, and all the other navel-strings and feeding tubes of his ego. The critic takes over where the poet leaves off, and criticism can hardly do without a kind of literary psychology connecting the poet with the poem. Part of this may be a psychological study of the poet, though this is useful chiefly in analysing the failures in his expression, the things in him which are still attached to his work. More important is the fact that every poet has his private mythology, his own spectroscopic band or peculiar formation of symbols, of much of which he is quite unconscious. In works with characters of their own, such as dramas and novels, the same psychological analysis may be extended to the interplay of characters, though of course literary psychology would analyse the behavior of such characters only in relation to literary convention.

There is still before us the problem of the formal cause of the poem, a problem deeply involved with the question of genres. We cannot say much about genres, for criticism does not know much about them. A good many critical efforts to grapple with such words as "novel" or "epic" are chiefly interesting as examples of the psychology of rumor. Two conceptions of the genre, however, are obviously fallacious, and as they are opposite extremes, the truth must lie somewhere between them. One is the pseudo-Platonic conception of genres as existing prior to and independently of creation, which confuses them with mere conventions of form like the sonnet. The other is that pseudo-biological conception of them as evolving species which turns up in so many surveys of the "development" of this or that form.

We next inquire for the origin of the genre, and turn first of all to the social conditions and cultural demands which produced it—in other words to the material cause of the work of art. This leads us into literary history, which differs from ordinary history in that its containing categories, "Gothic," "Baroque," "Romantic," and the like are cultural categories, of little use to the ordinary historian. Most literary history does not get as far as these categories, but even so we know more about it than about most kinds of critical scholarship. The historian treats literature and philosophy historically; the philosopher treats history and literature philosophically; and the so-called history of ideas approach marks the beginning of an attempt to treat history and philosophy from the point of view of an autonomous criticism.

But still we feel that there is something missing. We say that every poet has his own peculiar formation of images. But when so many poets use so many of the same images, surely there are much bigger critical problems involved than biographical ones. As Mr. Auden's brilliant essay *The Enchafèd Flood* shows, an important symbol like the sea cannot remain within the poetry of Shelley or Keats or Coleridge: it is bound to expand over many poets into an archetypal symbol of literature. And if the genre has a historical origin, why does the genre of drama emerge from medieval religion in a way so strikingly similar to the way it emerged from Greek religion centuries before? This is a problem of structure rather than origin, and suggests that there may be archetypes of genres as well as of images.

It is clear that criticism cannot be systematic unless there is a quality in literature which enables it to be so, an order of words corresponding to the order of nature in the natural sciences. An archetype should be not only a unifying category of criticism, but itself a part of a total form, and it leads us at once to the question of what sort of total form criticism can see in literature. Our survey of critical techniques has taken us as far as literary history. Total literary history moves from the primitive to the sophisticated, and here we glimpse the possibility of seeing literature as a complication of a relatively restricted and simple group of formulas that can be studied in primitive culture. If so, then the search for archetypes is a kind of literary anthropology, concerned with the way that literature is informed by pre-literary categories such as ritual, myth and folk tale. We next realize that the relation between these categories and literature is by no means purely one of descent, as we find them reappearing in the greatest classics—in fact there seems to be a general tendency on the part of great classics to revert to them. This coincides with a feeling that we have all had: that the study of mediocre works of art, however energetic, obstinately remains a random and peripheral form of critical experience, whereas the profound masterpiece seems to draw us to a point at which we can see an enormous number of converging patterns of significance. Here we begin to wonder if we cannot see literature, not only as complicating itself in time, but as spread out in conceptual space from some unseen center.

This inductive movement towards the archetype is a process of backing up, as it were, from structural analysis, as we back up from a painting if we want to see composition instead of brush-work. In the foreground of the grave-digger scene in *Hamlet*, for instance, is an intricate verbal texture, ranging from the puns of the first clown to the *danse macabre* of the Yorick soliloquy, which we study in the printed text. One step back, and we are in the Wilson Knight and Spurgeon group of critics, listening to the steady rain of images of corruption and decay. Here too, as the sense of the place of this scene in the whole play begins to dawn on us, we are in the network of psychological relationships which were the main interest of Bradley. But after all, we say, we are forgetting the genre: *Hamlet* is a play, and an Elizabethan play. So we take another step back into the Stoll and Shaw group and see the scene conventionally as part of its dramatic context. One step more, and we can begin to glimpse the archetype of the scene, as the hero's *Liebestod* and first unequivocal declaration of his love, his struggle with Laertes and the sealing of his own fate, and the sudden sobering of his mood that marks the transition to the final scene, all take shape around a leap into and return from the grave that has so weirdly yawned open on the stage.

At each stage of understanding this scene we are dependent on a certain kind of scholarly organization. We need first an editor to clean up the text for us, then the rhetorician and philologist, then the literary psychologist. We cannot study the genre without the help of the literary social historian, the literary philosopher and the student of the "history of ideas," and for the archetype we need a literary anthropologist. But now that we have got our central pattern of criticism established, all these interests are seen as converging on literary criticism instead of receding from it into psychology and history and the rest. In particular, the literary anthropologist who chases the source of the Hamlet legend from the pre-Shakespeare play to Saxo, and from Saxo to nature-myths, is not running away from Shakespeare: he is drawing closer to the archetypal form which Shakespeare recreated. A minor result of our new perspective is that contradictions among critics, and assertions that this and not that critical approach is the right one, show a remarkable tendency to dissolve into unreality. Let us now see what we can get from the deductive end.

III

Some arts move in time, like music; others are presented in space, like painting. In both cases the organizing principle is recurrence, which is called rhythm when it is temporal and pattern when it is spatial. Thus we speak of the rhythm of music and the pattern of painting; but later, to show off our sophistication, we may begin to speak of the rhythm of painting and the pattern of music. In other words, all arts may be conceived both temporally and spatially. The score of a musical composition may be studied all at once; a picture may be seen as the track of an intricate dance of the eye. Literature seems to be intermediate between music and painting: its words form rhythms which approach a musical sequence of sounds at one of its boundaries, and form patterns which approach the hieroglyphic or pictorial image at the other. The attempts to get as near to these boundaries as possible form the main body of what is called experimental writing. We may call the rhythm of literature the narrative, and the pattern, the simultaneous mental grasp of the verbal structure, the meaning or significance. We hear or listen to a narrative, but when we grasp a writer's total pattern we "see" what he means.

The criticism of literature is much more hampered by the representational fallacy than even the criticism of painting. That is why we are apt to think of narrative as a sequential representation of events in an outside "life," and of meaning as a reflection of some external "idea." Properly used as critical terms, an author's narrative is his linear movement; his meaning is the integrity of his completed form. Similarly an image is not merely a verbal replica of an external object, but any unit of a verbal structure seen as part of a total pattern or rhythm. Even the letters an author spells his words with form part of his imagery, though only in special cases (such as alliteration) would they call for critical notice. Narrative and meaning thus become respectively, to borrow musical terms, the melodic and harmonic contexts of the imagery.

Rhythm, or recurrent movement, is deeply founded on the natural cycle, and everything in nature that we think of as having some analogy with works of art, like the flower or the bird's song, grows out of a profound synchronization between an organism and the rhythms of its environment, especially that of the solar year.

With animals some expressions of synchronization, like the mating dances of birds, could almost be called rituals. But in human life a ritual seems to be something of a voluntary effort (hence the magical element in it) to recapture a lost rapport with the natural cycle. A farmer must harvest his crop at a certain time of year, but because this is involuntary, harvesting itself is not precisely a ritual. It is the deliberate expression of a will to synchronize human and natural energies at that time which produces the harvest songs, harvest sacrifices and harvest folk customs that we call rituals. In ritual, then, we may find the origin of narrative, a ritual being a temporal sequence of acts in which the conscious meaning or significance is latent: it can be seen by an observer, but is largely concealed from the participators themselves. The pull of ritual is toward pure narrative, which, if there could be such a thing, would be automatic and unconscious repetition. We should notice too the regular tendency of ritual to become encyclopedic. All the important recurrences in nature, the day, the phases of the moon, the seasons and solstices of the year, the crises of existence from birth to death, get rituals attached to them, and most of the higher religions are equipped with a definitive total body of rituals suggestive, if we may put it so, of the entire range of potentially significant actions in human life.

Patterns of imagery, on the other hand, or fragments of significance, are oracular in origin, and derive from the epiphanic moment, the flash of instantaneous comprehension with no direct reference to time, the importance of which is indicated by Cassirer in *Myth and Language*. By the time we get them, in the form of proverbs, riddles, commandments and etiological folk tales, there is already a considerable element of narrative in them. They too are encyclopedic in tendency, building up a total structure of significance, or doctrine, from random and empiric fragments. And just as pure narrative would be unconscious act, so pure significance would be an incommunicable state of consciousness, for communication begins by constructing narrative.

The myth is the central informing power that gives archetypal significance to the ritual and archetypal narrative to the oracle. Hence the myth *is* the archetype, though it might be convenient to say myth only when referring to narrative, and archetype when speaking of significance. In the solar cycle of the day, the seasonal cycle of the year, and the organic cycle of human life, there is a single pattern of significance, out of which myth constructs a central narrative around a figure who is partly the sun, partly vegetative fertility and partly a god or archetypal human being. The crucial importance of this myth has been forced on literary critics by Jung and Frazer in particular, but the several books now available on it are not always systematic in their approach, for which reason I supply the following table of its phases:

1 The dawn, spring and birth phase. Myths of the birth of the hero, of revival and resurrection, of creation and (because the four phases are a cycle) of the defeat of the powers of darkness, winter and death. Subordinate characters: the father and the mother. The archetype of romance and of most dithyrambic and rhapsodic poetry.

2 The zenith, summer, and marriage or triumph phase. Myths of apotheosis, of the sacred marriage, and of entering into Paradise. Subordinate characters: the companion and the bride. The archetype of comedy, pastoral and idyll.

3 The sunset, autumn and death phase. Myths of fall, of the dying god, of violent death and sacrifice and of the isolation of the hero. Subordinate characters: the traitor and the siren. The archetype of tragedy and elegy.

4 The darkness, winter and dissolution phase. Myths of the triumph of these powers; myths of floods and the return of chaos, of the defeat of the hero, and Götterdämmerung myths. Subordinate characters: the ogre and the witch. The archetype of satire (see, for instance, the conclusion of *The Dunciad*).

The quest of the hero also tends to assimilate the oracular and random verbal structures, as we can see when we watch the chaos of local legends that results from prophetic epiphanies consolidating into a narrative mythology of departmental gods. In most of the higher religions this in turn has become the same central quest-myth that emerges from ritual, as the Messiah myth became the narrative structure of the oracles of Judaism. A local flood may beget a folk tale by accident, but a comparison of flood stories will show how quickly such tales become examples of the myth of dissolution. Finally, the tendency of both ritual and epiphany to become encyclopedic is realized in the definitive body of myth which constitutes the sacred scriptures of religions. These sacred scriptures are consequently the first documents that the literary critic has to study to gain a comprehensive view of his subject. After he has understood their structure, then he can descend from archetypes to genres, and see how the drama emerges from the ritual side of myth and lyric from the epiphanic or fragmented side, while the epic carries on the central encyclopedic structure.

Some words of caution and encouragement are necessary before literary criticism has clearly staked out its boundaries in these fields. It is part of the critic's business to show how all literary genres are derived from the quest-myth, but the derivation is a logical one within the science of criticism: the quest-myth will constitute the first chapter of whatever future handbooks of criticism may be written that will be based on enough organized critical knowledge to call themselves "introductions" or "outlines" and still be able to live up to their titles. It is only when we try to expound the derivation chronologically that we find ourselves writing pseudo-prehistorical fictions and theories of mythological contract. Again, because psychology and anthropology are more highly developed sciences, the critic who deals with this kind of material is bound to appear, for some time, a dilettante of those subjects. These two phases of criticism are largely undeveloped in comparison with literary history and rhetoric, the reason being the later development of the sciences they are related to. But the fascination which *The Golden Bough* and Jung's book on libido symbols have for literary critics is not based on dilettantism, but on the fact that these books are primarily studies in literary criticism, and very important ones.

In any case the critic who is studying the principles of literary form has a quite different interest from the psychologist's concern with states of mind or the anthropologist's with social institutions. For instance: the mental response to narrative is mainly passive; to significance mainly active. From this fact Ruth Benedict's *Patterns of Culture* develops a distinction between "Apollonian" cultures based on obedience to ritual and "Dionysiac" ones based on a tense exposure of the prophetic mind to epiphany. The critic would tend rather to note how popular literature which appeals to the inertia of the untrained mind puts a heavy emphasis on narrative values, whereas a sophisticated attempt to disrupt the connection between the poet and his environment produces the Rimbaud type of *illumination,* Joyce's solitary epiphanies, and Baudelaire's conception of nature as a source of oracles. Also how literature, as it develops from the primitive to the self-conscious, shows a gradual shift of the poet's attention from narrative to significant values, this shift of attention being the basis of Schiller's distinction between naive and sentimental poetry.

The relation of criticism to religion, when they deal with the same documents, is more complicated. In criticism, as in history, the divine is always treated as a human artifact. God for the critic, whether he finds him in *Paradise Lost* or the Bible, is a character in a human story; and for the critic all epiphanies are explained, not in terms of the riddle of a possessing god or devil, but as mental phenomena closely associated in their origin with dreams. This once established, it is then necessary to say that nothing in criticism or art compels the critic to take the attitude of ordinary waking consciousness towards the dream or the god. Art deals not with the real but with the conceivable; and criticism, though it will eventually have to have some theory of conceivability, can never be justified in trying to develop, much less assume, any theory of actuality. It is necessary to understand this before our next and final point can be made.

We have identified the central myth of literature, in its narrative aspect, with the quest-myth. Now if we wish to see this central myth as a pattern of meaning also, we have to start with the workings of the subconscious where the epiphany originates, in other words in the dream. The human cycle of waking and dreaming corresponds closely to the natural cycle of light and darkness, and it is perhaps in this correspondence that all imaginative life begins. The correspondence is largely an antithesis: it is in daylight that man is really in the power of darkness, a prey to frustration and weakness; it is in the darkness of nature that the "libido" or conquering heroic self awakes. Hence art, which Plato called a dream for awakened minds, seems to have as its final cause the resolution of the antithesis, the mingling of the sun and the hero, the realizing of a world in which the inner desire and the outward circumstance coincide. This is the same goal, of course, that the attempt to combine human and natural power in ritual has. The social function of the arts, therefore, seems to be closely connected with visualizing the goal of work in human life. So in terms of significance, the central myth of art must be the vision of the end of social effort, the innocent world of fulfilled desires, the free human society. Once this is understood, the integral place of criticism among the other social sciences, in interpreting and systematizing the vision of the artist, will be easier to see. It is at this point that we can see how religious conceptions of the final cause of human effort are as relevant as any others to criticism.

The importance of the god or hero in the myth lies in the fact that such characters, who are conceived in human likeness and yet have more power over nature, gradually build up the vision of an omnipotent personal community beyond an indifferent nature. It is this community which the hero regularly enters in his apotheosis. The world of this apotheosis thus begins to pull away from the rotary cycle of the quest in which all triumph is temporary. Hence if we look at the quest-myth as a pattern of imagery, we see the hero's quest first of all in terms of its fulfillment. This gives us our central pattern of archetypal images, the vision of innocence which sees the world in terms of total human intelligibility. It corresponds to, and is usually found in the form of, the vision of the unfallen world or heaven in religion. We may call it the comic vision of life, in contrast to the tragic vision, which sees the quest only in the form of its ordained cycle.

We conclude with a second table of contents, in which we shall attempt to set forth the central pattern of the comic and tragic visions. One essential principle of archetypal criticism is that the individual and the universal forms of an image are identical, the reasons being too complicated for us just now. We proceed according to the general plan of the game of Twenty Questions, or, if we prefer, of the Great Chain of Being:

1 In the comic vision the *human* world is a community, or a hero who represents the wish-fulfillment of the reader. The archetype of images of symposium, communion, order, friendship and love. In the tragic vision the human world is a tyranny or anarchy, or an individual or isolated man, the leader with his back to his followers, the bullying giant of romance, the deserted or betrayed hero. Marriage or some equivalent consummation belongs to the comic vision; the harlot, witch and other varieties of Jung's "terrible mother" belongs to the tragic one. All divine, heroic, angelic or other superhuman communities follow the human pattern.

2 In the comic vision the *animal* world is a community of domesticated animals, usually a flock of sheep, or a lamb, or one of the gentler birds, usually a dove. The archetype of pastoral images. In the tragic vision the animal world is seen

in terms of beasts and birds of prey, wolves, vultures, serpents, dragons and the like.

3   In the comic vision the *vegetable* world is a garden, grove or park, or a tree of life, or a rose or lotus. The archetype of Arcadian images, such as that of Marvell's green world or of Shakespeare's forest comedies. In the tragic vision it is a sinister forest like the one in *Comus* or at the opening of the *Inferno*, or a heath or wilderness, or a tree of death.

4   In the comic vision the *mineral* world is a city, or one building or temple, or one stone, normally a glowing precious stone—in fact the whole comic series, especially the tree, can be conceived as luminous or fiery. The archetype of geometrical images: the "starlit dome" belongs here. In the tragic vision the mineral world is seen in terms of deserts, rocks and ruins, or of sinister geometrical images like the cross.

5   In the comic vision the *unformed* world is a river, traditionally fourfold, which influenced the Renaissance image of the temperate body with its four humors. In the tragic vision this world usually becomes the sea, as the narrative myth of dissolution is so often a flood myth. The combination of the sea and beast images gives us the leviathan and similar water-monsters.

Obvious as this table looks, a great variety of poetic images and forms will be found to fit it. Yeats's "Sailing to Byzantium," to take a famous example of the comic vision at random, has the city, the tree, the bird, the community of sages, the geometrical gyre and the detachment from the cyclic world. It is, of course, only the general comic or tragic context that determines the interpretation of any symbol: this is obvious with relatively neutral archetypes like the island, which may be Prospero's island or Circe's.

Our tables are, of course, not only elementary but grossly oversimplified, just as our inductive approach to the archetype was a mere hunch. The important point is not the deficiencies of either procedure, taken by itself, but the fact that, somewhere and somehow, the two are clearly going to meet in the middle. And if they do meet, the ground plan of a systematic and comprehensive development of criticism has been established.

≥ Myth, Fiction, and Displacement

"MYTH" IS A CONCEPTION WHICH RUNS THROUGH MANY AREAS of contemporary thought: anthropology, psychology, comparative religion, sociology, and several others. What follows is an attempt to explain what the term means in literary criticism today. Such an explanation must begin with the question: Why did the term ever get into literary criticism? There can be only one legitimate answer to such a question: because myth is and has always been an integral element of literature, the interest of poets in myth and mythology having been remarkable and constant since Homer's time.

There are two broad divisions of literary works, which may be called the fictional and the thematic. The former comprises works of literature with internal characters, and includes novels, plays, narrative poetry, folk tales, and everything that tells a story. In thematic literature the author and the reader are the only characters involved: this division includes most lyrics, essays, didactic poetry and oratory. Each division has its own type of myth, but we shall be concerned here only with the fictional part of literature, and with myth in its more common and easily recognized form as a certain kind of narrative.

When a critic deals with a work of literature, the most natural thing for him to do is to freeze it, to ignore its movement in time and look at it as a completed pattern of words, with all its parts existing simultaneously. This approach is common to nearly all types of critical techniques: here new and old-fashioned critics are at one. But in the direct experience of literature, which is something distinct from criticism, we are aware of what we may call the persuasion of continuity, the power that keeps us turning the pages of a novel and that holds us in our seats at the theatre. The continuity may be logical, or pseudo-logical, or psychological, or rhetorical: it may reside in the surge and thunder of epic verse or in some donkey's carrot like the identity of the murderer in a detective story or the first sexual act of the heroine in a romance. Or we may feel afterwards that the sense of continuity was pure illusion, as though we had been laid under a spell.

The continuity of a work of literature exists on different rhythmical levels. In the foreground, every word, every image, even every sound made audibly or inaudibly by the words, is making its tiny contribution to the total movement. But it would take a portentous concentration to attend to such details in direct experience: they belong to the kind of critical study that is dealing with a simultaneous unity. What we are conscious of in direct experience is rather a series of larger groupings, events and scenes that make up what we call the story. In ordinary English the word "plot" means this latter sequence of gross events. For a term that would include the total movement of sounds and images, the word "narrative" seems more natural than "plot," though the choice is a matter of usage and not of inherent correctness. Both words translate Aristotle's *mythos*, but Aristotle meant mainly by *mythos* what we are calling plot: narrative, in the above sense, is closer to his *lexis*. The plot, then, is like the trees and houses that we focus our eyes on through a train window: the narrative is more like the weeds and stones that rush by in the foreground.

We now run into a curious difficulty. Plot, Aristotle says, is the life and soul of tragedy (and by implication of fiction generally): the essence of fiction, then, is plot or imitation of action, and characters exist primarily as functions of the plot. In our direct experience of fiction we feel how central is the importance of the steady progression of events that holds and guides our attention. Yet afterwards, when we try to remember or think about what we have seen, this sense of continuity is one of the most difficult things to recapture. What stands out in our minds is a vivid characterization, a great speech or striking image, a detached scene, bits and pieces of unusually convincing realization. A summary of a plot, say of a Scott novel, has much the same numbing effect on a hearer as a summary of last night's dream. That is not how we remember the book; or at least not why we remember it. And even with a work of fiction that we know thoroughly, such as *Hamlet*, while we keep in mind a sequence of scenes, and know that the ghost comes at the beginning and the duel with Laertes at the end, still there is something oddly discontinuous about our possession of it. With the histories this disappearance of continuity is even more striking. *The Oxford Companion to English Literature* is an invaluable reference work largely because it is so good at summarizing all the fictional plots that one has forgotten, but here is its summary of *King John*:

The play, with some departures from historical accuracy, deals with various events in King John's reign, and principally with the tragedy of young Arthur. It ends with the death of John at Swinstead Abbey. It is significant that no mention of Magna Carta appears in it. The tragic quality of the play, the poignant grief of Constance, Arthur's mother, and the political complications depicted, are relieved by the wit, humour, and gallantry of the Bastard of Faulconbridge.

This is, more or less, how we remember the play. We remember Faulconbridge and his great speech at the end; we remember the death scene of Prince Arthur; we remember Constance; we remember nothing about Magna Carta; we remember in the background the vacillating, obstinate, defiant king. But what *happened* in the play? What were the incidents that made it an imitation of an action? Does it matter? If it doesn't matter, what becomes of the principle that the characters exist for the sake of the action, the truth of which we felt so vividly while watching the play? If it does matter, are we going to invent some silly pedantic theory of unity that would rule out *King John* as legitimate drama?
Whatever the final answer, we may tentatively accept the principle that, in the direct experience of fiction, continuity is the center of our attention; our later memory, or what I call the possession of it, tends to become discontinuous. Our attention shifts from the sequence of incidents to another focus: a sense of what the work of fiction was all *about*, or what criticism usually calls its theme. And we notice that as we go on to study and reread the work of fiction, we tend, not to reconstruct the plot, but to become more conscious of the theme, and to see all incidents as manifestations of it. Thus the incidents themselves tend to remain, in our critical study of the work, discontinuous, detached from one another and regrouped in a new way. Even if we know it by heart this is still true, and if we are writing or lecturing on it, we usually start with something other than its linear action.
Now in the conception "theme," as in the conception "narrative," there are a number of distinguishable elements. One of them is "subject," which criticism can usually express by some kind of summarized statement. If we are asked what Arthur Miller's *The Crucible* is about, we say that it is about—that is, its subject is—the Salem witch trials. Similarly, the subject of *Hamlet* is Hamlet's attempt at revenge on an uncle who has murdered his father and married his mother. But the Olivier movie of *Hamlet* began with

the statement (quoted from an unreliable memory): "This is the story of a man who could not make up his mind." Here is a quite different conception of theme: it expresses the theme in terms of what we may call its allegorical value. To the extent that it is an adequate statement of the theme of *Hamlet*, it makes the play into an allegory and the chief character into a personification of Indecision. In his illuminating study of *The Ancient Mariner*, Robert Penn Warren says that the poem is written out of, and about, the general belief that the truth is implicit "in the poetic act as such, that the moral concern and the aesthetic concern are aspects of the same activity, the creative activity, and that this activity is expressive of the whole mind" (italicized in the original). Here again is allegorization, of a kind that takes the theme to be what Aristotle appears to have meant primarily by *dianoia*, the "thought" or sententious reflexion that the poem suggests to a meditative reader.

It seems to me that a third conception of "theme" is possible, less abstract than the subject and more direct than an allegorical translation. It is also, however, a conception for which the primitive vocabulary of contemporary criticism is ill adapted. Theme in this third sense is the *mythos* or plot examined as a simultaneous unity, when the entire shape of it is clear in our minds. In *Anatomy of Criticism* I use *dianoia* in this sense: an extension of Aristotle's meaning, no doubt, but in my opinion a justifiable one. The theme, so considered, differs appreciably from the moving plot: it is the same in substance, but we are now concerned with the details in relation to a unity, not in relation to suspense and linear progression. The unifying factors assume a new and increased importance, and the smaller details of imagery, which may escape conscious notice in direct experience, take on their proper significance. It is because of this difference that we find our memory of the progression of events dissolving as the events regroup themselves around another center of attention. Each event or incident, we now see, is a manifestation of some underlying unity, a unity that it both conceals and reveals, as clothes do the body in *Sartor Resartus*.

Further, the plot or progress of events as a whole is also a manifestation of the theme, for the same story (i.e., theme in our sense) could be told in many different ways. It is, of course, impossible to say how extensive the changes of detail would have to be before we had a different theme, but they can be surprisingly extensive. Chaucer's *Pardoner's Tale* is a folk tale that started in India and must have reached Chaucer from some West-European source. It also stayed in India, where Kipling picked it up and put it into the *Second Jungle Book*. Everything is different—setting, details, method of treatment—yet I think any reader, on whatever level of sophistication, would say that it was recognizably the same "story" —story as theme, that is, for the linear progression is what is different. More often we have only smaller units in common, of a kind that students of folklore call motifs. Thus in Hawthorne's *The Marble Faun* we have the motif of the two heroines, one dark and one light, that we have in *Ivanhoe* and elsewhere; in *Lycidas* we have the motif of the "sanguine flower inscrib'd with woe," the red or purple flower that turns up everywhere in pastoral elegy, and so on. These smaller units I have elsewhere called archetypes, a word which has been connected since Plato's time with the sense of a pattern or model used in creation.

In most works of fiction we are at once aware that the *mythos* or sequence of events which holds our attention is being shaped into a unity. We are continually, if often unconsciously, attempting to construct a larger pattern of simultaneous significance out of what we have so far read or seen. We feel confident that the beginning implies an end, and that the story is not like the soul in natural theology, starting off at an arbitrary moment in time and going on forever. Hence we often keep on reading even a tiresome novel "to see how it turns out." That is, we expect a certain point near the end at which linear suspense is resolved and the unifying shape of the whole design becomes conceptually visible. This point was called *anagnorisis* by Aristotle, a term for which "recognition" is a better rendering than "discovery." A tragic or comic plot is not a straight line: it is a parabola following the shapes of the mouths on the conventional masks. Comedy has a U-shaped plot, with the action sinking into deep and often potentially tragic complications, and then suddenly turning upward into a happy ending. Tragedy has an inverted U, with the action rising in crisis to a peripety and then plunging downward to catastrophe through a series of recognitions, usually of the inevitable consequences of previous acts. But in both cases what is recognized is seldom anything new; it is something which has been there all along, and which, by its reappearance or manifestation, brings the end into line with the beginning.

Recognition, and the unity of theme which it manifests, is often symbolized by some kind of emblematic object. A simple example is in the sixteenth-century play, *Gammer Gurton's Needle*, the action of which is largely a great to-do over the loss of the needle, and which ends when a clown named Hodge gets it stuck in his posterior, bringing about what *Finnegans Wake* would call a culious epiphany. Fans, rings, chains and other standard props of comedy are emblematic talismans of the same kind. Nearly always, however, such an emblem has to do with the identification of a chief character. Birthmarks and their symbolic relatives have run through fiction from Odysseus' scar to the scarlet letter, and from the brand of Cain to the rose tattoo. In Greek romance and its descendants we have infants of noble birth exposed on a hillside with birth-tokens beside them; they are found by a shepherd or farmer and brought up in a lower station of life, and the birth-tokens are produced when the story has gone on long enough. In more complex fiction the emblem may be an oblique comment on a character, as with Henry James's golden bowl; or, if it is only a motif, it may serve as what T. S. Eliot calls an objective correlative.

In any case, the point of recognition seems to be also a point of identification, where a hidden truth about something or somebody emerges into view. Besides the emblem, the hero may discover who his parents or children are, or he may go through some kind of ordeal (*basanos*) that manifests his true character, or the villain may be unmasked as a hypocrite, or, as in a detective story, identified as a murderer. In the Chinese play *The Chalk Circle* we have almost every possible form of recognition in the crucial scene. A concubine bears her master a son and is then accused of having murdered him by the wife, who has murdered him herself, and who also claims the son as her own. The concubine is tried before a foolish judge and condemned to death, then tried again before a wise one, who performs an experiment in a chalk circle resembling that of the judgment of Solomon in the Bible, and which proves that the concubine is the mother. Here we have: (a) the specific emblematic device which gives the play its name; (b) an ordeal or test which reveals character; (c) the reunion of the mother with her rightful child; and (d) the recognition of the true moral natures of concubine and wife. There are several other elements of structural importance, but these will do to go on with.

So far, however, we have been speaking of strictly controlled forms, like comedy, where the end of the linear action also manifests the unity of the theme. What shall we find if we turn to other works where the author has just let his imagination go? I put the question in the form of this very common phrase because of the way that it illustrates a curious critical muddle. Usually, when we think of "imagination" psychologically, we think of it in its Renaissance sense as a faculty that works mainly by association and out-side the province of judgment. But the associative faculty is not the creative one, though the two are frequently confused by neurotics. When we think of imagination as the power that pro-duces art, we often think of it as the designing or structural principle in creation, Coleridge's "esemplastic" power. But imagina-tion in this sense, left to itself, can only design. Random fantasy is exceedingly rare in the arts, and most of what we do have is a clever simulation of it. From primitive cultures to the *tachiste* and action paintings of today, it has been a regular rule that the unin-hibited imagination, in the structural sense, produces highly con-ventionalized art.

This rule implies, of course, that the main source of inhibitions is the need to produce a credible or plausible story, to come to terms with things as they are and not as the story-teller would like them to be for his convenience. Removing the necessity for telling a credible story enables the teller to concentrate on its structure, and when this happens, characters turn into imaginative projec-tions, heroes becoming purely heroic and villains purely villainous. That is, they become assimilated to their functions in the plot. We see this conventionalizing of structure very clearly in the folk tale. Folk tales tell us nothing credible about the life or manners of any society; so far from giving us dialogue, imagery or complex be-havior, they do not even care whether their characters are men or ghosts or animals. Folk tales are simply abstract story-patterns, un-complicated and easy to remember, no more hampered by barriers of language and culture than migrating birds are by customs officers, and made up of interchangeable motifs that can be counted and indexed.

Nevertheless, folk tales form a continuum with other literary fictions. We know, vaguely, that the story of Cinderella has been retold hundreds of thousands of times in middle-class fiction, and that nearly every thriller we see is a variant of Bluebeard. But it is seldom explained why even the greatest writers are interested in such tales: why Shakespeare put a folk-tale motif into nearly every comedy he wrote; why some of the most intellectualized fiction of our day, such as the later works of Thomas Mann, are based on them. Writers are interested in folk tales for the same reason that painters are interested in still-life arrangements: because they illus-trate essential principles of storytelling. The writer who uses them then has the technical problem of making them sufficiently plausible or credible to a sophisticated audience. When he succeeds, he produces, not realism, but a distortion of realism in the interests of structure. Such distortion is the literary equivalent of the tendency in painting to assimilate subject-matter to geometrical form, which we see both in primitive painting and in the sophisticated primitivism of, say, Léger or Modigliani.

What we see clearly in the folk tale we see less clearly in popular fiction. If we want incident for its own sake, we turn from the standard novelists to adventure stories, like those of Rider Haggard or John Buchan, where the action is close to if not actually across the boundary of the credible. Such stories are not looser or more flexible than the classical novels, but far tighter. Gone is all sense of the leisurely acquiring of incidental experience, of exploring all facets of a character, of learning something about a specific society. A hazardous enterprise is announced at the beginning and everything is rigorously subordinated to that. In such works, while characters exist for the sake of the action, the two aspects of the action which we have defined as plot and theme are very close together. The story could hardly have been told in any other narrative shape, and our attention has so little expanding to do when it reaches the recognition that we often feel that there would be no point in reading it a second time. The subordination of character to linear action is also a feature of the detective story, for the fact that one of the characters is capable of murder is the concealed clue on which every detective story turns. Even more striking is the subordinating of moral attitude to the conventions of the story. Thus in Robert Louis Stevenson's tale, *The Body-Snatcher*, which is about the smuggling of corpses from cemeteries into medical classrooms, we read of bodies being "exposed to uttermost indignities before a class of gaping boys," and much more to the same effect. It is irrelevant to inquire whether this is really Stevenson's attitude to the use of cadavers in medical study or whether he expects it to be ours. The more sinister the crime can be felt to be, the more thrilling the thriller, and the moral attitude is being deliberately talked up to thicken the atmosphere.

The opposite extreme from such conventionalized fiction is represented by Trollope's *Last Chronicle of Barset*. Here the main story line is a kind of parody of a detective novel—such parodies of suspense are frequent in Trollope. Some money has been stolen, and suspicion falls on the Reverend Josiah Crawley, curate of Hogglestock. The point of the parody is that Crawley's character is clearly and fully set forth, and if you imagine him capable of stealing money you are simply not attending to the story. The action, therefore, appears to exist for the sake of the characters, reversing Aristotle's axiom. But this is not really true. Characters still exist only as functions of the action, but in Trollope the "action" resides in the huge social panorama that the linear events build up. Recognition is continuous: it is in the texture of characterization, the dialogue and the comment itself, and needs no twist in the plot to dramatize a contrast between appearance and reality. And what is true of Trollope is roughly true of most mimetic fiction between Defoe and Arnold Bennett. When we read Smollett or Jane Austen or Dickens, we read them for the sake of the texture of characterization, and tend to think of the plot, when we think of it at all, as a conventional, mechanical, or even (as occasionally in Dickens) absurd contrivance included only to satisfy the demands of the literary market.

The requirement of plausibility, then, has the apparently paradoxical effect of limiting the imagination by making its design more flexible. Thus in a Dutch realistic interior the painter's ability to render the sheen of satin or the varnish of a lute both limits his power of design (for a realistic painter cannot, like Braque or Juan Gris, distort his object in the interest of pictorial composition) and yet makes that design less easy to take in at a glance. In fact we often "read" Dutch pictures instead of looking at them, absorbed by their technical virtuosity but unaffected by much conscious sense of their total structure.

By this time the ambiguity in our word "imagination" is catching up with us. So far we have been using it in the sense of a structural power which, left to itself, produces rigorously predictable fictions. In this sense Bernard Shaw spoke of the romances of Marie Corelli as illustrating the triumph of imagination over mind. What is implied by "mind" here is less a structural than a reproductive power, which expresses itself in the texture of characterization and imagery. There seems no reason why this should not be called imagination too: in any case, in reading fiction there are two kinds of recognition. One is the continuous recognition of credibility, fidelity to experience, and of what is not so much lifelikeness as life-liveliness. The other is the recognition of the identity of the total design, into which we are initiated by the technical recognition in the plot.

The influence of mimetic fiction has thrown the main emphasis in criticism on the former kind of recognition. Coleridge, as is well known, intended the climax of the *Biographia Literaria* to be a demonstration of the "esemplastic" or structural nature of the imagination, only to discover when the great chapter arrived that he was unable to write it. There were doubtless many reasons for this, but one was that he does not really think of imagination as a constructive power at all. He means by imagination what we have called the reproductive power, the ability to bring to life the texture of characterization and imagery. It is to this power that he applies his favorite metaphor of an organism, where the unity is some mysterious and elusive "vitality." His practical criticism of work he admires is concerned with texture: he never discusses the total design, or what we call the theme, of a Shakespeare play. It is really fancy which is his "esemplastic" power, and which he tends to think of as mechanical. His conception of fancy as a mode of memory, emancipated from time and space and playing with fixities and definites, admirably characterizes the folk tale, with its remoteness from society and its stock of interchangeable motifs. Thus Coleridge is in the tradition of critical naturalism, which bases its values on the immediacy of contact between art and nature that we continuously feel in the texture of mimetic fiction.

There is nothing wrong with critical naturalism, as far as it goes, but it does not do full justice to our feelings about the total design of a work of fiction. We shall not improve on Coleridge, however, by merely reversing his perspective, as T. E. Hulme did, and giving our favorable value-judgments to fancy, wit, and highly conventionalized forms. This can start a new critical trend, but not develop the study of criticism. In the direct experience of a new work of fiction we have a sense of its unity which we derive from its persuasive continuity. As the work becomes more familiar, this sense of continuity fades out, and we tend to think of it as a discontinuous series of episodes, held together by something which eludes critical analysis. But that this unity is available for critical study as well seems clear when it emerges as a unity of "theme," as we call it, which we can study all at once, and to which we are normally initiated by some crucial recognition in the plot. Hence we need a supplementary form of criticism which can examine the total design of fiction as something which is neither mechanical nor of secondary importance.

By a myth, as I said at the beginning, I mean primarily a certain type of story. It is a story in which some of the chief characters are gods or other beings larger in power than humanity. Very seldom is it located in history: its action takes place in a world above or prior to ordinary time, *in illo tempore*, in Mircea Eliade's phrase.

Hence, like the folk tale, it is an abstract story-pattern. The characters can do what they like, which means what the story-teller likes: there is no need to be plausible or logical in motivation. The things that happen in myth are things that happen only in stories; they are in a self-contained literary world. Hence myth would naturally have the same kind of appeal for the fiction writer that folk tales have. It presents him with a ready-made framework, hoary with antiquity, and allows him to devote all his energies to elaborating its design. Thus the use of myth in Joyce or Cocteau, like the use of folk tale in Mann, is parallel to the use of abstraction and other means of emphasizing design in contemporary painting; and a modern writer's interest in primitive fertility rites is parallel to a modern sculptor's interest in primitive woodcarving.

The differences between myth and folk tale, however, also have their importance. Myths, as compared with folk tales, are usually in a special category of seriousness: they are believed to have "really happened," or to have some exceptional significance in explaining certain features of life, such as ritual. Again, whereas folk tales simply interchange motifs and develop variants, myths show an odd tendency to stick together and build up bigger structures. We have creation myths, fall and flood myths, metamorphosis and dying-god myths, divine-marriage and hero-ancestry myths, etiological myths, apocalyptic myths; and writers of sacred scriptures or collectors of myth like Ovid tend to arrange these in a series. And while myths themselves are seldom historical, they seem to provide a kind of containing form of tradition, one result of which is the obliterating of boundaries separating legend, historical reminiscence, and actual history that we find in Homer and the Old Testament.

As a type of story, myth is a form of verbal art, and belongs to the world of art. Like art, and unlike science, it deals, not with the world that man contemplates, but with the world that man creates. The total form of art, so to speak, is a world whose content is nature but whose form is human; hence when it "imitates" nature it assimilates nature to human forms. The world of art is human in perspective, a world in which the sun continues to rise and set long after science has explained that its rising and setting are illusions. And myth, too, makes a systematic attempt to see nature in human shape: it does not simply roam at large in nature like the folk tale.

The obvious conception which brings together the human form and the natural content in myth is the god. It is not the connexion of the stories of Phaethon and Endymion with the sun and moon that makes them myths, for we could have folk tales of the same kind: it is rather their attachment to the body of stories told about Apollo and Artemis which gives them a canonical place in the growing system of tales that we call a mythology. And every developed mythology tends to complete itself, to outline an entire universe in which the "gods" represent the whole of nature in humanized form, and at the same time show in perspective man's origin, his destiny, the limits of his power, and the extension of his hopes and desires. A mythology may develop by accretion, as in Greece, or by rigorous codifying and the excluding of unwanted material, as in Israel; but the drive toward a verbal circumference of human experience is clear in both cultures.

The two great conceptual principles which myth uses in assimilating nature to human form are analogy and identity. Analogy establishes the parallels between human life and natural phenomena, and identity conceives of a "sun-god" or a "tree-god." Myth seizes on the fundamental element of design offered by nature—the cycle, as we have it daily in the sun and yearly in the seasons—and assimilates it to the human cycle of life, death, and (analogy again) rebirth. At the same time the discrepancy between the world man lives in and the world he would like to live in develops a dialectic in myth which, as in the New Testament and Plato's *Phaedo*, separates reality into two contrasting states, a heaven and a hell.

Again, myths are often used as allegories of science or religion or morality: they may arise in the first place to account for a ritual or a law, or they may be *exempla* or parables which illustrate a particular situation or argument, like the myths in Plato or Achilles' myth of the two jars of Zeus at the end of the Iliad. Once established in their own right, they may then be interpreted dogmatically or allegorically, as all the standard myths have been for centuries, in innumerable ways. But because myths are stories, what they "mean" is inside them, in the implications of their incidents. No rendering of any myth into conceptual language can serve as a full equivalent of its meaning. A myth may be told and retold: it may be modified or elaborated, or different patterns may be discovered in it; and its life is always the poetic life of a story, not the homiletic life of some illustrated truism. When a system of myths loses all connexion with belief, it becomes purely literary, as Classical myth did in Christian Europe. Such a development would be impossible unless myths were inherently literary in structure. As it makes no difference to that structure whether an interpretation of the myth is believed in or not, there is no difficulty in speaking of a Christian mythology.

Myth thus provides the main outlines and the circumference of a verbal universe which is later occupied by literature as well. Literature is more flexible than myth, and fills up this universe more completely: a poet or novelist may work in areas of human life apparently remote from the shadowy gods and gigantic story-outlines of mythology. But in all cultures mythology merges insensibly into, and with, literature. The Odyssey is to us a work of literature, but its early place in the literary tradition, the importance of gods in its action, and its influence on the later religious thought of Greece, are all features common to literature proper and to mythology, and indicate that the difference between them is more chronological than structural. Educators are now aware that any effective teaching of literature has to recapitulate its history and begin, in early childhood, with myths, folk tales and legends.

We should expect, therefore, that there would be a great many literary works derived directly from specific myths, like the poems by Drayton and Keats about Endymion which are derived from the myth of Endymion. But the study of the relations between mythology and literature is not confined to such one-to-one relationships. In the first place, mythology as a total structure, defining as it does a society's religious beliefs, historical traditions, cosmological speculations—in short, the whole range of its verbal expressiveness—is the matrix of literature, and major poetry keeps returning to it. In every age poets who are thinkers (remembering that poets think in metaphors and images, not in propositions) and are deeply concerned with the origin or destiny or desires of mankind—with anything that belongs to the larger outlines of what literature can express—can hardly find a literary theme that does not coincide with a myth. Hence the imposing body of explicitly mythopoeic poetry in the epic and encyclopaedic forms which so many of the greatest poets use. A poet who accepts a mythology as valid for belief, as Dante and Milton accepted Christianity, will naturally use it; poets outside such a tradition turn to other mythologies as suggestive or symbolic of what might be believed, as in the adaptations of Classical or occult mythological systems made by Goethe, Victor Hugo, Shelley, or Yeats.

Similarly, the structural principles of a mythology, built up from analogy and identity, become in due course the structural principles of literature. The absorption of the natural cycle into mythology provides myth with two of these structures; the rising movement that we find in myths of spring or the dawn, of birth, marriage and resurrection, and the falling movement in myths of death, metamorphosis, or sacrifice. These movements reappear as the structural principles of comedy and tragedy in literature. Again, the dialectic in myth that projects a paradise or heaven above our world and a hell or place of shades below it reappears in literature as the idealized world of pastoral and romance and the absurd, suffering, or frustrated world of irony and satire.

The relation between myth and literature, therefore, is established by studying the genres and conventions of literature. Thus the convention of the pastoral elegy in *Lycidas* links it to Virgil and Theocritus, and thence with the myth of Adonis. Thus the convention of the foundling plot, which is the basis of *Tom Jones* and *Oliver Twist*, goes back to Menandrine comedy formulas, thence to Euripides, and so back to such myths as the finding of Moses and Perseus. In myth criticism, when we examine the theme or total design of a fiction, we must isolate that aspect of the fiction which is conventional, and held in common with all other works of the same category. When we begin, say, *Pride and Prejudice*, we can see at once that a story which sustains that particular mood or tone is most unlikely to end in tragedy or melodrama or mordant irony or romance. It clearly belongs to the category represented by the word "comedy," and we are not surprised to find in it the conventional features of comedy, including a foolish lover, with some economic advantages, encouraged by one of the parents, a hypocrite unmasked, misunderstandings between the chief characters eventually cleared up and happy marriages for those who deserve them. This conventional comic form is in *Pride and Prejudice* somewhat as the sonata form is in a Mozart symphony. Its presence there does not account for any of the merits of the novel, but it does account for its conventional, as distinct from its individual, structure. A serious interest in structure, then, ought naturally to lead us from *Pride and Prejudice* to a study of the comic form which it exemplifies, the conventions of which have presented much the same features from Plautus to our own day. These conventions in turn take us back into myth. When we compare the conventional plot of a play of Plautus with the Christian myth of a son appeasing the wrath of a father and redeeming his bride, we can see that the latter is quite accurately described, from a literary point of view, as a divine comedy.

Whenever we find explicit mythologizing in literature, or a writer trying to indicate what myths he is particularly interested

FABLES OF IDENTITY

in, we should treat this as confirmatory or supporting evidence for our study of the genres and conventions he is using. Meredith's *The Egoist* is a story about a girl who narrowly escapes marrying a selfish man, which makes many references, both explicitly and indirectly in its imagery, to the two best-known myths of female sacrifice, the stories of Andromeda and Iphigeneia. Such allusions would be pointless or unintelligible except as indications by Meredith of an awareness of the conventional shape of the story he is telling. Again, it is as true of poetry as it is of myth that its main conceptual elements are analogy and identity, which reappear in the two commonest figures of speech, the simile and the metaphor. Literature, like mythology, is largely an art of misleading analogies and mistaken identities. Hence we often find poets, especially young poets, turning to myth because of the scope it affords them for uninhibited poetic imagery. If Shakespeare's *Venus and Adonis* had been simply a story about a willing girl and an unwilling boy, all the resources of analogy and identity would have been left unexplored: the fanciful imagery appropriate to the mythical subject would have been merely tasteless exaggeration. Especially is this true with what may be called sympathetic imagery, the association of human and natural life:

> No flower was nigh, no grass, herb, leaf, or weed,
> But stole his blood and seem'd with him to bleed.

The opposite extreme from such deliberate exploiting of myth is to be found in the general tendency of realism or naturalism to give imaginative life and coherence to something closely resembling our own ordinary experience. Such realism often begins by simplifying its language, and dropping the explicit connexions with myth which are a sign of an awareness of literary tradition. Wordsworth, for example, felt that in his day Phoebus and Philomela were getting to be mere trade slang for the sun and the nightingale, and that poetry would do better to discard this kind of inorganic allusion. But, as Wordsworth himself clearly recognized, the result of turning one's back on explicit myth can only be the reconstructing of the same mythical patterns in more ordinary words:

> Paradise, and groves
> Elysian, Fortunate Fields—like those of old
> Sought in the Atlantic Main—why should they be
> A history only of departed things,
> Or a mere fiction of what never was?
> For the discerning intellect of Man,

When wedded to this goodly universe
In love and holy passion, shall find these
A simple produce of the common day.

To this indirect mythologizing I have elsewhere given the name of displacement. By displacement I mean the techniques a writer uses to make his story credible, logically motivated or morally acceptable—lifelike, in short. I call it displacement for many reasons, but one is that fidelity to the credible is a feature of literature that can affect only content. Life presents a continuum, and a selection from it can only be what is called a *tranche de vie:* plausibility is easy to sustain, but except for death life has little to suggest in the way of plausible conclusions. And even a plausible conclusion does not necessarily round out a shape. The realistic writer soon finds that the requirements of literary form and plausible content always fight against each other. Just as the poetic metaphor is always a logical absurdity, so every inherited convention of plot in literature is more or less mad. The king's rash promise, the cuckold's jealousy, the "lived happily ever after" tag to a concluding marriage, the manipulated happy endings of comedy in general, the equally manipulated ironic endings of modern realism—none of these was suggested by any observation of human life or behavior: all exist solely as story-telling devices. Literary shape cannot come from life; it comes only from literary tradition, and so ultimately from myth. In sober realism, like the novels of Trollope, the plot, as we have noted, is often a parody plot. It is instructive to notice, too, how strong the popular demand is for such forms as detective stories, science fiction, comic strips, comic formulas like the P. G. Wodehouse stories, all of which are as rigorously conventional and stylized as the folk tale itself, works of pure "esemplastic" imagination, with the recognition turning up as predictably as the caesura in minor Augustan poetry.

One difficulty in proceeding from this point comes from the lack of any literary term which corresponds to the word "mythology." We find it hard to conceive of literature as an order of words, as a unified imaginative system that can be studied as a whole by criticism. If we had such a conception, we could readily see that literature as a whole provides a framework or context for every work of literature, just as a fully developed mythology provides a framework or context for each of its myths. Further, because mythology and literature occupy the same verbal space, so to speak, the framework or context of every work of literature can be found in mythology as well, when its literary tradition is understood. It is relatively easy to see the place of a myth in a mythology, and one of the main uses of myth criticism is to enable us to understand the corresponding place that a work of literature has in the context of literature as a whole.

Putting works of literature in such a context gives them an immense reverberating dimension of significance. (If anyone is worrying about value-judgments, I should add that establishing such a context tends to make the genuine work of literature sublime and the pinchbeck one ridiculous.) This reverberating significance, in which every literary work catches the echoes of all other works of its type in literature, and so ripples out into the rest of literature and thence into life, is often, and wrongly, called allegory. We have allegory when one literary work is joined to another, or to a myth, by a certain interpretation of meaning rather than by structure. Thus *The Pilgrim's Progress* is related allegorically to the Christian myth of redemption, and Hawthorne's story, *The Bosom Serpent*, is related allegorically to various moral serpents going back to the Book of Genesis. Arthur Miller's *The Crucible*, already mentioned, deals with the Salem witch trials in a way that suggested McCarthyism to most of its original audience. This relation in itself is allegorical. But if *The Crucible* is good enough to hold the stage after McCarthyism has become as dead an issue as the Salem trials, it would be clear that the theme of *The Crucible* is one which can always be used in literature, and that any social hysteria can form its subject matter. Social hysteria, however, is the content and not the form of the theme itself, which belongs in the category of the purgatorial or triumphant tragedy. As so often happens in literature, the only explicit clue to its mythical shape is provided by the title.

To sum up. In the direct experience of a new work of literature, we are aware of its continuity or moving power in time. As we become both more familiar with and more detached from it, the work tends to break up into a discontinuous series of felicities, bits of vivid imagery, convincing characterization, witty dialogue, and the like. The study of this belongs to what we have called critical naturalism or continuous recognition, the sense of the sharply focused reproduction of life in the fiction. But there was a feeling of unity in the original experience which such criticism does not recapture. We need to move from a criticism of "effects" to what we may call a criticism of causes, specifically the formal cause which holds the work together. The fact that such unity is available for critical study as well as for direct experience is normally symbolized by a crucial recognition, a point marking a real and not merely apparent unity in the design. Fictions like those of Trollope which appeal particularly to critical naturalism often play down or even parody such a device, and such works show the highest degree of displacement and the least conscious or explicit relationship to myth.

If, however, we go on to study the theme or total shape of the fiction, we find that it also belongs to a convention or category, like those of comedy and tragedy. With the literary category we reach a dead end, until we realize that literature is a reconstructed mythology, with its structural principles derived from those of myth. Then we can see that literature is in a complex setting what a mythology is in a simpler one: a total body of verbal creation. In literature, whatever has a shape has a mythical shape, and leads us toward the center of the order of words. For just as critical naturalism studies the counterpoint of literature and life, words and things, so myth criticism pulls us away from "life" toward a self-contained and autonomous literary universe. But myth, as we said at the beginning, means many things besides literary structure, and the world of words is not so self-contained and autonomous after all.

❧ Nature and Homer

IN THE FIRST PART OF THE *Essay on Criticism* POPE DEALS WITH A
critical principle and a group of critical facts. The principle is
that a work of art is an imitation of nature. The facts are dealt with
by being reduced to the principle. The method of arguing is typi-
cally youthful, even granting that Pope was an incredibly pre-
cocious youth. It is a fact that a poet observes certain literary con-
ventions, but these are really nature methodized. It is a fact that a
poet works with a specific mental quality which Pope calls wit, but
then wit is really nature to advantage dressed. Above all, it is a fact
that a poem is an imitation of other poems. It is possible that Virgil
imitated nature; it is certain that he imitated Homer. This ob-
trusively stubborn fact has to be hammered down a little before
it is on a level with the principle:

> When first young Maro in his youthful mind
> A work t' outlast immortal Rome designed,
> Perhaps he seemed above the critic's law,
> And but from Nature's fountains scorned to draw:
> But when t' examine ev'ry part he came,
> Nature and Homer were, he found, the same.

The traditional view of the relation of art to nature, as enun-
ciated by Aristotle, broadened by the late Classical rhetoricians,
and developed by Christianity, preserves a distinction that is much
less clear in Pope. In this view there are two levels of nature. The
lower one is the ordinary physical world, which is theologically
"fallen"; the upper is divinely sanctioned order, existing in Eden
before the Fall, and mirrored in the Classical and Boethian myth
of the Golden Age. To this upper world we may attain by means
of education, obedience to law, and the habit of virtue; or, as the
Elizabethans said, by adding nurture to nature. The upper world
is the world of "art," and though art may be represented by a
bewildering variety of things, such as magic in *The Tempest* or
the grafting of a tree in *The Winter's Tale*, still it usually includes
what we mean by art, and poetry, for all its Renaissance defenders,
is one of the most important of the educational and regenerative

agents that lead us up to the world of art. When Sidney says: "(Nature's) world is brazen; the poets only deliver a golden," he means by nature the ordinary or fallen world. When he says that art "doth grow in effect a second nature," he is saying that the upper level is also within the natural order. As Burke was to say later, "art is man's nature." The educated and virtuous man is as natural as the animal, but he lives in a world of specifically human nature, where moral goodness is natural. Thus in *Comus* the Lady brushes off Comus's argument that her chastity is unnatural by saying that nature "Means her provision only to the good." This conception of art as not "artificial" in the modern sense but as identical with nature conceived as a morally intelligible order is the basis of Pope's reductive argument—the art itself is nature, as Polixenes says in *The Winter's Tale*.

The two levels are further subdivided into four. The lower level has in its basement the world of sin and moral corruption, which is strictly speaking unnatural, though it often appears to be an intensification of ordinary nature, as it does in *Comus*. The ordinary physical world above it, the nature of animals and plants, is morally neutral, and hence not a resting place for man. Man is in this nature but not of it; he must either go downward into sin or upward into his proper human world. The upper level has above it a supernatural order, which operates in this one as the economy of grace, providence, and salvation. The supernatural world is often associated, as in the *Nativity Ode,* with the world above the moon, the starry spheres that suffer no change or decay. Of course even this is still nature, and its relation to the world of God's actual presence symbolic only, but the symbolizing of the higher by the lower "heaven" has been traditional throughout the Christian period. The last stanza of Spenser's *Mutabilitie Cantoes* is a familiar English example.

The four worlds may also be thought of as concentric, as they are in Dante, where hell is at the centre of the earth, paradise is in the surrounding world of the planets, and purgatory, the world of moral education in which we move upward to our original unfallen nature in Eden, fills the space between the ordinary world and paradise. Thus, in its medieval and Renaissance formulation, art, including poetry, belongs in a world of its own, a world which is, from one point of view at least, *bigger* than ordinary nature, and contains and comprehends it on all sides. If Dante's Eden revolved, like the moon, it would form a sphere containing the inhabited world. Bigger is a physical metaphor, and it was certainly easier to conceive the metaphor when the Ptolemaic universe provided the physical analogies for it that Dante's poem affords. In Pope's anxiety to reduce everything to nature we can see the later tendency to think of art as a specialized development or by-product of nature, sitting precariously in the middle of nature and trying to draw support from its surroundings. As it seems even more self-evident to us than it did to Pope that nature is "bigger" than the world of art, we must return to the fundamental distinction on which all literary criticism has, at least historically, been founded.

In Plato's *Republic* there are four levels too, of a different though significantly related kind. There are two major divisions, the ideal or intelligible world and the physical or objective world. On the upper level of the intelligible world, there is *nous*, the knowledge *of* reality in which the subjective form, or human soul, is united with the objective form or idea. Below it is *dianoia*, knowledge *about* reality, of the kind given us by mathematics. Below this, in the upper level of the lower division, is *pistis*, or knowledge *of* the physical world, the knowledge of bodies which the human body is equipped to receive, and at the bottom is *eikasia*, or opinion, knowledge *about* the physical world, whose relation to *pistis* corresponds to the relation of *dianoia* to *nous*. The first three levels correspond roughly to the analogy between reason, will and appetite in the mind and the ruler, guard, and artisan in the just state on which the whole scheme of the *Republic* turns. *Eikasia* corresponds to the work of the artist who imitates the physical world, and, though not necessarily erroneous in itself, it is a potential source of error, and is unnecessary in a just state.

The equation of art and *eikasia* is implicit only in the *Republic*, as Socrates evidently intends his argument about poets to be tentative, or perhaps paradoxical. Let the poets and their defenders, he says, refute it if they can, and we shall listen to them with respect. Plato himself, in other dialogues, gives the art he approves of a much higher rating, and Plato's influence has been strongest on such critics as Shelley who have claimed the maximum for their art. But the art Plato approves of is hardly, in his terms, an imitation of nature at all, and if we are to keep the conception of imitation the only answer to the argument in the *Republic* is the one that Aristotle's *Poetics* first made possible. The relation of art to nature is not an external relation of reproduction to model, but an internal relation of form to content. Art does not reflect nature; it contains nature, for the essence of content is to be contained. Hence art, no less than mathematics, is, in Plato's terminology, a mode of (at least) *dianoia*, not of *eikasia*. Of course nature is the environment as well as the content of art, and in that respect will always be external to it. That is why the figure of the mirror has been so frequently employed to illustrate the relationship. But the indispensable axiom that, as long as we are talking about art, nature is inside art as its content, not outside it as its model, was written once for all into the critic's handbook by Longinus when he identified the "sublime," not with size, but with the mental capacity that appreciates the vastness of nature and, in the stock but expressive phrase, "takes it in." Thus art is, unlike Alice, as natural as life, but twice as large:

> What is it they saw, those godlike writers who in their work aim at what is greatest and overlook precision in every detail? This, among other things: that nature judged man to be no lowly or ignoble creature when she brought us into this life and into the whole universe as into a great celebration, to be spectators of her whole performance and most ambitious actors. She implanted at once into our souls an invincible love for all that is great and more divine than ourselves. That is why the whole universe gives insufficient scope to man's power of contemplation and reflection, but his thoughts often pass beyond the boundaries of the surrounding world (tr. G. M. A. Grube, Library of Liberal Arts, p. 47).

We are not concerned here with the later versions of the relation of art to nature, but only with the critical confusions caused by the notion that art is somehow formed by its content. The terms nature, life, reality, experience, are all interchangeable in the primitive language of criticism: they are all synonyms for content. Hence life or experience cannot be the formal cause of art; the impulse to give a literary shape to something can only come from previous contact with literature. The forms of literature cannot exist outside literature, and a writer's technical ability, his power to construct a literary form, depends more on his literary scholarship than on any other factor—a point of some importance for universities that teach writing courses. Of course experience may turn up something with an accidental resemblance to literary form—in fact literary criticism badly needs a term corresponding to "picturesque," such as the "literatesque" suggested by Bagehot. Failing such a term, we express the idea very vaguely: if a man is killed in the street by a car, it is a horrifying experience to see, but it is not a "tragedy" any more than it is a novel or an epic. Every writer is constantly on the lookout for experiences that seem to have a story or poem in them, but the story or poem is not in them; it is in the writer's grasp of the literary tradition and his power of assimilating experience to it.

When Henry James was asked about the part played by experience in writing, he could only say that one should be the kind of writer on whom no experience is lost, that is, a writer with enough technical knowledge of literature to be constantly absorbing his experience into literary forms and conventions. Such a maxim hardly sounds controversial, yet much bewilderment has been caused by using terms of content as metaphors for form. If we are examining the sketch books of two artists and find that B appeals to us much more than A, we may say: A is dead and lifeless; B's drawings are full of life: or, A is dull and uninspired; B has the fire of imagination in him: or, A thinks only of his drawing; B is looking at the subject. But all these are secondary and rationalized ways of saying "B draws better." If he draws better, his command of drawing is the primary fact, not his relation to life or imagination or nature, all of which are haphazard guesses about him.

Critics who stress the imitation of nature usually have a strong respect for tradition: critics who stress the "original," like Edward Young, usually prefer to speak of the poet as inspired or creative. But no matter how we think of the poetic process, its end is to produce a new member of a class of things called poems or novels or plays which is already in existence. The parents of a new baby are proud of its novelty; they may even speak of it as unique; but the source of their pride is the fact that it is a recognizable human being, and conforms to a prescribed convention. The same principle holds when a new work of art is called "original." In literature, as in life, the unconventionally new is a monstrosity, as critics from Horace onward have constantly insisted. Such terms as original and inspired are value-judgments, and as my position on the role of value-judgments has been a good deal discussed and often misunderstood, I may summarize it here in four points. (1) Every value-judgment contains within it an antecedent categorical judgment, as we obviously cannot tell how good a thing is until we know what it is. (2) Inadequate value-judgments nearly always owe their inadequacy to an insufficient knowledge of what the categories of literature are. (3) Categorical judgments are based on a knowledge that can be learned and which should constantly increase; value-judgments are based on a skill derived only from such knowledge as we already have. (4) Therefore, knowledge, or scholarship, has priority to value-judgments, constantly corrects their perspective, and always has the power of veto over them, whereas subordinating knowledge to value-judgments leads to impossible pedantries. Rymer's value-judgment of *Othello* as nothing but a bloody farce is not bad criticism; it is logical criticism based on narrow scholarship.

It seems to be difficult for the modern mind to take in the conception of a formal cause which follows most of its effects. The efficient cause of a poem may be the poet; its material cause may be nature, life, reality, experience, or whatever is being shaped. But its formal cause, the literary shape itself, is inside poetry, poetry being, not a simple aggregate of poems, but a body of forms and categories to which every new poem attaches itself somewhere. The difficulty in understanding this is, of course, increased by the law of copyright and the false analogy it suggests between writing and other forms of marketing. In Young's *Conjectures on Original Composition*, already glanced at, we can see a hazy mercantile analogy taking shape between the original writer and the entrepreneur, and between the plagiary and the mere worker. When Young comes to the unshakable fact of the imitation of earlier poems by poets, he draws a distinction (of rhetorical origin, going back to Longinus) between the poem and its author: the true original, he says, imitates not the *Iliad* but Homer, the poem being assumed to be the by-product of a personality. But a poet's personality is either unconnected with his work or part of its convention. Two Romantic poets with very remarkable personalities were Byron and Landor. Landor's personality is not integral with his poetry: it is so different as to have suggested Yeats's theory of the mask, or the poetic personality as the *opposite* of the actual one, and his personality has consequently survived only as a biographical curiosity. With Byron the personality is, so to speak, built in to the poetry, which means that Byron's personality has poetic importance because it conforms to a literary convention. This coincidence of a poetic personality with a fictional archetype is as old as Homer (for the legendary blind bard comes apparently from Homer's own Demodocus) and new enough to account for the cult of Scott Fitzgerald in our day.

Another form of the confusion between literary and personal experience is easier to recognize, though its sources are harder to identify: the confusion between literary and personal sincerity. If a poet is really in love, his Muse may well desert him; if he is a

Courtly Love poet writing sonnets to an aging and irascible duchess informing her that he is her devoted slave for life, that her eyes have struck him irremediably with Cupid's dart, that he must die unless she accords him grace—all of which means, in terms of personal sincerity, that he wants a job tutoring her children—he may break out into passionate eloquence. It is not the experience of love but practice in writing love sonnets that releases the floods of poetic emotion. Every so often Shakespeare criticism is invaded by eager amateurs proving that Shakespeare must have been a lawyer or soldier to speak with such authority about law or soldiering: there are probably books somewhere proving that he must have been a murderer to have written *Macbeth,* or that he must have gone to Italy incognito and spent years as a Renaissance prince to understand so well the psychology of royalty. Here again what is in itself an elementary fallacy often operates under cover in more sophisticated criticism.

For instance: one of the main sources of the confusion is the fact that the *profession* of personal sincerity is itself a literary convention. A Courtly Love poet may be as second-hand in inspiration as you please, but the one thing he is sure to transcribe from his sources is the statement that while most of his predecessors have got their emotions out of books, he really means what he says. The first sonnet of *Astrophel and Stella* ends with the famous line: "Fool, said my Muse to me, look in thy heart and write," which means, as biographical fact, that Sidney has been looking into Petrarch. In the fifteenth sonnet Sidney ridicules his inferiors thus:

> You that poor Petrarch's long deceased woes
> With new-born sighs and den'zened wit do sing:
> You take wrong ways . . .

But he is in a position to say this, not because he is doing something different, but because he is doing the same thing better. All this we may readily concede, as Courtly Love conventions are remote enough from us to be recognized as conventions. But when Wordsworth informs us in the prefaces and poems of the *Lyrical Ballads* that he is letting nature and experience be his teacher, he is using precisely the same convention of professing personal sincerity that Sidney is using. He may have believed it himself; so may Sidney; there is no reason why so much higher a proportion of his readers should have believed *him.* Personal sincerity in the poet is like virtue in Machiavelli's prince: the reality of it is of no consequence; the appearance of it may be.

Because works of literature form a verbal society, and because the forms of literature can only be derived from other literary forms, literature is allusive, not externally or incidentally allusive, but substantially and integrally so. To start with a simple example: G. K. Chesterton's poem *The Donkey*, after describing the grotesque appearance and miserable life of the animal, ends with the quatrain:

> Fools! For I also had my hour,
> One far fierce hour and sweet:
> There was a shouting round my ears,
> And palms before my feet.

The allusion to the first Palm Sunday is not incidental to the poem: it is the whole point of the poem: it is, once again, its formal cause. The Bible is, of course, central to many things in our experience besides literature, but a purely literary allusion may play an informing role equally well, as an allusion to Agamemnon does at the end of Eliot's *Sweeney among the Nightingales* or in Yeats's *Leda*. Agamemnon is one of the founding fathers of our literary society: that is why an allusion to him has the tremendous evocative authority of our whole literary tradition behind it. It is possible to carry the same principle a step further. When Byron writes:

> The mountain looks on Marathon,
> And Marathon looks on the sea

we are reminded of Longinus and his comment on a speech of Demosthenes, that the orator "turns what is essentially an argument into a supremely great and passionate passage" by a reference to Marathon. It is true that both Demosthenes and Byron are talking about the freedom of Greece; but Marathon carries this evocative ring *to us* because it is a battle of literary importance. As events become history, they disappear into books, and are absorbed into the conventions of books. As time goes on, and historical tradition becomes more tenuous, only the events with conventional poetic associations can carry the thrilling magic of a great name. When Lincoln said of the heroes of Gettysburg: "The world will little note nor long remember what we say here, but it can never forget what they did here," he was using one of the oldest literary conventions in the business, the so-called *topos* of modesty, which is even older than the profession of sincerity. He was rhetorically right in using it, and yet what he said is not really true: it is almost impossible to remember the names and dates of battles unless there is some literary reason for doing so, and if the name "Gettysburg" evokes strong feelings when it is as far away from us as we are from Marathon, it will do so only because of whatever literary tradition may have begun with Lincoln's speech.

I do not deny the reality of the sense of the unexpected, the shocking or radically novel, about the original writer, but the difference between the original and the derivative writer does need restating, on the basis of the fact that the original writer is derivative at a deeper level. There are many aspects to the subject of originality in literature, but I have space to deal with only one.

There are no primitives today, and no way of tracing the origin of the impulse to put things into literary form. Everyone, however, lives in continuous contact with words. Much of this contact is with words used descriptively, i.e., to convey information, or what passes as such. But there is a residual contact with words used for entertainment in the broadest sense. For literary people a good deal or most of this contact is with literature, in the conventional modes of books and plays. For people with no consistent literary taste it takes various sub-literary forms: reading the comics, watching television, staying up with detective stories, listening to funny stories, gossiping, and the like. And however thickly covered up with commercial formulas such experience may be today, it is continuous with the popular literary experience of the past. By popular literature I mean roughly the imaginative verbal experience of those with no specifically literary training or interest. The popular in this sense is the contemporary primitive, and it tends to become primitive with the passing of time. Much of it is rubbish, though occasionally a very good work of literature may become popular in the sense of affording a key to imaginative experience for the untrained: *Huckleberry Finn* and some of Dickens's novels are nineteenth-century examples. In simpler societies popular literature consists largely of ballads, myths, folk tales, and similar forms which persist in recognizable disguises to our own day, especially in the nursery rhymes and fairy tales of childhood.

Literature often becomes superficially or inorganically conventional. This usually happens when it follows the narrowing dialectic of a cultural elite belonging to a class which is culturally ascendant but is losing its social effectiveness. The drama of the late Caroline private theatre tended to narrow its appeal in this way, until a social revolution that seemed oddly to coincide with an inner collapse of vitality swept it out in 1642. The original writer in such a situation is likely to do something that will be decried by this elite as vulgar, and hailed by a later generation as turning from literary convention to experience. Thus at the end of the eighteenth century, with so many poets ringing the changes on what Cowper calls Philomela's "mechanick woe," Blake's *Songs of Innocence* and Wordsworth's *Lyrical Ballads* are a breath of fresh air. Hence our readiness to accept Wordsworth's statement that he is ignoring bookish models and making a direct contact with life. As usual, this account is over-simplified. What Blake and Wordsworth also did was to set up a new series of literary echoes: keepsake poems, broadside ballads, moralizing tales for children, were suddenly shown to have an undreamed-of potentiality in their trite formulas.

It is difficult to think of any new and startling development in literature that has not bestowed glass slippers and pumpkin coaches on some subliterary Cinderella. The most obvious example is Elizabethan popular drama, the flower and fruit of what ran to seed with Carlell and Glapthorne. However great the difference in value between *King Lear* and *King Cambyses*, it is hardly likely that Shakespeare would have got as far as *King Lear* if he had not been shrewd enough to see literary possibilities in *King Cambyses* that more highbrow contemporaries did not see. The same practical shrewdness is evident in his exploiting of the formulas of primitive romance and *commedia dell' arte* improvisations in his last period.

The same principle affects many aspects of modern literature. I am not thinking so much of, say, Yeats's interest in the legends and superstitions of the Irish peasantry, which is a usual enough type of interest in popular literary experience: I am thinking rather of the exploiting of a squalid lower-middle-class sub-culture in *Ulysses*, of Yeats's own use of an equally dingy type of occult literature, of the newspaper verse idioms in Auden, of the way in which experimental drama has been affected by primitive and archaic types of popular drama from *Sweeney Agonistes* to *Waiting for Godot*, the latter being of course a frozen vaudeville act. Graham Greene has spoken with great contempt of "books to read while you wait for the bus," but such "entertainments" as *Brighton Rock* and *The Ministry of Fear* are literary developments of precisely the formulas of such books. Wherever we turn in literature it is the same story: every fresh contact with "life" involves also a reshaping of literary convention. Wordsworth's attempt "to choose incidents and situations from common life . . . as far as was possible in a selection of language really used by men" echoes the similar attempt with which Spenser in the *Shepheards Calender* revitalized

Tudor poetry, described by E. K. as bringing "great grace, and, as one would say, auctoritie to the verse." Let us compare two passages from representative poems of the turn of this century, one from a lyric in *A Shropshire Lad* and the other from John Davidson's *Thirty Bob a Week*:

> "Rest you so from trouble sore,
> Fear the heat o' the sun no more,
> Nor the snowing winter wild,
> Now you labour not with child.
>
> "Empty vessel, garment cast,
> We that wore you long shall last.
> —Another night, another day."
> So my bones within me say.

> I step into my heart and there I meet
>   A god-almighty devil singing small,
> Who would like to shout and whistle in the street,
>   And squelch the passers flat against the wall;
> If the whole world was a cake he had the power to take,
>   He would take it, ask for more, and eat it all.
>
> And I meet a sort of simpleton beside,
>   The kind that life is always giving beans;
> With thirty bob a week to keep a bride
>   He fell in love and married in his teens:
> At thirty bob he stuck; but he knows it isn't luck:
>   He knows the seas are deeper than tureens.

The first reaction of a student coming upon these two poems might well be to say that the Housman poem was exquisite and the Davidson one noisy and sentimental doggerel. His second reaction might well be to swing to the opposite extreme and say that one is mere literature and the other a transcription from life, so shattering in its impact as to make it impossible for us to think of Housman as a serious poet at all by comparison. His next duty is to get the assumptions behind these value-judgments sorted out in his mind. Housman's poetry is steeped in conventions that are themselves deeply absorbed in the literary tradition, conventions ranging from the ballad to the sentimental nineteenth-century lyric, and including a deliberate echo of Shakespeare. The Davidson poem uses the idiom and rhythm of a music-hall song to express the kind of life that the music hall indirectly reflects. Housman is deliberately erudite in his use of convention; Davidson deliberately the reverse; but they are equally conventional. By that time, the student will be experienced enough in criticism to have stopped wanting to make comparative value-judgments.

There is no question of finding a primitive or popular core of literary experience in every work of literature: I am dealing here only with the special case in which literature may give, to a hasty observer, the illusion of turning away from books to "life." In our age, as in every age of literature, there are certain assumptions held by our cultural elite that need to be examined with detachment and catholicity of taste. In the Renaissance it was assumed that epic and tragedy were the aristocrats of literary forms, and that major poets would normally devote themselves to these genres. The assumption produced many dull epics and pedantic tragedies, but it also encouraged the genius of Spenser and Milton, of Marlowe and not impossibly of Shakespeare. At the same time we keep a sharp eye out for such diversifiers of literary experience as Donne and Marvell, or, to go further afield, as Deloney, Dorothy Osborne, or Samuel Pepys. In our day it is assumed that the "creative" writer devotes himself to poetry, fiction, and drama, and a great deal of the creative energy of our writing will undoubtedly run through these genres. To press the assumption too far, to assume not only that all "creative" writers would work in these genres but that all who do work in them are creative people, would be ascribing an inherently creative quality to the genres themselves, which is clearly nonsense. It is possible that a substantial proportion of our genuinely "creative" writers may work in such peripheral genres as journalism, popular science, criticism, comic strips, or biography. If so, they will not be turning from literature to life, but exploring different literary conventions.

The opposite extreme from elite standards is the anti-intellectual fallacy of sentimentalizing sub-literary experience in itself. All of us, even the most highbrow, spend much time in the sub-literary world; all of us derive many surreptitious pleasures from it; but this world is, from the point of view of actual literature, mainly a babbling chaos, waiting for the creative word to brood over it and bring it to literary life. In itself it is made up of the most rigidly stylized conventions: the primitive, like the decadent, is inorganically conventional, and what it suggests to the artist is not new content, but new possibilities in the treatment of convention. In short, it is not the world of ordinary life or raw experience, but a suburban literary world.

The critic, once he understands this, may derive much pleasure and profit from attempting to unify his literary experience on all levels, without confusing his value-judgments. If he has a passion for detective stories, he may study the way in which the readability of this genre is increased by the rigidity of its conventions: it is almost a literary development of an important genre of sub-literary experience, the word-puzzle. If he has a special fondness for P. G. Wodehouse, he may discover not only that Wodehouse is the most conventionalized of modern comic writers, but that the conventions used are identical with those of Plautus. If he is moved in spite of himself by a sentimental movie or magazine story, he may recognize the same devices that move him on a different level in *Pericles* or *The Winter's Tale*. Wherever he goes in his imaginative verbal experience, the conventions of literature contain the experience; their formal laws hold everywhere; and from this point of view there is no difference between the scholarly and the popular in the world of words. Nature and Homer are, we find, the same.

❧ New Directions from Old

I N HIS ESSAY ON EDGAR ALLAN POE'S *Eureka*, PAUL VALÉRY SPEAKS of cosmology as one of the oldest of literary arts. Not many people have clearly understood that cosmology is a literary form, not a religious or scientific one. It is true of course that religion and science have regularly been confused with, or more accurately confused by, cosmological structures. In the Middle Ages the Ptolemaic universe had close associations with contemporary theology and science as well as with poetry. But as science depends on experiment and religion on experience, neither is committed to a specific cosmology, or to any cosmology at all. Science blew up the Ptolemaic universe, and Christianity, after feeling itself cautiously all over, discovered that it had survived the explosion. The situation is very different in poetry. It is a gross error to study the cosmology of the *Commedia* or *Paradise Lost* as extraneous obsolete science, for the cosmology of these poems is not simply a part of their subject-matter, but inseparably a part of their total form, the framework of their imagery. Dante's love of symmetry, of which so many critics speak, is not a personal predilection, but an essential part of his poetic craftsmanship.

Even in times when science gives little encouragement for it, poetry shows a tendency to return to the older cosmological structures, as Poe's *Eureka* itself shows. In chemistry the periodical table of elements may have replaced the old tetrad of fire, air, water, and earth, but it is the traditional four that reappear in the Eliot Quartets. The universe of Dylan Thomas's "Altarwise by owl-light" sonnets is still geocentric and astrological; the structure of *Finnegans Wake* is held together by occult correspondence; no reputable scientist has had the influence on the poetry of the last century that Swedenborg or Blavatsky has had. Critics have often remarked on the archaic, even the atavistic, tendencies of poets, and nowhere are these tendencies better illustrated than in the reckless cosmological doodling that may be traced in poetry from Dante's *Convivio* to Yeats's *Vision*. A principle of some importance is involved here, nothing less in fact than the whole question of poetic thought, as distinct from other kinds of thought. Either Peacock's thesis is correct, that poets are a barbaric survival in a scientific age that has outgrown them, or there are requirements in poetic thinking that have never been carefully studied by critics. The graduate-school cliché that Dante's *Commedia* is the metaphysical system of St. Thomas translated into imagery is a melancholy example of how helpless criticism is to deal with one of its own subjects.

We are all familiar with the Aristotelian argument about the relation of poetry to action. Action, or *praxis*, is the world of events; and history, in the broadest sense, may be called a verbal imitation of action, or events put into the form of words. The historian imitates action directly: he makes specific statements about what happened, and is judged by the truth of what he says. What really happened is the external model of his pattern of words, and he is judged by the adequacy with which his words reproduce that model.

The poet, in dramas and epics at least, also imitates actions in words, like the historian. But the poet makes no specific statements of fact, and hence is not judged by the truth or falsehood of what he says. The poet has no external model for his imitation, and is judged by the integrity or consistency of his verbal structure. The reason is that he imitates the universal, not the particular; he is concerned not with what happened but with what happens. His subject-matter is the kind of thing that does happen, in other words the typical or recurring element in action. There is thus a close analogy between the poet's subject-matter and those significant actions that men engage in simply because they are typical and recurring, the actions that we call rituals. The verbal imitation of ritual is myth, and the typical action of poetry is the plot, or what Aristotle calls *mythos*, so that for the literary critic the Aristotelian term *mythos* and the English word myth are much the same thing. Such plots, because they describe typical actions, naturally fall into typical forms. One of these is the tragic plot, with its desis and lysis, its peripety and catastrophe, as charted in the *Poetics*. Another is the comic plot with its happy ending; another is the romance plot with its adventures and its final quest; another is the ironic plot, usually a parody of romance. The poet finds increasingly that he can deal with history only to the extent that history supplies him with, or affords a pretext for, the comic, tragic, romantic or ironic myths that he actually uses.

We notice that when a historian's scheme gets to a certain point of comprehensiveness it becomes mythical in shape, and so approaches the poetic in its structure. There are romantic historical myths based on a quest or pilgrimage to a City of God or a classless society; there are comic historical myths of progress through evolution or revolution; there are tragic myths of decline and fall, like the works of Gibbon and Spengler; there are ironic myths of recurrence or casual catastrophe. It is not necessary, of course, for such a myth to be a universal theory of history, but merely for it to be exemplified in whatever history is using it. A Canadian historian, F. H. Underhill, writing on Toynbee, has employed the term "metahistory" for such works. We notice that metahistory, though it usually tends to very long and erudite books, is far more popular than regular history: in fact metahistory is really the form in which most history reaches the general public. It is only the metahistorian, whether Spengler or Toynbee or H. G. Wells or a religious writer using history as his source of *exempla,* who has much chance of becoming a best-seller.

We notice also that the historian proper tends to confine his verbal imitations of action to human events. His instinct is to look always for the human cause; he avoids the miraculous or the providential; he may assess various non-human factors such as climate, but he keeps them in his "background." The poet, of course, is under no such limitation. Gods and ghosts may be quite as important characters for him as human beings; actions may be cause by *hybris* or nemesis, and the "pathetic fallacy" may be an essential part of his design. Here again metahistory resembles poetry. Metahistorical themes often assume an analogy, or even an identity, with natural processes. Spengler's *Decline of the West* is based on the analogy of historical cultures and vegetable life; Toynbee's "withdrawal and return" theme turns on the analogy of the natural cycle; most theories of progress during the last century have claimed some kind of kinship with evolution. All deterministic histories, whether the determining force is economics or geography or the providence of God, are based on an analogy between history and something else, and so are metahistorical.

The historian works inductively, collecting his facts and trying to avoid any informing patterns except those that he sees, or is honestly convinced he sees, in the facts themselves. The poet, like the metahistorian, works deductively. If he is going to write a tragedy, his decision to impose a tragic pattern on his subject is prior, in importance at least, to his decision to choose a specific historical or legendary or contemporary theme. The remark of Menander that so impressed Matthew Arnold, that his new play was finished and he had only to write it, is typical of the way the poet's mind works. No fact, however interesting, no image, however vivid, no phrase, however striking, no combination of sounds, however resonant, is of any use to a poet unless it fits: unless it appears to spring inevitably out of its context.

A historian in the position of Menander, ready to write his book, would say that he had finished his research and had only to put it into shape. He works toward his unifying form, as the poet works from it. The informing pattern of the historian's book, which is his *mythos* or plot, is secondary, just as detail to a poet is secondary. Hence the first thing that strikes us about the relation of the poet to the historian is their opposition. In a sense the historical is the opposite of the mythical, and to tell a historian that what gives shape to his book is a myth would sound to him vaguely insulting. Most historians would prefer to believe, with Bacon, that poetry is "feigned history," or, at least, that history is one thing and poetry another, and that all metahistory is a bastard combination of two things that will not really combine. But metahistory is too large and flourishing a growth to be so easily weeded out, and such oversimplifying would eliminate Tacitus and Thucydides equally with Buckle and Spengler. It would be better to recognize that metahistory has two poles, one in history proper and the other in poetry. Historians, up to a point, know what the province of history is and what its dependable methods are; but literary critics know so little of the province or methods of either poetry or criticism that it is natural for the historian to feel that one pole of metahistory is real and the other imaginary, and that whatever is poetic in a historical work destroys its value as history. This is to assume that poetry is simply a form of permissible lying, but that is an assumption which critics have never done much to refute.

Because of its concern with the universal rather than the particular, poetry, Aristotle says, is more philosophical than history. Aristotle never followed up this remark, to the extent at least of working out the relation of poetry to conceptual thought. Perhaps, however, we can reconstruct it along lines similar to his discussion of the relation of poetry to action. We may think, then, of literature as an area of verbal imitation midway between events and ideas, or, as Sir Philip Sidney calls them, examples and precepts. Poetry faces, in one direction, the world of *praxis* or action, a world of events occurring in time. In the opposite direction, it faces the world of *theoria*, of images and ideas, the conceptual or visualizable world spread out in space, or mental space. This world may be imitated in a variety of ways, most commonly in words, though composers, painters, mathematicians and others do not think primarily in words. Still, there is a large area of discursive writing, or works of science and philosophy, which makes up the primary verbal imitation of thought. The discursive writer puts ideas and images into words directly. Like the historian, he makes specific statements, or predications; and, like the historian, he is judged by the truth of what he says, or by the adequacy of his verbal reproduction of his external model.

The poet, similarly, is concerned, not with specific or particular predications, but with typical or recurring ones: "What oft was thought," in other words. The truism, the sententious axiom, the proverb, the *topos* or rhetorical commonplace, the irresistibly quotable phrase—such things are the very life-blood of poetry. The poet seeks the new expression, not the new content, and when we find profound or great thoughts in poetry we are usually finding a statement of a common human situation wittily or inevitably expressed. "The course of true love never did run smooth" is from a Shakespearean comedy, and such sententious comments have been a conventional feature of comedy at least since Menander, whose stock of them was raided by St. Paul. The pleasure we get from quoting such axioms is derived from the versatility with which they fit a great variety of situations with an unexpected appositeness. There are serious works on theology and economics that use a quotation from *Alice in Wonderland* as a motto for each chapter.

Again the poet has more in common with the constructive elements in thought, and less in common with its descriptive elements. Versified science, whether obsolete or up to date, as we have it in various encyclopedic poems from medieval times onward, never seems able to get beyond a certain point of poetic merit. It is not that the poets are unskillful, but that there is something wrong with the organizing form of the poem. The unifying theme of the *Ormulum* or *The Pastime of Pleasure* is not itself poetic in outline. We may compare the versified historical chronicles of Robert of Gloucester or William Warner, in which we also retain only a languid literary interest, and for the same reason. Poetry seems to have a good deal more affinity with speculative systems, which from Lucretius to *The Testament of Beauty* have consistently shown a more poetic shape. It looks as though there were something of the same kind of affinity between poetry and metaphysics that there is between poetry and metahistory. Of late

FABLES OF IDENTITY

years we have become much more impressed with the element of *construct* in metaphysical systems, with the feature in them that seems most closely to resemble the poetic. There are logicians who regard metaphysics as bastard logic, just as there are historians who regard metahistory as bastard history. Everything is most properly symmetrical.

The only defect in the symmetry is that metaphysics seems to work mainly with abstractions, and poetry has a limited tolerance for abstractions. Poetry is, in Milton's words, more simple, sensuous and passionate than philosophy. Poetry seeks the image rather than the idea, and even when it deals with ideas it tends to seek the latent basis of concrete imagery in the idea. A discursive nineteenth-century writer will talk of progress and advance in history without noticing, or deliberately ignoring, the fact that his idea has been suggested by the invention of the railway. Tennyson will say "Let the great world spin for ever down the ringing grooves of change," getting his mechanical facts wrong, as poets will, but hitting his conceptual target straight in its sensational bullseye. Literary criticism finds a good deal of difficulty in dealing with such works as *Sartor Resartus*, which appear to employ philosophical concepts and seem to be stating propositions, and yet are clearly something else than actual philosophy. *Sartor Resartus* takes the structure of German Romantic philosophy and extracts from it a central metaphor in which the phenomenal is to the noumenal world as clothing is to the naked body: something which conceals it, and yet, by enabling it to appear in public, paradoxically reveals it as well.

The "ideas" the poets use, therefore, are not actual propositions, but thought-forms or conceptual myths, usually dealing with images rather than abstractions, and hence normally unified by metaphor, or image-phrasing, rather than by logic. The mechanical or diagrammatic image referred to above is a clear example of the poetic element in thought. We sometimes get explicit diagrams in philosophical thought, such as Plato's divided line and Aristotle's middle way, but the great chain of being is more typically a poetic conceptual myth, because it is a device for classifying images. The chain is only one of a great variety of mechanical models in poetic thought, some of them preceding by centuries the machines that embody them. There are the wheels of fate and fortune, mirrors (the word "reflection" indicates how deeply rooted the conceptual world is in the mechanism of the eye), internal combustion or vital spark metaphors, the geared machinery of so much nineteenth-century scientism, the thermostat and feedback metaphors which. since at least Burke's time and certainly long before "cybernetics," have organized most democratic political thought.

Just as we are initially aware of an opposition between the historical and the mythical, so we are initially aware of an opposition between the scientific and the systematic. The scientist starts out empirically, and tries to avoid hampering himself with such gigantic constructs as "universe" or "substance." Similarly, the idea "God," taken as a scientific hypothesis, has never been anything but a nuisance to science. God himself, in the Book of Job, is represented as warning man of this when he points out to Job that the conception "creation," as an objective fact, is not and never can be contained by human experience. Such constructive concepts are at least metaphysical, and metaphysics, as its etymology indicates, comes after physical science. In theology the deductive tendency has completely taken over, as there can hardly be such a thing as empirical theology. The next step brings us to poetic mythology, the concrete, sensational, figurative, anthropomorphic basis out of which the informing concepts of discursive thought come.

II

In its use of images and symbols, as in its use of ideas, poetry seeks the typical and recurring. That is one reason why throughout the history of poetry the basis for organizing the imagery of the physical world has been the natural cycle. The sequence of seasons, times of day, periods of life and death, have helped to provide for literature the combination of movement and order, of change and regularity, that is needed in all the arts. Hence the importance, in poetic symbolism, of the mythical figure known as the dying god, whether Adonis or Proserpine or their innumerable allotropic forms, who represents the cycle of nature.

Again, for poets, the physical world has usually been not only a cyclical world but a "middle earth," situated between an upper and a lower world. These two worlds reflect in their form the heavens and hells of the religions contemporary with the poet, and are normally thought of as abodes of unchanging being, not as cyclical. The upper world is reached by some form of ascent, and is a world of gods or happy souls. The most frequent images of ascent are the mountain, the tower, the winding staircase or ladder, or a tree of cosmological dimensions. The upper world is often symbolized by the heavenly bodies, of which the one nearest us is the moon. The lower world, reached by descent through a cave or under water, is more oracular and sinister, and as a rule is or includes a place of torment and punishment. It follows that there would be two points of particular significance in poetic symbolism. One is the point, usually the top of a mountain just below the moon, where the upper world and this one come into alignment, where we look up to the heavenly world and down on the turning cycle of nature. The other is the point, usually in a mysterious labyrinthine cave, where the lower world and this one come into alignment, where we look down to a world of pain and up to the turning cycle of nature. This upward perspective sees the same world, though from the opposite pole, as the downward perspective in the vision of ascent, and hence the same cyclical symbols may be employed for it.

The definitive literary example of the journey of ascent is in the last half-dozen cantos of Dante's *Purgatorio*. Here Dante, climbing a mountain in the form of a winding stair, purges himself of his last sin at the end of Canto 26, and then finds that he has recovered his lost youth, not his individual but his generic youth as a child of Adam, and hence is in the garden of Eden, the Golden Age of Classical mythology, a lower Paradise directly below the moon, where Paradise proper begins. This point is as far up as Virgil can go, and after Virgil leaves Dante the great apocalyptic vision of the Word and the Church begins. We are told in Canto 28 that Eden is a *locus amoenus*, a place of perpetually temperate climate, from which the seeds of vegetable life in the world below proceed, and to which they return—in other words Eden is at the apex of the natural cycle. In Eden Dante sees the maiden Matilda, who, he says in the same canto, makes him remember where and what Proserpine was, when her mother lost her and she lost the spring flowers. Earlier, in Canto 27, the dying god's conventional emblem, the red or purple flower, is dropped into the imagery with a reference to Pyramus and Thisbe. As a garden is a place of trees, the tree itself is, like the mountain-top, a natural symbol of the vision of ascent, and enters Dante's vision, first in Canto 29 in the form of the seven candlesticks, which look like golden trees at a distance, and later in Canto 32 as the tree of knowledge, which turns purple in color.

The Gardens of Adonis episode in Book Three of *The Faerie Queene* is a familiar English example of *locus amoenus* symbolism. The Gardens of Adonis are spoken of as a "Paradise," and are, again, a place of seed from which the forms of life in the cycle of nature proceed, and to which they return. In Spenser we have the dying god Adonis, the purple flower amaranthus (associated with Sidney, whose fatal thigh-wound made him a favorite historical embodiment of Adonis) and a grove of myrtle trees on top of a mountain. One of Spenser's earliest and acutest critics, Henry Reynolds, suggests, in the easy-going fashion of his time, an etymological connection between Adonis and Eden, but Spenser does not make any explicit link between this garden and Eden, which is the kingdom of Una's parents in Book One. Nor does he explicitly locate the Gardens at the apex of the cyclical world just below the moon, though he does speak of Adonis as "eterne in mutabilitie," which reminds us of the *Mutabilitie Cantoes* and of the dispute between Mutability and Jove, held in the sphere of the moon at the boundary of Jove's world. In this poem the evidence brought forward by Mutability in her favor, which consists of various aspects of the natural cycle, proves Jove's case instead, because it is evidence of a principle of stability in flux. In any case the upper location of the Gardens of Adonis seems to be in Milton's mind when in *Comus* he introduces the Attendant Spirit as coming from the Gardens of Adonis, which according to the opening line are "Before the starry threshold of Jove's Court." Milton also places Eden on a mountain-top, protected by a "verdurous wall," and the world into which Adam is exiled is spoken of as a "subjected plain."

In Biblical typology the relation between Eden and the wilderness of Adam's exile is closely parallel to the relation between the Promised Land and the wilderness of the law. Here again the Promised Land is thought of as being "above" the wilderness, its capital being Jerusalem, the center of the world and the city on the mountain, "whither the tribes go up." The same kind of language enters the prophetic visions: Ezekiel's wilderness vision of dry bones is in a valley, while the panorama of the restored Jerusalem with which the prophecy concludes begins with the prophet seated "upon a very high mountain." In *Paradise Regained* Christ's temptation in the wilderness is really a descent into hell, or the domain of Satan, terminated by his successful stand on the pinnacle of Jerusalem, which prefigures his later conquest of the lower world of death and hell, much as Satan prefigures his own success in Eden when he sits "like a cormorant," in the tree of life, the highest point in the garden. Christ's victory over Satan also, Milton says, "raised" Eden in the wilderness. The forty days of the temptation are commemorated in Lent, which is immediately followed in the calendar by Easter; they also correspond to the forty years of wilderness wandering under the law, which was terminated by the conquest of the Promised Land by Joshua, who has the same name as Jesus (cf. *Paradise Lost* xii, 307-314).

T. S. Eliot's *Ash Wednesday* is a poem founded on Dante's *Purgatorio* which at the same time glances at these Biblical and liturgical typologies. The central image of the poem is the winding stair of Dante's mountain, which leads to a Paradisal garden. Overtones of Israel in the wilderness ("This is the land. We have our inheritance."), of Ezekiel's valley of dry bones, and of course of Lent, are also present. As the poet is preoccupied with ascent, we get only fitful glimpses of the natural cycle on the way up: "a slotted window bellied like the fig's fruit," "hawthorn blossom," and a "broadbacked figure drest in blue and green," the last reappearing in a subdued form as a silent "garden god" in the *locus amoenus* above. In the final section the poet returns from the universal past to the individual past, from "the violet and the violet" of the garden to a nostalgia symbolized among other things by "lost lilacs."

In view of the explicit and avowed debt of this poem to the *Purgatorio,* the parallels in imagery may not seem very significant. It is all the more interesting to compare the treatment of the "winding stair" image in Yeats, as there, whatever influence from Dante there may be, the attitude taken towards the ascent is radically different. Two of Yeats's poems, *A Dialogue of Self and Soul* and *Vacillation,* turn on a debate between a "soul" who wants only to ascend the stair to some ineffable communion beyond, and a "self" or "heart" who is fascinated by the downward vision into nature, even to the point of accepting rebirth in its cycle. In the former poem the "self" focuses its gaze on the dying-god symbol of the Japanese ceremonial sword wrapped in silk embroidered with flowers of "heart's purple." In *Vacillation* the symbol of ascent and separation from the cycle, the uncorrupted body of the saint, is contrasted with the cycle itself of death and corruption and rebirth, represented by the lion and honeycomb of Samson's riddle. Here, however, it is the symbol of the tree, associated with "Attis' image" and somewhat like Dante's candlestick vision, "half all glittering flame and half all green," that dominates the poem, and that seems to combine in itself the images of ascent and cycle. Similarly in *Among School Children* the contrast between the nun and the mother, the "bronze repose" of direct ascent and the cyclical "honey of generation," is resolved in the image of the chestnut tree.

There are other examples of the green world at the top of the natural cycle in modern poetry. Wallace Stevens, for instance, gives us a very clear description of it in *Credences of Summer:*

> It is the natural tower of all the world,
> The point of survey, green's green apogee,
> But a tower more precious than the view beyond,
> A point of survey squatting like a throne,
> Axis of everything.

But in the twentieth century, on the whole, images of descent are, so to speak, in the ascendant. These derive mainly from the sixth book of the Aeneid, and its progenitor in the eleventh book of the Odyssey. Here also one is confronted with two levels, a lower world of unending pain, the world of Tantalus and Sisyphus and Ixion, and an upper world more closely connected with the natural cycle. In Virgil there is a most elaborate development of cyclical and rebirth symbolism, introducing speculations of a type that are rarely encountered again in Western poetry before at least Romantic times. In the vision of descent, where we enter a world of darkness and mystery, there is more emphasis on initiation, on learning the proper rites, on acquiring effective talismans like the golden bough. The main figures have a strongly parental aura about them: in Virgil the prophet of the future of Rome is Aeneas' father, and the maternal figure is represented by the Sibyl. In Homer, Odysseus' mother appears, and the figure corresponding to Virgil's Sibyl is Circe, whom Homer calls *potnia,* which means something like reverend. At the top of the winding stair one normally attains direct knowledge or vision, but the reward of descent is usually oracular or esoteric knowledge, concealed or forbidden to most people, often the knowledge of the future.

In romance, where descent themes are very common, the hero often has to kill or pacify a dragon who guards a secret hoard of wealth or wisdom. The descent is also often portrayed as a mimic, temporary or actual death of the hero; or he may be swallowed by the dragon, so that his descent is into the monster's belly. In medieval treatments of the Christian story some of these themes reappear. Between his death on the cross and his resurrection Jesus descends into hell, often portrayed, especially in fresco, as the body of a huge dragon or shark, which he enters by the mouth, like his prototype Jonah. Again there are two levels in the lower world: hell proper, a world of endless torment, and the upper limbo which is "harrowed," and from which the redeemed, among whom the parental figures Adam and Eve have an honored place, return to the upper world. The monster's open mouth recurs in *Ash Wednesday* as "the toothed gullet of an agèd shark," and as the symbol of the "blue rocks" or Symplegades, whose clashing together has similar overtones.

For obvious reasons, visions of descent in medieval and Renaissance poetry are usually infernal visions, based on Virgil but ignoring his interest in rebirth. Only with Romantic poetry do we begin to get once more the oracular or quest descent, where the hero gets something more from his descent than a tragic tale or an inspection of torments. In Keats's *Endymion* there are adventures in both upward and downward directions, the upward ones being mainly quests for beauty and the downward ones quests for truth. The Gardens of Adonis in this poem seem to be down rather than up, as they do at the conclusion of Blake's *Book of Thel,* though in that conclusion there is a sudden reversal of perspective. Shelley's *Prometheus Unbound* is a more striking example of a cosmology in which the beneficial comes mainly from below, and the sinister from above. The contrast here with the cosmology of Dante and Milton is so striking that it deserves more examination.

In Dante, in Spenser, in Milton, the foreground of symbols and images seems to be portrayed against a background of roughly four levels of existence. I need a word for this background, and am strongly tempted to steal "topocosm" from Theodor H. Gaster's *Thespis,* though he uses it in a quite different sense. The top level is the place of the presence of God, the empyreal heaven, which operates in this world as the order of grace and providence. The next level is that of human nature properly speaking, represented by the garden of Eden or the Golden Age before the Fall, and now a world to be regained internally by moral and intellectual effort. Third is the level of physical nature, morally neutral but theologically fallen, which man is born into but can never adjust to, and fourth is the level of sin, death and corruption, which since the Fall has permeated the third level too. Throughout this period it was traditional to symbolize the top level by the starry spheres, the spiritual by the physical heaven. Dante's upper Paradise is located in the planetary spheres, and in Milton's *Nativity Ode* the music of the spheres, symbol of the understanding of unfallen man, is in counterpoint to the chorus of descending angels.

After the rise of Copernican astronomy and Newtonian physics, the starry sky becomes a less natural and a more perfunctory and literary metaphor for the spiritual world. The stars look increasingly less like vehicles of angelic intelligences, and come to suggest rather a mechanical and mindless revolution. This shift of perspective is of course already present in a famous passage in Pascal, but it does not make its full impact on poetry until much later. A deity at home in such a world would seem stupid or malignant, at best a kind of self-hypnotized Pangloss. Hence the variety of stupid sky-gods in Romantic poetry: Blake's Urizen, Shelley's Jupiter, Byron's Arimanes, Hardy's Immanent Will, perhaps the God of the Prologue to *Faust*. Blake, the closest of this group to the orthodox Christian tradition, points out that there is more Scriptural evidence for Satan as a sky god than for Jesus. Even more significant for poetic symbolism is the sense of the mechanical complications of starry movement as the projection or reflection of something mechanical and malignant in human nature. In other words, the Frankenstein theme of actualizing human death-impulses in some form of fateful mechanism has a strong natural connection with the sky or "outer space," and in modern science fiction is regularly attached to it. At the same time poets in the Romantic period tend to think of nature less as a structure or system, set over against the conscious mind as an object, and more as a body of organisms from which the human organism proceeds, nature being the underlying source of humanity, as the seed is of the plant.

Hence with Romanticism another "topocosm," almost the reverse of the traditional one, begins to take shape. On top is the bleak and frightening world of outer space. Next comes the level of ordinary human experience, with all its anomalies and injustices. Below, in the only place left for any *locus amoenus*, is the buried original form of society, now concealed under the historical layers of civilization. With a modern Christian poet this would be the old unfallen world, or its equivalent: thus in Auden's *For the Time Being* the "garden" world is hidden within or concealed by the "wilderness" of ordinary life. With a poet closer to Rousseau this buried society would be the primitive society of nature and reason, the sleeping beauty that a revolutionary act of sufficient courage would awaken. On the fourth level, corresponding to the traditional hell or world of death, is the mysterious reservoir of power and life out of which both nature and humanity proceed. This world is morally ambivalent, being too archaic for distinctions of good and evil, and so retains some of the sinister qualities of its predecessor. Hence the insistence in Romantic culture of the ambivalent nature of "genius," or an unusual degree of natural creative power, which may destroy the poet's personality or drive him to various forms of evil or suffering, as in the Byronic hero, the *poète maudit*, the compulsive sinner of contemporary Christian and existential fiction, and other varieties of Romantic agony.

Against this "topocosm" the action of *Prometheus Unbound* seems logical enough. In the sky is Jupiter, the projection of human superstition with its tendency to deify a mechanical and subhuman order. Below is the martyred Prometheus; below him Mother Earth (in whose domain is included the world of death, which has a mysterious but recurring connection with the *locus amoenus* in Shelley), and at the bottom of the whole action is the oracular cave of Demogorgon, who calls himself Eternity, and from whom the power proceeds that rejuvenates Earth, liberates Prometheus, and annihilates Jupiter.

The Romantic "topocosm," like its predecessor, is, for the poet, simply a way of arranging metaphors, and does not in itself imply any particular attitudes or beliefs or conceptions. The traditional infernal journey naturally persists: Eliot's *Waste Land* and the first of Pound's *Cantos* are closely related examples, the former having many Aeneid echoes and the latter being based on the Odyssey. In Pound the characteristic parental figure is Aphrodite, called "venerendam," an echo of Homer's *potnia*, who bears the "golden bough of Argicida," in other words of Hermes the psychopomp. In Eliot the parallel figure to this combination of Hermes and Aphrodite is the hermaphroditic Teiresias, the seer who was the object of Odysseus' descent.

The "topocosm" of Dante was closely related to contemporary religious and scientific constructs, and to a much lesser degree the same is true of the post-Romantic one. We get our "up" metaphors from the traditional forms: everything that is uplifting or aspiring about the spiritual quest, such as the wings of angels or the ascension of Christ or the phrase "lift up your hearts," is derived from the metaphorical association of God and the sky. Even as late as the nineteenth century, progress and evolution were still going up as well as on. In the last century or so there has been a considerable increase in the use of approving "down" metaphors: to get "down" to bedrock or brass tacks or the basic facts is now the sign of a proper empirical procedure. Descent myths are also deeply involved in the social sciences, especially psychology, where we have a subconscious or unconscious mind assumed, by a spatial metaphor, to be underneath the consciousness, and into this mind we descend in quest of parental figures. The Virgilian inspiration of modern scientific mythology is not hard to see: the golden bough of the sixth book of the Aeneid supplies the title and theme for Frazer, and the famous line spoken by Juno in the seventh, that if she cannot prevail on the high gods she will stir up hell (fletere si nequeo superos, Acheronta movebo), is the apt motto of Freud's *Interpretation of Dreams*. But now that politics and science at least are beginning to focus once more on the moon, it is possible that a new construct will be formed, and a new table of metaphors organize the imagery of our poets.

≥ The Structure of Imagery in
The Faerie Queene

THE *Faerie Queene*, LONG AS IT IS, IS NOT NEARLY AS LONG AS THE poem that Spenser intended to write, according to his letter to Raleigh and two of the *Amoretti* sonnets. It therefore at once raises the problem of whether the poem as it now stands is unfinished or merely uncompleted. If merely uncompleted, then it still may be a unity, like a torso in sculpture; if unfinished, then, as in Dickens' *Mystery of Edwin Drood,* certain essential clues to the total meaning are forever withheld from us.

Many readers tend to assume that Spenser wrote the poem in the same way that they read it, starting at the beginning and keeping on until he collapsed with exhaustion. But while *The Faerie Queene* probably evolved in a much more complicated way than that, there is no evidence of exhaustion. In the eightieth *Amoretti* sonnet he sounds winded, but not bored; and of course he is not the kind of poet who depends on anything that a Romantic would call inspiration. He is a professional poet, learned in rhetoric, who approaches his sublime passages with the nonchalance of a car-driver shifting into second gear. All the purple patches in Spenser —the temptations of Despair and Acrasia, the praise of Elizabeth in *Colin Clouts Come Home Again,* the "Bellona" passage in *The Shepheards Calendar*—are deliberate rhetorical exercises. There may be passages in *The Faerie Queene* that *we* find dull, but there are very few in which Spenser's own standards are not met. In some cantos of the fifth book, perhaps, he sounds tired and irritable, as though he were preoccupied with his anxieties instead of his subject, and in these cantos there are lapses into muddled argument, tasteless imagery, and cacophonous doggerel. But on the whole no poem in English of comparable scope is more evenly sustained. Further, Spenser is not, like Coleridge, a poet of fragments. Just as there is a touch of Pope himself in Pope's admiration for "The spider's touch, how exquisitely fine!," so there is a touch of Spenser himself in Spenser's admiration for the honey bee "Working her formal rooms in wexen frame." He thinks inside regular frameworks—the twelve months, the nine muses, the seven deadly sins—and he goes on filling up his frame even when his scheme is mistaken from the beginning, as it certainly is in *The Tears of the Muses*.

What can be said is that, as one virtue is likely to involve others, Spenser's scheme was bound to foreshorten as he went on. In the historical allegory he still had the Armada to deal with, but in the moral allegory there is already a good deal of inorganic repetition, especially in the symbols of evil (for example, the Occasion-Ate-Sclaunder sequence and the reduplicative foul monsters). In the first book he uses up so much of the structure of Biblical typology that he could hardly have written a second book in the area of revelation; and chastity and justice, each of which is described as the supreme virtue, almost exhaust the sources of plausible compliments to Elizabeth. Spenser may well have ended his sixth book realizing that he might not write any more of it, and designed its conclusion for either possibility. He provides himself, of course, with opportunities for carrying on the story. Apart from Prince Arthur himself, we have a fresh set of characters; a seventh book would doubtless have got some clothes on Serena, who is left nude and shivering at the end of the eighth canto; the poet hints that the baby rescued by Calepine may grow up to be the hero of a future legend; he allows the Blatant Beast to escape again. But there are many such dropped stitches in the plots of the other five books, and they do not interfere with our sense of their unity. At the same time the appearance of Spenser's "signature" in Colin Clout and two other symbols from *The Shepheards Calendar*, the four Graces and the envious beast that barks at poets, make the end of the sixth book also a summing up and conclusion for the entire poem and for Spenser's poetic career. There is, at least, nothing in the poem as we now have it that seems to depend for its meaning on anything unwritten.

I shall assume, as a working hypothesis, that the six books we have form a unified epic structure, regardless of how much might have been added that wasn't. There are six books, and Spenser has a curious fondness for mentioning the number six: there are six counsellors of Lucifera, six couples in the masque of Cupid, two groups of six knights fighting Britomart, six judges at Cambell's tournament, six partisans of Marinell at Florimell's tournament, six grooms of Care, and so on. In most of these groups there is a crucial seventh, and perhaps the *Mutabilitie Cantos* have that function in the total scheme of the epic. We shall probably never know on what manuscript evidence the publisher of the Folio numbered the two cantos of this poem six and seven. What we can see is that the *Mutabilitie Cantos* are certainly not a fragment: they constitute a single beautifully shaped poem that could not have had a more logical beginning, development, and end. It is entirely impossible that the last two stanzas could have been the opening stanzas of an eighth unfinished canto, as the rubric suggests. Nor is it possible that in their present form these cantos could have been the "core" of a seventh book, unless that book was inconceivably different in its structure from the existing ones. The poem brings us to the poet's "Sabbath's sight" after his six great efforts of creation, and there is nothing which at any point can be properly described as "unperfite."

To demonstrate a unity in *The Faerie Queene*, we have to examine the imagery of the poem rather than its allegory. It is Spenser's habitual technique, developing as it did out of the emblematic visions he wrote in his nonage, to start with the image, not the allegorical translation of it, and when he says at the beginning of the final canto of Book II:

> Now ginnes this goodly frame of Temperaunce
> Fayrely to rise

one feels that the "frame" is built out of the characters and places that are clearly announced to be what they are, not out of their moral or historical shadows. Spenser prefaces the whole poem with sonnets to possible patrons, telling several of them that they are in the poem somewhere, not specifying where: the implication is that for such readers the allegory is to be read more or less *ad libitum*. Spenser's own language about allegory, "darke conceit," "clowdily enwrapped," emphasizes its deliberate vagueness. We know that Belphoebe refers to Elizabeth: therefore, when Timias speaks of "her, whom the hevens doe serve and sew," is there, as one edition suggests, a reference to the storm that wrecked the Armada? I cite this only as an example of how subjective an allegorical reading can be. Allegory is not only often uncertain, however, but in the work of one of our greatest allegorical poets it can even be addled, as it is in *Mother Hubberds Tale,* where the fox and the ape argue over which of them is more like a man, and hence more worthy to wear the skin of a lion. In such episodes as the legal decisions of Artegall, too, we can see that Spenser, unlike Milton, is a poet of very limited conceptual powers, and is helpless without some kind of visualization to start him thinking. I am far from urging that we should "let the allegory go" in reading Spenser, but it is self-evident that the imagery is prior in importance to it. One cannot begin to discuss the allegory without using the imagery, but one could work out an exhaustive analysis of the imagery without ever mentioning the allegory.

Our first step is to find a general structure of imagery in the poem as a whole, and with so public a poet as Spenser we should hardly expect to find this in Spenser's private possession, as we might with Blake or Shelley or Keats. We should be better advised to look for it in the axioms and assumptions which Spenser and his public shared, and which form the basis of its imaginative communication. Perhaps the *Mutabilitie Cantos,* which give us so many clues to the sense of *The Faerie Queene* as a whole, will help us here also.

The action of the *Mutabilitie Cantos* embraces four distinguishable levels of existence. First is that of Mutability herself, the level of death, corruption, and dissolution, which would also be, if this poem were using moral categories, the level of sin. Next comes the world of ordinary experience, the nature of the four elements, over which Mutability is also dominant. Its central symbol is the cycle, the round of days, months, and hours which Mutability brings forth as evidence of her supremacy. In the cycle there are two elements: becoming or change, which is certainly Mutability's, and a principle of order or recurrence within which the change occurs. Hence Mutability's evidence is not conclusive, but could just as easily be turned against her. Above our world is upper nature, the stars in their courses, a world still cyclical but immortal and unchanged in essence. This upper world is all that is now left of nature as God originally created it, the state described in the Biblical story of Eden and the Classical myth of the Golden Age. Its regent is Jove, armed with the power which, in a world struggling against chaos and evil, is "the right hand of justice truly hight." But Jove, however he may bluster and threaten, has no authority over Mutability; that authority belongs to the goddess Nature, whose viceroy he is. If Mutability could be cast out of the world of ordinary experience, lower and upper nature would be reunited, man would re-enter the Golden Age, and the reign of "Saturn's son" would be replaced by that of Saturn. Above Nature is the real God, to whom Mutability appeals when she brushes Jove out of her way, who is invoked in the last stanza of the poem, and who appears in the reference to the Transfiguration of Christ like a mirage behind the assembly of lower gods.

Man is born into the third of these worlds, the order of physical

nature which is theologically "fallen" and under the sway of Muta-
bility. But though in this world he is not of it: he really belongs
to the upper nature of which he formed part before his fall. The
order of physical nature, the world of animals and plants, is
morally neutral: man is confronted from his birth with a moral
dialectic, and must either sink below it into sin or rise above it into
his proper human home. This latter he may reach by the practice
of virtue and through education, which includes law, religion, and
everything the Elizabethans meant by art. The question whether
this "art" included what we mean by art, poetry, painting, and
music, was much debated in Spenser's day, and explains why so
much of the criticism of the period took the form of apologetic.
As a poet, Spenser believed in the moral reality of poetry and in
its effectiveness as an educating agent; as a Puritan, he was sensitive
to the abuse and perversion of art which had raised the question
of its moral value in the first place, and he shows his sense of the
importance of the question in his description of the Bower of Bliss.

Spenser means by "Faerie" primarily the world of realized hu-
man nature. It is an "antique" world, extending backward to Eden
and the Golden Age, and its central figure of Prince Arthur was
chosen, Spenser tells us, as "furthest from the daunger of envy, and
suspition of present time." It occupies the same space as the ordi-
nary physical world, a fact which makes contemporary allusions
possible, but its time sequence is different. It is not timeless: we
hear of months or years passing, but time seems curiously fore-
shortened, as though it followed instead of establishing the rhythm
of conscious life. Such foreshortening of time suggests a world of
dream and wishfulfilment, like the fairylands of Shakespeare's
comedies. But Spenser, with his uneasy political feeling that the
price of authority is eternal vigilance, will hardly allow his virtu-
ous characters even to sleep, much less dream, and the drowsy
narcotic passages which have so impressed his imitators are asso-
ciated with spiritual peril. He tells us that sleep is one of the three
divisions of the lowest world, the other two being death and hell;
and Prince Arthur's long tirade against night (III, iv) would be
out of proportion if night, like its seasonal counterpart winter, did
not symbolize a lower world than Faerie. The vision of Faerie may
be the *author's* dream, as the pilgrimage of Christian is presented
as a dream of Bunyan, but what the poet dreams of is the strenu-
ous effort, physical, mental, and moral, of waking up to one's true
humanity.

In the ordinary physical world good and evil are inextricably confused; the use and the abuse of natural energies are hard to distinguish, motives are mixed and behaviour inconsistent. The perspective of Faerie, the achieved quest of virtue, clarifies this view. What we now see is a completed moral dialectic. The mixed-up physical world separates out into a human moral world and a demonic one. In this perspective heroes and villains are purely and simply heroic and villainous; characters are either white or black, for the quest or against it; right always has superior might in the long run, for we are looking at reality from the perspective of man as he was originally made in the image of God, unconfused about the difference between heaven and hell. We can now see that physical nature is a source of energy, but that this energy can run only in either of two opposing directions: toward its own fulfilment or towards its own destruction. Nature says to Mutability: "For thy decay thou seekst by thy desire," and contrasts her with those who, struggling out of the natural cycle, "Doe worke their owne perfection so by fate."

Spenser, in Hamlet's language, has no interest in holding the mirror up to nature unless he can thereby show virtue her own feature and scorn her own image. His evil characters are rarely converted to good, and while there is one virtuous character who comes to a bad end, Sir Terpine in Book V, this exception proves the rule, as his fate makes an allegorical point about justice. Sometimes the fiction writer clashes with the moralist in Spenser, though never for long. When Malbecco offers to take Hellenore back from the satyrs, he becomes a figure of some dignity as well as pathos; but Spenser cannot let his dramatic sympathy with Malbecco evolve. Complicated behaviour, mixed motives, or the kind of driving energy of character which makes moral considerations seem less important, as it does in all Shakespeare's heroes, and even in Milton's Satan—none of this could be contained in Spenser's framework.

The Faerie Queene in consequence is necessarily a romance, for romance is the genre of simplified or black and white characterization. The imagery of this romance is organized on two major principles. One is that of the natural cycle, the progression of days and seasons. The other is that of the moral dialectic, in which symbols of virtue are parodied by their vicious or demonic counterparts. Any symbol may be used ambivalently, and may be virtuous or demonic according to its context, an obvious example being the symbolism of gold. Cyclical symbols are subordinated to dialectical ones; in other words the upward turn from darkness to dawn or from winter to spring usually symbolizes the lift in perspective from physical to human nature. Ordinary experience, the morally neutral world of physical nature, never appears as such in *The Faerie Queene*, but its place in Spenser's scheme is symbolized by nymphs and other elemental spirits, or by the satyrs, who may be tamed and awed by the sight of Una or more habitually stimulated by the sight of Hellenore. Satyrane, as his name indicates, is, with several puns intended, a good-natured man, and two of the chief heroes, Redcrosse and Artegall, are explicitly said to be natives of this world and not, like Guyon, natives of Faerie. What this means in practice is that their quests include a good deal of historical allegory.

In the letter to Raleigh Spenser speaks of a possible twenty-four books, twelve to deal with the private virtues of Prince Arthur and the other twelve with the public ones manifested after he was crowned king. But this appalling spectre must have been exorcized very quickly. If we look at the six virtues he did treat, we can see that the first three, holiness, temperance, and chastity, are essentially private virtues, and that the next three, friendship, justice, and courtesy, are public ones. Further, that both sets seem to run in a sort of Hegelian progression. Of all public virtues, friendship is the most private and personal; justice the most public and impersonal, and courtesy seems to combine the two, Calidore being notable for his capacity for friendship and yet able to capture the Blatant Beast that eluded Artegall. Similarly, of all private virtues, holiness is most dependent on grace and revelation, hence the imagery of Book I is Biblical and apocalyptic, and introduces the theological virtues. Temperance, in contrast, is a virtue shared by the enlightened heathen, a prerequisite and somewhat pedestrian virtue (Guyon loses his horse early in the book and does not get it back until Book V), hence the imagery of Book II is classical, with much drawn from the *Odyssey* and from Platonic and Aristotelian ethics. Chastity, a virtue described by Spenser as "farre above the rest," seems to combine something of both. The encounter of Redcrosse and Guyon is indecisive, but Britomart, by virtue of her enchanted spear, is clearly stronger than Guyon, and hardly seems to need Redcrosse's assistance in Castle Joyeous.

We note that in Spenser, as in Milton's *Comus*, the supreme private virtue appears to be chastity rather than charity. Charity, in the sense of Christian love, does not fit the scheme of *The Faerie Queene*: for Spenser it would primarily mean, not man's love for God, but God's love for man, as depicted in the *Hymn of*

Heavenly Love. Charissa appears in Book I, but her main con-
nexions are with the kindliness that we associate with "giving to
charity"; Agape appears in Book IV, but is so minor and so dim-
witted a character that one wonders whether Spenser knew the
connotations of the word. Hence, though Book I is the only book
that deals explicitly with Christian imagery, it does not follow that
holiness is the supreme virtue. Spenser is not dealing with what
God gives to man, but with what man does with his gifts, and
Redcrosse's grip on holiness is humanly uncertain.

In one of its aspects *The Faerie Queene* is an educational treatise,
based, like other treatises of its time, on the two essential social facts
of the Renaissance, the prince and the courtier. The most impor-
tant person in Renaissance society to educate was the prince, and
the next most important was the courtier, the servant of the prince.
Spenser's heroes are courtiers who serve the Faerie Queene and
who metaphorically make up the body and mind of Prince Arthur.
To demonstrate the moral reality of poetry Spenser had to assume
a connexion between the educational treatise and the highest forms
of literature. For Spenser, as for most Elizabethan writers, the
highest form of poetry would be either epic or tragedy, and the
epic for him deals essentially with the actions of the heroic prince
or leader. The highest form of prose, similarly, would be either a
Utopian vision outlined in a Platonic dialogue or in a romance like
Sidney's *Arcadia,* or a description of an ideal prince's ideal educa-
tion, for which the classical model was Xenophon's *Cyropaedia.*
Spenser's preference of Xenophon's form to Plato's is explicit in
the letter to Raleigh. This high view of education is inseparable
from Spenser's view of the relation between nature and art. For
Spenser, as for Burke centuries later, art is man's nature. Art is
nature on the human plane, or what Sidney calls a second nature,
a "golden" world, to use another phrase of Sidney's, because essen-
tially the same world as that of the Golden Age, and in contrast
to the "brazen" world of physical nature. Hence art is no less
natural than physical nature—the art itself is nature, as Polixenes
says in *The Winter's Tale*—but it is the civilized nature appro-
priate to human life.

Private and public education, then, are the central themes of *The
Faerie Queene.* If we had to find a single word for the virtue un-
derlying all private education, the best word would perhaps be
fidelity: that unswerving loyalty to an ideal which is virtue, to a
single lady which is love, and to the demands of one's calling
which is courage. Fidelity on the specifically human plane of

endeavour is faith, the vision of holiness by which one lives; on the natural plane it is temperance, or the ability to live humanely in the physical world. The corresponding term for the virtue of public education is, perhaps, concord or harmony. On the physical plane concord is friendship, again the ability to achieve a human community in ordinary life; on the specifically human plane it is justice and equity, the foundation of society.

In the first two books the symbolism comes to a climax in what we may call a "house of recognition," the House of Holiness in Book I and the House of Alma in Book II. In the third the climax is the vision of the order of nature in the Gardens of Adonis. The second part repeats the same scheme: we have houses of recognition in the Temple of Venus in Book IV and the Palace of Mercilla in Book V, and a second *locus amoenus* vision in the Mount Acidale canto of Book VI, where the poet himself appears with the Graces. The sequence runs roughly as follows: fidelity in the context of human nature; fidelity in the context of physical nature; fidelity in the context of nature as a whole; concord in the context of physical nature; concord in the context of human nature; concord in the context of nature as a whole. Or, abbreviated: human fidelity, natural fidelity, nature; natural concord, human concord, art. Obviously, such a summary is unacceptable as it stands, but it may give some notion of how the books are related and of how the symbolism flows out of one book into the next one.

The conception of the four levels of existence and the symbols used to represent it come from Spenser's cultural tradition in general and from the Bible in particular. The Bible, as Spenser read it for his purposes, describes how man originally inhabited his own human world, the Garden of Eden, and fell out of it into the present physical world, which fell with him. By his fall he lost the tree and water of life. Below him is hell, represented on earth by the kingdoms of bondage, Egypt, Babylon, and Rome, and symbolized by the serpent of Eden, otherwise Satan, otherwise the huge water-monster called Leviathan or the dragon by the prophets. Man is redeemed by the quest of Christ, who after overcoming the world descended to hell and in three days conquered it too. His descent is usually symbolized in art as walking into the open mouth of a dragon, and when he returns in triumph he carries a banner of a red cross on a white ground, the colours typifying his blood and flesh. At the end of time the dragon of death is finally destroyed, man is restored to Eden, and gets back the water and tree of life. In Christianity these last are symbolized by the two sacraments accepted by the Reformed Church, baptism and the Eucharist.

The quest of the Redcrosse knight in Book I follows the symbolism of the quest of Christ. He carries the same emblem of a red cross on a white ground; the monster he has to kill is "that old dragon" (quatrain to Canto xi; cf. Rev. xii, 9) who is identical with the Biblical Satan, Leviathan, and serpent of Eden, and the object of killing him is to restore Una's parents, who are Adam and Eve, to their kingdom of Eden, which includes the entire world, now usurped by the dragon. The tyranny of Egypt, Babylon, and the Roman Empire continues in the tyranny of the Roman Church, and the Book of Revelation, as Spenser read it, prophesies the future ascendancy of that church and its ultimate defeat in its vision of the dragon and Great Whore, the latter identified with his Duessa. St. George fights the dragon for three days in the garden of Eden, refreshed by the water and tree of life on the first two days respectively.

But Eden is not heaven: in Spenser, as in Dante, it is rather the summit of purgatory, which St. George goes through in the House of Holiness. It is the world of recovered human nature, as it originally was and still can be when sin is removed. St. George similarly is not Christ, but only the English people trying to be Christian, and the dragon, while he may be part of Satan, is considerably less Satanic than Archimago or Duessa, who survive the book. No monster, however loathsome, can really be evil: for evil there must be a perversion of intelligence, and Spenser drew his dragon with some appreciation of the fact mentioned in an essay of Valéry, that in poetry the most frightful creatures always have something rather childlike about them:

> So dreadfully he towards him did pas,
> Forelifting up aloft his speckled brest,
> And often bounding on the brused gras,
> As for great ioyance of his newcome guest. (I, xi, 15)

Hence the theatre of operations in the first book is still a human world. The real heaven appears only in the vision of Jerusalem at the end of the tenth canto and in a few other traces, like the invisible husband of Charissa and the heavenly music heard in the background of the final betrothal. Eden is within the order of nature but it is a new earth turned upward, or sacramentally aligned with a new heaven. The main direction of the imagery is also upward: this upward movement is the theme of the House of

Holiness, of the final quest, and of various subordinate themes like the worship of Una by the satyrs.

We have spoken of the principle of symbolic parody, which we meet in all books of *The Faerie Queene*. Virtues are contrasted not only with their vicious opposites, but with vices that have similar names and appearances. Thus the golden mean of temperance is parodied by the golden means provided by Mammon; "That part of justice, which is equity" in Book V is parodied by the anarchistic equality preached by the giant in the second canto, and so on. As the main theme of Book I is really faith, or spiritual fidelity, the sharpest parody of this sort is between Fidelia, or true faith, and Duessa, who calls herself Fidessa. Fidelia holds a golden cup of wine and water (which in other romance patterns would be the Holy Grail, though Spenser's one reference to the Grail shows that he has no interest in it); Duessa holds the golden cup of the Whore of Babylon. Fidelia's cup also contains a serpent (the redeeming brazen serpent of Moses typifying the Crucifixion); Duessa sits on the dragon of the Apocalypse who is metaphorically the same beast as the serpent of Eden. Fidelia's power to raise the dead is stressed; Duessa raises Sansjoy from the dead by the power of Aesculapius, whose emblem is the serpent. Of all such parodies in the first book the most important for the imagery of the poem as a whole is the parody of the tree and water of life in Eden. These symbols have their demonic counterparts in the paralysed trees of Fradubio and Fraelissa and in the paralysing fountain from which St. George drinks in the seventh canto.

Thus the first book shows very clearly what we have called the subordinating of cyclical symbols to dialectical ones: the tree and water of life, originally symbols of the rebirth of spring, are here symbols of resurrection, or a permanent change from a life in physical nature above the animals to life in human nature under God. The main interest of the second book is also dialectical, but in the reverse direction, concerned with human life in the ordinary physical world, and with its separation from the demonic world below. The Bower of Bliss is a parody of Eden, and just as the climax of Book I is St. George's three-day battle with the dragon of death, so the narrative climax of Book II is Guyon's three-day endurance in the underworld. It is the climax at least as far as Guyon's heroism is concerned, for it is Arthur who defeats Maleger and it is really the Palmer who catches Acrasia.

We should expect to find in Book II, therefore, many demonic parodies of the symbols in Book I, especially of the tree and water of life and its symbolic relatives. At the beginning we note that Acrasia, like Duessa, has a golden cup of death, filled, like Fidelia's, with wine and water ("Bacchus with the nymph"). There follows Ruddymane, with his bloody hands that cannot be washed. Spenser speaks of Redcrosse's hands as "baptised" after he falls back into the well of life, and the Ruddymane incident is partly a reference to original sin, removable only by baptism or bathing in a "liuing well." The demonic counterparts of both sacraments appear in the hell scene in the cave of Mammon, in connexion with Pilate and Tantalus. Pilate, forever washing his hands in vain, repeats the Ruddymane image in its demonic context, and Tantalus is the corresponding parody of the Eucharist. These figures are preceded by the description of the golden appletree in the garden of Proserpina and the river Cocytus. Images of trees and water are considerably expanded in the description of the Bower of Bliss.

The fact that the fountain of Diana's nymph refuses to cleanse Ruddymane's hands indicates the rather subordinate role of Diana in Spenser's symbolism. It is clear, if we compare the description of Venus in Book IV with the description of Nature in the *Mutabilitie Cantos*, that Venus represents the whole order of nature, in its higher human as well as its lower physical aspect. What Diana stands for is the resistance to corruption, as symbolized by unchastity, which is the beginning, and of course always an essential part, of moral realization. Hence Diana in Spenser is a little like the law in Milton, which can discover sin but not remove it. In the *Mutabilitie Cantos* the glimpsing of Diana's nakedness by Faunus is parallel, on a small scale, to the rebellion of the lower against the higher nature which is also represented by Mutability's thrusting herself into heaven at the place of Cynthia, who is another form of Diana. Naturally Elizabeth's virginity compelled Spenser to give a high place to Diana and her protégé Belphoebe, but for symbolic as well as political reasons he preferred to make the Faerie Queene a young woman proceeding toward marriage, like Britomart. Meanwhile it is the virginal Faerie Queene whose picture Guyon carries on his shield, Guyon being in his whole moral complex something of a male Diana.

Temperance in Spenser is a rather negative virtue, being the resistance of consciousness to impulsive action which is necessary in order to know whether the action is going up or down in the moral dialectic. Conscious action is real action, Aristotle's proairesis; impulsive action is really pseudo-action, a passion which increasingly becomes passivity. Human life in the physical world has something of the feeling of an army of occupation about it, symbolized by the beleaguered castle of Alma. The House of Alma possesses two things in particular: wealth, in Ruskin's sense of well-being, and beauty, in the sense of correct proportion and ordering of parts. Its chief enemies are "Beauty, and money," the minions of Acrasia and Mammon, the external or instrumental possessions which the active mind uses and the passive mind thinks of as ends in themselves. Temperance is also good temperament, or the balancing of humours, and Guyon's enemies are mainly humours in the Elizabethan sense, although the humours are usually symbolized by their corresponding elements, as the choleric Pyrochles is associated with fire and the phlegmatic Cymochles with water. The battleground between the active and the passive mind is the area of sensation, the steady rain of impressions and stimuli coming in from the outer world which the active mind organizes and the passive mind merely yields to. Normally the sanguine humour predominates in the active mind; the passive one becomes a victim of melancholy, with its progressive weakening of will and of the power to distinguish reality from illusion. In Spenser's picture of the mind the fancy (Phantastes) is predisposed to melancholy and the influence of "oblique Saturne"; it is not the seat of the poetic imagination, as it would be in a nineteenth-century Romantic. The title of George Macdonald's *Phantastes,* the author tells us, comes not from Spenser but from Phineas Fletcher, who differs from Spenser in making Phantastes the source of art. Maleger, the leader of the assault on Alma, is a spirit of melancholy, and is sprung from the corresponding element of earth.

Having outlined the dialectical extremes of his imagery, Spenser moves on to consider the order of nature on its two main levels in the remaining books. Temperance steers a middle course between care and carelessness, jealousy and wantonness, miserliness and prodigality, Mammon's cave and Acrasia's bower. Acrasia is a kind of sinister Venus, and her victims, Mordant wallowing in his blood, Cymochles, Verdant, have something of a dead, wasted, or frustrated Adonis about them. Mammon is an old man with a daughter, Philotime. Much of the symbolism of the third book is based on these two archetypes. The first half leads up to the description of the Gardens of Adonis in Canto vi by at least three repetitions of the theme of Venus and Adonis. First we have the tapestry in the Castle Joyeous representing the story, with a longish description attached. Then comes the wounding of Marinell on his "precious shore" by Britomart (surely the most irritable heroine known to romance), where the sacrificial imagery, the laments of the nymphs, the strewing of flowers on the bier are all conventional images of Adonis. Next is Timias, discovered by Belphoebe wounded in the thigh with a boar-spear. Both Belphoebe and Marinell's mother Cymoent have pleasant retreats closely analogous to the Gardens of Adonis. In the second half of the book we have three examples of the old man and young woman relationship: Malbecco and Hellenore, Proteus and Florimell, Busirane and Amoret. All these are evil: there is no idealized version of this theme. The reason is that the idealized version would be the counterpart to the vision of charity in the *Hymn of Heavenly Love*. That is, it would be the vision of the female Sapience sitting in the bosom of the Deity that we meet at the end of the *Hymn to Heavenly Beauty*, and this would take us outside the scope of *The Faerie Queene*, or at any rate of its third book.

The central figure in the third book and the fourth is Venus, flanked on either side by Cupid and Adonis, or what a modern poet would call Eros and Thanatos. Cupid and Venus are gods of natural love, and form, not a demonic parody, but a simple analogy of Christian love, an analogy which is the symbolic basis of the *Fowre Hymnes*. Cupid, like Jesus, is lord of gods and creator of the cosmos, and simultaneously an infant, Venus' relation to him being that of an erotic Madonna, as her relation to Adonis is that of an erotic Pièta. Being androgynous, she brings forth Cupid without male assistance (see *Colin Clouts Come Home Again*, 800 ff.); she loses him and goes in search of him, and he returns in triumph in the great masque at the end as lord of all creation.

The Garden of Adonis, with its Genius and its temperate climate, is so carefully paralleled to the Bower of Bliss that it clearly represents the reality of which the Bower is a mirage. It presents the order of nature as a cyclical process of death and renewal, in itself morally innocent, but still within the realm of Mutability, as the presence of Time shows. Like Eden, it is a paradise: it is nature as nature would be if man could live in his proper human world, the "antique" Golden Age. It is a world where substance is constant but where "Forms are variable and decay"; and hence it is closely connected with the theme of metamorphosis, which is the central symbol of divine love as the pagans conceived it.

Such love naturally has its perverted form, represented by the possessive jealousy of Malbecco, Busirane, and Proteus, all of whom enact variants of the myth of Tithonus and Aurora, the aged lover and the struggling dawn. Hellenore escapes into the world of satyrs, a world too "natural" to be wholly sinful. The torturing of Amoret by Busirane, representing the anguish of jealous love, recurs in various images of bleeding, such as the "long bloody river" in the tapestry of Cupid. Painful or not, it is love that makes the world go round, that keeps the cycle of nature turning, and it is particularly the love of Marinell and Florimell, whose names suggest water and vegetation, that seems linked to the natural cycle. Florimell is imprisoned under the sea during a kind of symbolic winter in which a "snowy" Florimell takes her place. Marinell is not cured of his illness until his mother turns from "watry gods" to the sun, and when he sees Florimell he revives

> As withered weed through cruell winters tine,
> That feels the warmth of sunny beam's reflection
> Lifts up his head, that did before decline
> And gins to spread his leaf before the fair sunshine.
>   (IV, xii, 34)

Book IV is full of images of natural revival, some in very unlikely places, and it comes to a climax with the symbolism of the tree and water of life in their natural context. At the temple of Venus, we are told, "No tree, that is of count . . . But there was planted," and the next canto is a tremendous outburst of water. The wedding of the Thames and the Medway takes place in Proteus' hall, and Proteus, in the mythological handbooks, is the spirit of metamorphosis, the liquid energy of substance driving through endless varieties of form.

The impulse in sexual love is toward union in one flesh, which is part of the symbolism of Christian marriage. The original conclusion to Book III leaves Scudamour and Amoret locked in an embrace which makes them look like a single hermaphrodite. The reason for this curious epithet becomes clear in Book IV, where we learn that Venus herself is hermaphroditic, and of course all embracing lovers are epiphanies of Venus. Naturally this image lends itself to demonic parody, as in the incestuous birth of Oliphant and Argante. Britomart watches Scudamour and Amoret rather enviously, making a mental resolve to get herself into the same position as soon as she can run her Artegall to earth: for Britomart, though as chaste as Belphoebe, is not vowed to virginity. Perhaps it is her accessibility to human emotions that is symbolized by the bleeding wound she receives from an arrow in the first canto of Book III, an image repeated, with a symmetry unusual even in Spenser, in the last canto.

A slight extension of the same symbol of unity through love takes us into the area of social love, or friendship, the theme of the fourth book. Friendship shows, even more clearly than sexual passion, the power of love as a creative force, separating the elements from chaos by the attraction of like to like. The human counterpart of this ordering of elements is concord or harmony, for which Spenser uses various symbols, notably the golden chain, an image introduced into Book I and parodied by the chain of ambition in the cave of Mammon. We also have the image of two (or three) souls united in one body in the extremely tedious account of Priamond, Diamond, and Triamond. It is rather more interesting that Spenser seems to regard the poetic tradition as a community of friendship of a similar kind. In all six books of *The Faerie Queene* it is only in the fourth that Spenser refers *explicitly* to his two great models Chaucer and Ariosto, and his phrase about Chaucer is significant: "thine own spirit, which doth in me survive."

When we move from friendship, an abstract pattern of human community which only noble spirits can form, to justice, in which the base and evil must also be included, we return to historical allegory. Spenser's vision of history (III, ix) focuses on the legend of Troy: the first Troy is recalled by Hellenore and Paridell, and the second, or Rome, by Duessa, who reappears in Books IV and V. The third is of course England itself, which will not collapse in adultery or superstition if her leading poet can prevent it. In the prophecy of this third Troy we meet an image connected with the wedding of the Thames in Book IV:

> It [sc. London] Troynovant is hight, that with the waves
> Of wealthy Thamis washed is along,
> Upon whose stubborn neck, whereat he raves
> With roaring rage, and sore himself does throng,
> That all men fear to tempt his billows strong,
> She fastened hath her foot, which stands so high
> That it a wonder of the world is sung
> In foreign lands, and all which passen by,
> Beholding it from far, do think it threats the sky. (III, ix, 45)

I quote this poetically licentious description of the Thames because it is so closely linked with Spenser's conception of justice as the harnessing of physical power to conquer physical nature. In its lower aspects this power is mechanical, symbolized by the "yron man" Talus, who must be one of the earliest "science fiction" or technological symbols in poetry, and who kills without discrimination for the sake of discrimination, like a South African policeman.

In its higher aspects where justice becomes equity, or consideration of circumstances, the central image is this one of the virgin guiding the raging monster. We meet this image very early in the adventures of Una and the lion in Book I, and the same symbolic shape reappears in the Gardens of Adonis, where Venus enjoys Adonis with the boar imprisoned in a cave underneath. Next comes the training of Artegall (who begins his career by taming animals) by Astraea, identified with the constellation Virgo. Next is the vision of Isis, where Osiris and the crocodile correspond to Adonis and the boar earlier, but are here explicitly identified. Finally we have Mercilla and the lion under her throne, where Spenser naturally refrains from speculating on the lion's possible identity with a human lover. It may be the link with London on the Thames that lends such prominence in Book V to the image of the river washing away the filth of injustice. At the same time the virgin who dominates the beast is herself the servant of an invisible male deity, hence the figure of the female rebel is important in the last two books: Radigund the Amazon in Book V, who rebels against justice, and Mirabell in Book VI, who rebels against courtesy. Radigund is associated with the moon because she parodies Isis, and Isis is associated with the moon partly because Queen Elizabeth is, by virtue of Raleigh's name for her, Cynthia.

Just as Book III deals with the secular and natural counterpart of love, so Book VI deals with the secular and natural counterpart of grace. The word grace itself in all its human manifestations is a thematic word in this book, and when the Graces themselves appear on Mount Acidale we find ourselves in a world that transcends the world of Venus:

> These three to men all gifts of grace do graunt,
> And all that Venus in herself doth vaunt
> Is borrowed of them. (VI, x, 15)

The Graces, we are told, were begotten by Jove when he returned from the wedding of Peleus and Thetis. This wedding is referred to again in the *Mutabilitie Cantos* as the most festive occasion the gods had held before the lawsuit of Mutability. For it was at this wedding that Jove was originally "confirmed in his imperial see": the marriage to Peleus removed the threat to Jove's power coming from the son of Thetis, a threat the secret of which only Prometheus knew, and which Prometheus was crucified on a rock for not revealing. Thus the wedding also led, though Spenser does not tell us this, to the reconciling of Jove and Prometheus, and it was Prometheus, whose name traditionally means forethought or wisdom, who, according to Book II, was the originator of Elves and Fays—that is, of man's moral and conscious nature. There are still many demonic symbols in Book VI, especially the attempt to sacrifice Serena, where the custom of eating the flesh and giving the blood to the priests has obvious overtones of parody. But the centre of symbolic gravity, so to speak, in Book VI is a pastoral Arcadian world, where we seem almost to be entering into the original home of man where, as in the child's world of Dylan Thomas's *Fern Hill*, it was all Adam and maiden. It is no longer the world of Eros; yet the sixth book is the most erotic, in the best sense, of all the books in the poem, full of innocent nakedness and copulation, the surprising of which is so acid a test of courtesy, and with many symbols of the state of innocence and of possible regeneration like the Salvage Man and the recognition scene in which Pastorella is reunited to her parents.

Such a world is a world in which the distinction between art and nature is disappearing because nature is taking on a human form. In the Bower of Bliss the *mixing* of art and nature is what is stressed: on Mount Acidale the art itself is nature, to quote Polixenes again. Yet art, especially poetry, has a central place in the legend of courtesy. Grace in religion implies revelation by the Word, and human grace depends much on good human words. All through the second part of *The Faerie Queene*, slander is portrayed as the worst enemy of the human community: we have Ate and Sclaunder herself in Book IV, Malfont with his tongue nailed to a post in Mercilla's court, as an allegory of what ought to be done to *other* poets; and finally the Blatant Beast, the voice of rumour full of tongues. The dependence of courtesy on reasonable speech is emphasized at every turn, and just as the legend of justice leads us to the figure of the Queen, as set forth in Mercilla, who manifests the order of society, so the legend of courtesy leads us to the figure of the poet himself, who manifests the order of words.

When Calidore commits his one discourteous act and interrupts Colin Clout, all the figures dancing to his pipe vanish. In Elizabethan English a common meaning of art was magic, and Spenser's Colin Clout, like Shakespeare's Prospero, has the magical power of summoning spirits to enact his present fancies, spirits who disappear if anyone speaks and breaks the spell. Nature similarly vanishes mysteriously at the end of the *Mutabilitie Cantos*, just as the counterpart to Prospero's revels is his subsequent speech on the disappearance of all created things. Colin Clout, understandably annoyed at being suddenly deprived of the company of a hundred and four naked maidens, destroys his pipe, as Prospero drowns his book. Poetry works by suggestion and indirection, and conveys meanings out of all proportion to its words; but in magic the impulse to complete a pattern is very strong. If a spirit is being conjured by the seventy-two names of God as set forth in the *Schemhamphoras*, it will not do if the magician can remember only seventy-one of them. At the end of the sixth book the magician in Spenser had completed half of his gigantic design, and was ready to start on the other half. But the poet in Spenser was satisfied: he had done his work, and his vision was complete.

≥ How True a Twain

ANY CRITIC OF SHAKESPEARE'S SONNETS WILL, TO SOME EXTENT, TELL the world more about his own critical limitations than about his subject; and if he starts out with very marked limitations, the clear surface of the sonnets will faithfully reflect them. Many readers tend to assume that poetry is a record of a poet's experience. Those who tell us that Shakespeare must have been a lawyer to have known so much about law, or a nobleman in disguise to have known so much about aristocratic psychology, always start with this assumption as their major premise. The assumption is then used in value-judgments. First-hand experience in life and second-hand experience derived from books are correlated with good and less good poetry respectively. Poem A is very good; therefore a genuine experience must lie behind it; Poem B is duller, so it must be a "mere literary exercise," where the poet's "real feelings" are not involved. Included in these assumptions, of course, is the view that convention is the opposite of originality, and the mark of inferior writers. It is particularly the lyric that suffers from such notions, as nobody can do much about the fact that every *play* of Shakespeare's tells a story that he got out of a book. And while experienced critics would repudiate all this in theory, still Shakespeare was an expert in keeping his personal life out of our reach, and we find this so tantalizing that any hint of more information about that life is apt to lower the threshold of a critic's discretion. The sonnets, therefore, still have power to release the frustrated Baconian who is inside so many Shakespearean scholars.

The first point to get clear is that if we read the sonnets as transcripts of experience, we are not reading them realistically but allegorically, as a series of cryptic allusions in which a rival poet may be Chapman, a mortal moon Queen Elizabeth, and a man in hue somebody named Hughes. Now if we approach the sonnets in this crude allegorical way, they become "riddles" of a most peculiar kind. They begin with seventeen appeals to a beautiful youth to beget a son. Rationalizing readers tell us that the poet is urging the youth to marry, but only one of these sonnets—the eighth—has any serious treatment of marriage. True, the youth is urged to marry as the only legal means of producing offspring, but apparently any woman will do: it is not suggested that he should fall in love or that there is any possibility of his producing daughters or even a son who takes after his mother, which seems curious when the youth himself does. In real life, one would think, the only possible reply from the youth would be that of Christ to Satan in *Paradise Regained:* "Why art *thou* solicitous?"

The poet then drops his appeal and falls in love with the youth himself. We next observe that although the poet promises the youth immortality, and clearly has the power to confer it, he does not lift a metrical foot to make the youth a credible or interesting person. He repeats obsessively that the youth is beautiful, and sometimes true and kind, if not overvirtuous; but in real life one would think that a poet who loved him so much would delight in telling us at least about his accomplishments, if he had any. Could he carry on a conversation, make puns, argue about religion, ride to hounds, wear his clothes with a dash, sing in a madrigal? The world's greatest master of characterization will not give him the individualizing touch that he so seldom refuses to the humblest of his dramatic creations. Of course, if we are predetermined to see the Earl of Southampton or some other witty and cultivated person in the youth, we may ascribe qualities to him that the poet does not. But considering him as a real person, and reading only what is there, we are forced to conclude that Shakespeare has lavished a century of the greatest sonnets in the language on an unresponsive oaf as stupid as a doorknob and as selfish as a weasel. Shakespeare expected the Earl of Southampton to be amused by his somewhat indecorous tale of a sulky urchin who was beloved by Venus herself and would not rise to the occasion. But the youth of the sonnets is more like the Adonis of that poem than he is like any appreciative reader of it.

Besides—who exactly is given immortality by the sonnets? Well, there was this Mr. W. H., except that some people think he was H. W. and that he wasn't a Mr. And how do we learn about this Mr. W. H., or this not-Mr. H. W.? Through one floundering and illiterate sentence, to call it that by courtesy, which was not written by Shakespeare, not addressed to us, and no more likely to be an accurate statement of fact than any other commercial plug. We are also referred to a story told in *Willobie his Avisa* about a certain H. W., who, "being suddenly infected with the contagion of a fantastical fit, at the first sight of A(visa), pineth a while in secret grief, at length not able any longer to endure the burning heat of so fervent a humour, bewrayeth the secrecy of his disease unto his familiar friend W. S." In short, a very literary story. As an account of something happening in real life, Polonius might believe it, but hardly Rosalind. We are not told that the youth of the sonnets wanted immortality, but if he did he would have done better to marry and beget a son, as he was advised to do all along. About all that one can get out of the sonnets, considered as transcripts of experience, is the reflection that pederastic infatuations with beautiful and stupid boys are probably very bad for practicing dramatists.

This conclusion is so grotesque that one would expect any critic who reached it to retrace his steps at once. But we often find such critics merely trying to save the face of the ridiculous creature that they have themselves created. Benson, the compiler of the 1640 edition of the sonnets, simply altered pronouns, but this is a trifle robust for the modern conscience. Coleridge disapproved of homosexual sentiments in poetry, and sneered at Virgil as a second-rate poet all his life because Virgil wrote the Second Eclogue; but Coleridge had practically signed a contract to endorse everything that Shakespeare wrote, so what to do? Well: "It seems to me that the sonnets could only have come from a man deeply in love, and in love with a woman; and there is one sonnet which, from its incongruity, I take to be a purposed blind." Another critic urges that the sonnets *must* be regarded as Shakespeare's earliest work, written in time for him to have got this affair out of his system, for if they are later, Shakespeare's personality must be considered "unwholesome." And what critic urges this? Samuel Butler, author of *Erewhon Revisited*, that genial spoofing of the eternal human tendency to turn untidy facts into symmetrical myths!

The same fate seems to pursue even the details of the allegorical approach. The line in Sonnet 107, "The mortal moon hath her eclipse endur'd," sounds as though it referred to Queen Elizabeth. If so, it means either that she died or that she didn't die, in which case it was presumably written either in 1603 or some time before 1603. Unless, that is, it is a retrospective allusion, of a kind that dilatory poets are only too apt to make, or unless it doesn't refer to Elizabeth at all, in which case it could have been written at any time between 1603 and its publication in 1609. Once again we feel uneasily that "Shakespeare the man" is slipping out of our grasp.

We should be better advised to start with the assumption that the sonnets are poetry, therefore written within a specific literary tradition and a specific literary genre, both of which were developed for specifically literary reasons. The tradition had developed in the Middle Ages, but would hardly have had so much vitality in Shakespeare's day without a contemporary context. In the Renaissance, anyone who wanted to be a serious poet had to work at it. He was supposed to be what Gabriel Harvey called a "curious universal scholar" as well as a practical expert in every known rhetorical device—and Renaissance writers knew many more rhetorical devices than we do. But learning and expertise would avail him little if he didn't, as we say, "have it." Have what? Have a powerful and disciplined imagination, to use the modern term, which, by struggling with the most tempestuous emotions, had learned to control them like plunging horses and force them into the service of poetry. True, the greatest moments of poetic *furor* and *raptus* are involuntary, but they never descend on those who are not ready for them. Could one acquire such an imagination if one didn't have it? No, but one could develop it if one did have it. How? Well, the strongest of human emotions, love, was also the most easily available.

The experience of love thus had a peculiarly close relation to the training of the poet, a point of some importance for understanding Shakespeare's sonnets. Love was for the Renaissance poet a kind of creative yoga, an imaginative discipline in which he watched the strongest possible feelings swirling around sexual excitement, jealousy, obsession, melancholy, as he was snubbed, inspired, teased, ennobled, forsaken, or made blissful by his mistress. The Renaissance poet was not expected to drift through life gaining "experience" and writing it up in poetry. He was expected to turn his mind into an emotional laboratory and gain his experience there under high pressure and close observation. Literature provided him with a convention, and the convention supplied the literary categories and forms into which his amorphous emotions were to be poured. Thus his imaginative development and his reading and study of literature advanced together and cross-fertilized one another.

Of course the experience of love is a real experience. It is not assumed that the youth trying to be a poet talks himself into a certain state of mind; it is assumed that, if normal, he will feel the emotion of love at some time or other, and that, if destined to be a poet, he will not fall in love tepidly or realistically but head-over-heels. But the experience of love and the writing of love poetry do not necessarily have any direct connection. One is experience, the other craftsmanship. So if we ask, is there a real mistress or does the poet merely make it all up? the answer is that an either-or way of putting the question is wrong. Modern criticism has developed the term "imagination" precisely to get around this unreal dilemma. Poetry is not reporting on experience, and love is not an uncultivated experience; in both poetry and love, reality is what is created, not the raw material for the creation.

The typical emotions inspired in the poet by love are thus formed into the typical patterns of literary convention. When the conventions of love poetry developed, the model for most of these patterns was the spiritual discipline of Christianity. In Christianity one may, with no apparent cause, become spiritually awakened, conscious of sin and of being under the wrath of God, and bound to a life of unconditional service to God's will. Much courtly love poetry was based on a secular and erotic analogy of Christian love. The poet falls in love at first sight, involuntarily or even with reluctance. The God of Love, angry at being neglected, has walked into his life and taken it over, and is now his "lord." His days of liberty are over, and ahead of him is nothing but unquestioning devotion to Love's commands. The first thing he must do is supplicate his mistress for "grace," and a mistress who did not demand long sieges of complaint, prayers for mercy, and protests against her inflexible cruelty was a conventionally impossible female. The mock-religious language, so elaborately developed in the Middle Ages, was still going strong in Shakespeare's day: Spenser's twenty-second *Amoretti* sonnet, for instance, moves at once from the Christian Lent into the Temple of Venus, where we find "saint," "image," "priests," "altar," "sacrifice," "goddess," and "relics."

The secular and erotic counterpart of the Madonna and Child was Venus and Eros, or Cupid. Cupid was a little boy shooting arrows, and at the same time he was, like his Christian counterpart, the greatest of the gods and the creator of the universe, which had arisen from chaos by the "attraction" of like particles. The domain of Eros included heat, energy, desire, love, and subjective emotion; Venus had the complementary area of light, form, desirability, beauty, and objective proportion. In a sense all lovers are incarnations of Eros, and all loved ones incarnations of Venus. One may express this by simple metonymy: thus Ovid, in a passage in the *Amores* which certainly caught Shakespeare's eye, remarks that while he prefers blondes, he can also get interested in a "Venus" with dark hair:

> est etiam in fusco grata colore Venus.

The possible scale of themes in courtly love poetry is as broad as love itself, and may have any kind of relationship to its Christian model, from an integral part to a contrast or even a parody. We may divide the scale into "high" and "low" phases, using these terms diagrammatically and not morally. In the "high" phases love is a spiritual education and a discipline of the soul, which leads the lover upward from the sensible to the eternal world. In Dante, the love of Beatrice, announced in the *Vita Nuova*, is a spiritual education of this sort leading straight to its own logical fulfillment in the Christian faith. It not only survives the death of Beatrice, but in the *Commedia* the same love conveys the poet upward from the top of Purgatory into the divine presence itself. Dante's love for Beatrice was the emotional focus of his life, but at no point was it a sexual love or connected with marriage. The philosophy of Plato, where one moves from the body's attraction to the physical reflection of reality upward to the soul's union with the form of reality, provided a convenient framework for later treatments of the "high" version of the convention. We find this Platonized form of love in Michelangelo and in the speech of Cardinal Bembo at the end of Castiglione's *Courtier*.

Next comes what we may call the Petrarchan norm, a conflict of human emotions in which the main theme is still unswerving devotion and supplications for grace. In Petrarch the human situation in love is far more elaborately analyzed than in Dante, but as in Dante the poet's love survives the death of Laura and does not depend on sexual experience. In Christianity love for God is obviously its own reward, because God is love. The Petrarchan poet similarly often finds that it is love itself, not the female embodiment of it, which fulfills his desire, and such a love could logically survive the death of the beloved, or be content, as Herrick says his is, with a contact of almost unbearable refinement:

> Only to kiss the air
> That lately kissed thee.

In Petrarch, however, there is more emphasis placed on physical frustration than on spiritual fulfillment, and the same is true of most of his followers. At this point the relation between heavenly and earthly love begins to appear as a contrast, as it often does in

Petrarch himself. Thus Spenser writes his hymns to Heavenly Love (Christ) and Heavenly Beauty (the Wisdom of the Book of Proverbs) as an alleged palinode to his courtly love hymns to Eros and Venus, and Sidney indicates in his famous "Leave me, O Love" sonnet a "higher" perspective on the story told in *Astrophel and Stella*.

In the middle of the scale comes the mistress as potential wife: this was still a rather rare form in love poetry, though of course normal for drama and romance. It is represented in English literature by Spenser's *Amoretti* sequence. We then move into the "low" area of more concrete and human relations, sometimes called anti-Petrarchan, the centre of gravity of the *Songs and Sonnets* of Donne, who remarks:

> Love's not so pure and abstract, as they use
> To say, which have no mistress but their Muse.

Here the poet is less aware of the dialectic of Eros and Agape, and more aware of another kind of dialectic established in the normal opening of the convention, when the poet first falls in love. When the God of Love enters the poet's life, the poet may regret his lost liberty of not having to serve a mistress, or he may contrast the bondage of his passion with the freedom of reason. He finds that in this context his love is inseparable from hatred—not necessarily hatred of the mistress, except in cases of jealousy, but hatred of the emotional damage done to his life by love. The God of Love in this situation is a tyrant, and the poet cannot identify the god's will with his own desire. Such moods of despair are often attached to palinodes, or they may be understood to be necessary early stages, where the poet is still establishing his constancy. But in "lower" phases the poet may get fed up with having so much demanded of him by the code and renounce love altogether; or the mistress may be abused as a monster of frigidity who has brought about her lover's death; or the poet may flit from one mistress to another or plunge into cynical amours with women of easy virtue— in short, parody the convention. Ovid, who as far as Shakespeare was concerned was by long odds the world's greatest poet, had a good deal of influence on these "low" phases of courtly love, as Platonism had on the "higher" ones.

It does not follow that the "lower" one goes, the more realistic the treatment becomes. This happens only to a very limited extent. The mistress normally remains almost equally uncharacterized at all stages: the poet is preoccupied with the emotions in himself which the mistress has caused, and with her only as source and goal of these emotions. Similarly with Shakespeare's youth: he is not characterized, in any realistic sense, because the conventions and genres employed exclude that kind of characterization. It is interesting to contrast the sonnets from this point of view with the narrative poem *A Lover's Complaint*, which, whoever wrote it, follows the sonnets in the 1609 Quarto, and presents three characters roughly parallel to the three major characters of the sonnets. Here what belongs to the genre is not so much characterization as description, which is given in abundance.

It was assumed that the major poet would eventually move on to the major genres, epic and tragedy, and from the expression of his own emotions to the expression of heroic ones. The young professional poet learning his trade, and the amateur too high in social rank to become a professional, both tended to remain within the conventions and genres appropriate to love poetry. The appropriate genres included the love lyric and the pastoral. In the love lyric the source of love was a mistress descended from the line of Laura; in the pastoral, following the example of Virgil's Second Eclogue, the love of two men for one another was more frequent. Here again the influence of Plato, in whose conception of love there are no mistresses, but the love of an older man for a younger one, has to be allowed for. Spenser began his career with the pastoral poetry of *The Shepheardes Calender*, because, according to his editor E. K., he intended to go on to epic, and pastoral was a normal genre in which to serve his apprenticeship. In "January," the first eclogue, Spenser represents himself as the shepherd Colin Clout, in love with one Rosalind, but also dearly attached to another shepherd named Hobbinol. E. K. explains in a note that such an attachment has nothing to do with pederasty (just as love for a mistress has no necessary, or even frequent, connection with adulterous liaisons). Spenser devoted the third book of *The Faerie Queene* to chastity, which for him included both married love and courtly *Frauendienst*, and the fourth book to friendship. In the Temple of Venus, described in the tenth canto of the fourth book, pairs of male friends are given an honored place, as friendship has a disinterested factor in it which for Spenser puts it among the "high" forms of courtly love. Examples include Hercules and Hylas, David and Jonathan, and Damon and Pythias. Such friends are called lovers, and it was conventional for male friends to use the language of love, just as it was conventional for a lover to shed floods of tears when disdained by his mistress. Similarly in Shakeₚeare the relation of poet to youth is one of love, but it is assumed (in Sonnet 20 and elsewhere) that neither the youth nor the poet has any sexual interest except in women. The "homosexual" view of the sonnets disappears at once as soon as we stop reading them as bad allegory.

After all the research, the speculation, and the guesswork, our knowledge of what in the sonnets is direct biographical allegory remains precisely zero. Anything may be; nothing must be, and what has produced them is not an experience like ours, but a creative imagination very unlike ours. Our ignorance is too complete to be accidental. The establishing of a recognized convention is of enormous benefit to poets, as it enables them to split off personal sincerity from literary sincerity, and personal emotion from communicable emotion. When emotions are made communicable by being conventionalized, the characters on whom they are projected may expand into figures of universal scope and infinitely haunting variety. Thus every syllable of Campion's wonderful song, "When thou must home to shades of underground," is pure convention, and no knowledge of the women in Campion's life could possibly have the least relevance to it. But it is the convention that has enabled him to realize so vividly the figure of the sinister underworld queen who has run through literature from Ishtar to the *femmes fatales* of our own day. Anyone who thinks he can write a better poem out of a "real experience" is welcome to try, but he cannot read Campion's poem with any understanding unless he realizes that the convention is not working against the emotion, but has released the emotion. The same principle applies to characterization. By suppressing realistic characterization, convention develops another kind, an archetypal character who is not individualized, but becomes a focus of our whole literary experience.

In Shakespeare's sonnets, the beautiful-youth group tells a "high" story of devotion, in the course of which the poet discovers that the reality of his love is the love itself rather than anything he receives from the beloved. Here, as in Petrarch and Sidney, the love proves to be an ennobling discipline although the experience itself is full of suffering and frustration. The dark-lady group is "low" and revolves around the theme of *odi et amo*. In the beautiful-youth group Shakespeare has adopted the disturbing and strikingly original device of associating the loved one with Eros rather than Venus, a beautiful boy who, like the regular mistress, is primarily a source of love rather than a responding lover. Other familiar landmarks of the convention can be easily recognized. The poet is the slave of his beloved; he cannot sleep for thinking of him; their souls are in one another's breasts; the poet protests his constancy and alleges that he has no theme for verse except his love; he is struck dumb with shame and bashfulness in the presence of his love; he ascribes all his virtues and talents to his love; his verse will immortalize the beloved; his love is triumphant over death (as the love of Dante and Petrarch survived the death of Beatrice and Laura, respectively); yet he continually finds love a compulsory anguish.

It is a reasonable assumption that Sonnets 1 through 126 are in sequence. There is a logic and rightness in their order which is greatly superior to that of any proposed rearrangement (such as Sir Denys Bray's "rhyme-link" scheme), and this order is at least as likely to be the author's as the editor's, for Thorpe, unlike Benson, shows no signs of officious editorial meddling. Sonnet 126, a twelve-line poem in couplets containing a masterly summary of the themes and images of the beautiful-youth group, is inescapably the "envoy" of the series—any interpretation that attempts to remove it from this position must have something wrong with it. The repetition of "render," too, shows that it closely follows on the difficult but crucial Sonnet 125. If, then, Sonnets 1 through 126 are in sequence, the rationale of that sequence would be roughly as follows:

We begin with a prelude which we may call "The Awakening of Narcissus," where the poet urges the youth to beget a son in his own likeness. In Sonnet 17 this theme modulates into the theme of gaining eternal youth through the poet's verse instead of through progeny, and this in turn modulates into the main theme of the poet's own love for the youth. The poet then revolves around the youth in a series of three cycles, each of which apparently lasts for a year (Sonnet 104), and takes him through every aspect of his love, from the most ecstatic to the most woebegone. At the beginning of the first cycle the poet is confident of the youth's love and feels that his genius as a poet is being released by it, and the great roar of triumph in Sonnet 19 is its high point. Gradually the poet's reflections become more melancholy and more independent of his love. In Sonnet 30 the final couplet seems almost deliberately perfunctory, a perceptible tug pulling us back to the main theme. The poet's age begins to haunt him in 22; a sense of the inadequacy of his poetry enters in 32, and his fortunes seem to sink as the cycle progresses, until by 37 he is not only old but lame, poor, and despised. Already in 33 a tone of reproach has begun, and with reproach comes, in 36, a feeling of the necessity of separation. Reproach is renewed in 40, where we learn that the youth has stolen the poet's mistress. In 50 the poet has wandered far away from the youth, but in this and the following sonnet he is riding back to his friend on horseback.

The phrase "Sweet love, renew thy force" in 56 indicates that we are near the beginning of a second cycle, which starts in 52. The slightly effusive praise of the youth in 17 is repeated in 53; the feeling of confidence in the poet's verse, which we met in 19, returns in 55; and the sense of identification with the youth, glanced at in 22, returns in 62. As before, however, the poet's meditations become increasingly melancholy, as in 65 and 66, where again the final couplets seem to jerk us back with an effort to the theme of love. By 71 the poet is preoccupied with images of old age, winter, and death. His poetry, in 76, again seems to him sterile and barren, and in 78 the theme of the rival poet begins. This theme corresponds to that of the stolen mistress in the first cycle, and the two together form an ironic counterpoint to the theme of the opening sonnets. Instead of acquiring a wife and transferring his beauty to a successor, the youth has acquired the poet's mistress and transferred his patronage to a second poet. A bitter series of reproaches follows, with the theme of separation reappearing in 87. In 92, however, we have a hint of a different perspective on the whole subject:

> I see a better state to me belongs
> Than that, which on thy humour doth depend.

This second cycle ends in 96, and a third cycle abruptly begins in 97, with a great rush of coming-of-spring images. Once again, in 100 with its phrase "Return, forgetful Muse," the poet is restored to confidence in his poetry; once again, in 106, the youth is effusively praised; once again, in 107, the poet promises the youth immortality in his verse. Again more melancholy and introspective reflections succeed, but this time the poet does not go around the cycle. He replaces reproach with self-reproach, or, more accurately, he replaces disillusionment with self-knowledge, and gradually finds the possession of what he has struggled for, not in the youth as a separate person, but in the love that unites him with the youth. In 116 the poet discovers the immortality of love; in 123 his own love achieves immortality; in 124 the phrase "my dear love" refers primarily to the poet's love; in 125 the poet's heart is accepted as an "oblation," and in 126 the youth, now only a lovely mirage, is abandoned to nature and time. Thus the problem stated in the opening sonnets, of how to perpetuate the youth's beauty, has been solved by poetic logic. It is the poet's love, not the youth's marriage, which has created a new youth, and one capable of preserving his loveliness forever. This at any rate is the "argument" of these sonnets whether they are in sequence or not, and we reach the same conclusion if we disregard sequence and simply study the imagery.

If Shakespeare himself had identified a specific person with the beautiful youth of the sonnets, that person would have had much the same relation to the youth that Edward King has to Lycidas. Milton tells us that *Lycidas* was written to commemorate the drowning of a "learned friend." But *Lycidas*, as a poem, is a pastoral elegy about Lycidas, and Lycidas is a literary and mythological figure, whose relatives are the Adonis and Daphnis of classical pastoral elegies. Similarly, the beautiful youth, though human, incarnates a divine beauty, and so is a kind of manifestation of Eros: "A god in love, to whom I am confined." Just as other love poets were fond of saying that their mistress was a goddess to rival Venus or the Platonic form of beauty that had fallen by accident into the lower world, so the youth is the "rose" (in its Elizabethan sense of "primate") or "pattern" of beauty, a kind of erotic Messiah to whom all past ages have been leading up (17, 53, and 106, or what we have called the "effusive" sonnets), whose death will be "Truth and Beauty's doom and date." In short, he is a divine man urged, like other divine men, to set about transferring his divinity to a younger successor as soon as he reaches the height of his own powers. And whether the sonnets are in sequence or not, he is consistently associated with the spring and summer of the natural cycle, and winter and old age are associated with absence from him. His moral character has the same associations: it is spring or summer when he is lovable and winter when he is reproachable.

The poet cannot keep the resolution announced in Sonnet 21 of detaching the youth from nature. A human being is a microcosm of nature, and the most obvious and conspicuous form of nature is the cycle. In the cycle there are two elements of poetic importance. One is the fact that winter and summer, age and youth, darkness and light, are always a contrast. The other is the continual passing of one into the other, or the cycle proper. The first element suggests an ultimate separation of a world of youth, light, and "eternal summer" from its opposite. This can never happen in experience, but it would be nice to live in the paradisal *ver perpetuum* that the youth's beauty symbolizes (Sonnet 53), and poetry is based on what might be, not on what is. The second element suggests universal mutability and decay. Thus if a final separation of the two poles of the cycle is conceivable, the lower pole will be identical with the cycle as such, and the world of winter, darkness, and age will be seen as the wheel of time that carries all created things, including the blossoms of spring, away into itself.

Time is the enemy of all things in the sonnets, the universal devourer that reduces everything to nonexistence. It is associated with a great variety of eating metaphors, the canker eating the rose, the festering lily, the earth devouring its brood, and the like, which imply disappearance rather than digestion. Death is only a small aspect of time's power: what is really terrifying about time is its capacity for annihilation. Hence the financial metaphors of "lease," "audit," and similar bargains with time are continually associated with the more sinister images of "expense" and "waste." The phrase "wastes of time" in Sonnet 12 carries the heaviest possible weight of brooding menace. Nature itself, though a force making for life as time makes for death, is capable only of "temporary" or time-bound resistance to time. Behind the daily cycle of the sun, the yearly cycle of the seasons, the generation cycle of human life, are the slower cycles of empires that build up pyramids with newer might, and the cosmological cycles glanced at in Sonnets 60 and 64, with their Ovidian echoes. But though slower, they are making for the same goal.

Nature in the sonnets, as in many of the plays, is closely associated with fortune, and the cycle of nature with fortune's wheel. Those who think of fortune as more substantial than a wheel are the "fools of time," who, whatever they are in Sonnet 124, include the painful warrior who is defeated and forgotten and the makers of "policy, that heretic"—policy, in contrast to justice or statesmanship, being the kind of expediency that merely greases the wheel of fortune. Royal figures are also, in Sonnets 7, 33, and perhaps 107, associated with the cycle of nature: they pass into "eclipse" like the sun and moon turning down from the height of heaven.

The nadir of experience is represented by the terrible Sonnet 129, which, starting from the thematic words "expense" and "waste," describes what a life completely bound to time is like, with the donkey's carrot of passion jerking us along its homeless road, causing an agonizing wrench of remorse at every instant. Directly above is "the heaven that leads men to this hell," and which includes in its many mansions the fool's paradise in which the youth is living in the opening sonnets. Here we must distinguish the poet's tone, which is tender and affectionate, from his imagery, which is disconcertingly sharp. As Sonnet 94 explains in a bitterer context, the youth causes but does not produce love: he is a self-enclosed "bud," contracted to his own bright eyes like Narcissus. As with a child, his self-absorption is part of his charm. He does not need to seek a beauty in women which he already contains (Sonnet 20, where all the rhymes are "feminine"). He lacks nothing, so he is never in search: he merely attracts, even to the point of becoming, in Sonnet 31, a charnel-house of the poet's dead loves. He is therefore not on the side of nature with her interest in "increase," "store," and renewed life, but on the side of time and its devouring "waste." He is his own gradually fading reflection in water, not "A liquid prisoner pent in walls of glass," or a seed which maintains an underground resistance to time. The poet's arguments in Sonnets 1-17 are not intended to be specious, like the similar-sounding arguments of Venus to Adonis. The youth is (by implication at least) "the tomb of his self-love," which is really a hatred turned against himself, and has no future but "folly, age, and cold decay."

It would take a large book to work out in detail the complications of the imagery of eyes and heart, of shadow and substance, of picture and treasure, around which the argument of the beautiful-youth sonnets revolves. We can only try to give the main point of it. Above the self-enclosed narcissistic world of the youth of the opening sonnets, there appear to be three main levels of experience. There is the world of ordinary experience, a physical world of subject and object, a world where lover and beloved are essentially separated. This is the world associated with winter and absence, with the "lower" elements of earth and water (Sonnet 44), with the poet's age and poverty which increase the sense of separateness, with the reproach and scandal that separate them mentally and morally. This is also the world in which the poet is a busy actor-dramatist, with a capacity for subduing his nature to what it works in unrivalled in the history of culture, a career which leaves him not only without a private life but almost without a private personality.

Then there is a world above this of lover and beloved in contact, a quasi-paradisal world associated with the presence and kindness of the youth, with spring and summer, with air and fire in Sonnet 45, with content, ecstasy, forgiveness, and reconciliation. It is in this world that the youth appears like a god of love, associated with the sun and its gift of life, the spirit who appears everywhere in nature (Sonnet 113), the god of the spring flowers (99), all hues in his controlling. But even in this world he is still a separate person, contemplated and adored.

There is still another world above this, a world which is above time itself. This is the world in which lover and beloved are not simply in contact, but are identified. The union symbolized by the "one flesh" of Christian marriage is a sexual union: this is the kind of union expressed in the light-hearted paradoxes of *The Phoenix and the Turtle*, where reason is outraged by the fact that two souls are one and yet remain two. In the sonnets the union is a "marriage of true minds," but the symbolism and the paradoxes are much the same. All through the sonnets we meet metaphors of identification and exchange of souls: these are, of course, the regulation hyperboles of love poetry, and in their context (as in Sonnet 39) are often harshly contradicted by the reality of separation. But in the 116-125 group they begin to take on new significance as a genuine aspect of the experience.

Sonnet 125 begins with adoring the youth's external beauty, expressed in the metaphor of bearing the canopy, and thence moves into the youth's heart, where an "oblation" and an exchange of souls takes place. The final consummation carries with it the expulsion of the "informer" or accuser, the spirit of the winter-and-absence world of separation, with all its scandals and rumors and misunderstandings and reproaches. Thus the lower world is left behind, and the higher paradisal world still remaining is dismissed in its turn in Sonnet 126. Here the "lovely boy" is seen in the role of a mock king, invested with the regalia of time, and the poem ends in a somber warning tone. From our point of view it is not much of a threat: he is merely told that he will grow old and eventually die, like everyone else. But the lovely boy from this perspective has nothing to him but what is temporary: what faces him is the annihilation of his essence.

It is not hard to understand how the selfish youth of the winter-and-absence sonnets, whose beauty is as deceitful as "Eve's apple," can also be the divine and radiant godhead of Sonnet 105, an unexampled trinity of kind, true, and fair. Love and propinquity work this miracle every day in human life, and Sonnet 114 shows it at work in the poet's mind. But what relation does the youth have, if any, to the "marriage of true minds"? There is little enough in the sonnets to show that the youth *had* a mind, much less a true one. We can hardly answer such a question: even Christianity, with all its theological apparatus, cannot clearly express the relation of whatever it is in us that is worth redeeming to what we actually are. And Shakespeare is not turning his theme over to Christianity, as Dante does in the moment at the end of the *Paradiso* when Beatrice gives place to the Virgin Mary. In these sonnets the poet assumes the role of both redeemer and repentant prodigal son. His love enables him to transcend himself, but in the instant of fulfillment the *object* of his love vanishes, because it is no longer an object. A straight Platonic explanation would be that the lover leaves behind the beautiful object as he enters into union with the form or idea of love: this is true enough as far as it goes, but we should not infer that the poet has achieved only a subjective triumph (he is no longer a subject) or that the world he enters is devoid of a beloved personality. However that may be, one thing is made clear to us: the identity of love, immortality, and the poet's genius or essential self. As Chaucer says:

> The lyf so short, the craft so long to lerne,
> Th' assay so hard, so sharp the conquering,
> The dredful joye, that alwey slit so yerne,
> Al this mene I by love.

Just as Sonnet 129 is the nadir of experience as the sonnets treat it, so Sonnet 146 is its zenith. Here there is no youth, only the poet's soul, which is told, in the exact imagery of the opening sonnets, not to devote all its attention to its "fading mansion" which only "worms" will inherit, but (in an astonishing reversal of the eating metaphors) to feed on death until death disappears. The poet's soul in this sonnet is a *nobile castello* or House of Alma, to outward view a beleaguered fortress, but in itself, like the tower of love in Sonnet 124, "hugely politic," reaching clear of time into a paradise beyond its cycle, as the mountain of purgatory does in Dante. In this sonnet, near the end of the series, Shakespeare takes the perspective that Petrarch adopts in his first sonnet, where he looks down at the time when he was another man, when he fed his heart with error and reaped a harvest of shame. But Shakespeare is not writing a palinode: nothing in the previous sonnets is repudiated, or even regretted. Love is as strong as death: there is no wavering on that point, nor is there any tendency, so far as we can see, to change from Eros to a "higher" type of love in mid-climb.

The second group of sonnets, 127 through 154, though a unity, can hardly be in strict sequence. Two of the finest of them, 129 and 146, have already been discussed: they indicate the total range of the theme of love as Shakespeare handles it, including this group as well as its predecessor. Some seem expendable: the silly octo-syllabic jingle of 145 does not gain any significance from its context, nor do the last two, which really do come under the head of "mere literary exercise," and for which the models have been discovered. Two other sonnets in this group, 138 and 144, appeared in *The Passionate Pilgrim* in 1599, along with three poems from *Love's Labour's Lost*, two of which are also sonnets. *Love's Labour's Lost* is a play which cries out for—in fact practically announces—a sequel, and Meres' reference to a *Love's Labour's Won* suggests that a sequel was mooted, if not written. I sometimes wonder if these sonnets were not originally thought of as potentially useful for some such play: if so, Sonnet 144 may have become the germ of the two great cycles after the play was abandoned. Perhaps the conception of an original dramatic context might be stretched to accommodate that social climber Sonnet 145. Every writer on the sonnets is entitled to one free speculation.

Most of these sonnets, of course, revolve around a dark female figure, who, unlike the youth, can be treated with irony and detachment, even playfulness. The basis of the attachment here is sexual, and the slightly ribald tone of 138 and 151 is appropriate for it. This ribald tone never appears in the first group except in the close of Sonnet 20, an exception which clearly proves the rule. In the first group the youth takes over the poet's mistress, and the poet resigns her with a pathetic wistfulness ("And yet it may be said I loved her dearly") which is not heard in the second group. In the second group the poet has two loves, a fair youth and a dark lady, in which the former has the role of a "better angel"—hardly his role in the other group, though of course he could be called that by hyperbole. It is natural to associate the mistress of Sonnet 42 with the dark lady and the "man right fair" of 144 with the beautiful youth. But it is simpler, and not really in contradiction with this, to think of the two groups, not as telling the same story, but as presenting a contrast of two opposed attitudes to love, a contrast heightened by a number of deliberate resemblances—"Minding true things by what their mockeries be," as the chorus says in *Henry V*.

The word "fair" in modern English means both attractive and light-complexioned, and Shakespeare's "black" has a similar double meaning of brunette and ill-favored. The same pun occurs in *Love's Labour's Lost* in connection with the dark Rosaline, and in *The Two Gentlemen of Verona* the fickle Proteus says that his new love for Silvia makes his old mistress Julia seem like a "swarthy Ethiop," though Julia herself tells us that her hair is "perfect yellow." The uniting of the two meanings suggests an involuntary attachment: involuntary means against the will, and the theme of the imprisoned will leads to more puns on the poet's name.

The center of gravity of the dark-lady sonnets is Sonnet 130, which corresponds to Sonnet 21 in the other group, where the poet stresses the ordinary humanity of his beloved. As we saw, he could not keep this balance with the youth. The youth is either present or absent: when present he seems divine, when absent he turns almost demonic. In the dark-lady group the poet again cannot keep the human balance, and the tone of affectionate raillery in 130 (and in 128) is not heard again. In striking contrast to the earlier group, the dark lady is both present and sinister. She takes on divine attributes up to a point, but they are those of a "white goddess" or what Blake would call a female will. Like Blake's Gwendolen or Rahab, she can be fitfully maternal (143) and more than fitfully meretricious (142), but her relation to her love is ultimately destructive. Thus these sonnets deal with what we have called the "low" dialectic of bondage and freedom in its sharpest possible form, where the lover is held by a sexual fascination to a mistress whom he does not like or respect, so that he despises himself for his own fidelity.

The dark lady is an incarnation of desire rather than love; she tantalizes, turning away "To follow that which flies before her face," precisely because she is not loved. The youth's infidelities hurt more than hers, but they do not exasperate: they touch nothing in the poet that wants only to possess. The assertion that her "face hath not the power to make love groan" indicates that she is a projection of something self-destructive in the lover, a death as strong as love, a "becoming of things ill" which ends, not in a romantic *Liebestod*, but in a gradual desiccation of the spirit. It is a very Proustian relation (though the role of the captive is reversed), and it is significant that the imagery is almost entirely sterile, with nothing of the former group's emphasis on store, increase, and rebirth.

What one misses in Shakespeare's sonnets, perhaps, is what we find so abundantly in the plays that it seems to us Shakespeare's outstanding characteristic. This is the sense of human proportion, of the concrete situation in which all passion is, however tragically, farcically, or romantically, spent. If the sonnets were new to us, we should expect Shakespeare to remain on the human middle ground of Sonnets 21 and 130: neither the quasi-religious language of 146 nor the prophetic vision of 129 seems typical of him. Here again we must think of the traditions of the genre he was using. The human middle ground is the area of Ovid, but the courtly love tradition, founded as it was on a "moralized" adaptation of Ovid, was committed to a psychological quest that sought to explore the utmost limits of consciousness and desire. It is this tradition of which Shakespeare's sonnets are the definitive summing-up. They are a poetic realization of the whole range of love in the Western world, from the idealism of Petrarch to the ironic frustrations of Proust. If his great predecessor tells us all we need to know of the art of love, Shakespeare has told us more than we can ever fully understand of its nature. He may not have unlocked his heart in the sonnets, but the sonnets can unlock doors in our minds, and show us that poetry can be something more than a mighty maze of walks without a plan. From the plays alone we get an impression of an inscrutable Shakespeare, Matthew Arnold's sphinx who poses riddles and will not answer them, who merely smiles and sits still. It is a call to mental adventure to find, in the sonnets, the authority of Shakespeare behind the conception of poetry as a marriage of Eros and Psyche, an identity of a genius that outlives time and a soul that feeds on death.

❧ Recognition in
The Winter's Tale

IN STRUCTURE *The Winter's Tale*, LIKE *King Lear*, FALLS INTO
two main parts separated by a storm. The fact that they are also
separated by sixteen years is less important. The first part ends
with the ill-fated Antigonus caught between a bear and a raging
sea, echoing a passage in one of Lear's storm speeches. This first
part is the "winter's tale" proper, for Mamillius is just about to
whisper his tale into his mother's ear when the real winter strikes
with the entrance of Leontes and his guards. Various bits of
imagery, such as Polixenes' wish to get back to Bohemia for fear
of "sneaping winds" blowing at home and Hermione's remark dur-
ing her trial (reproduced from *Pandosto*) that the emperor of
Russia was her father, are linked to a winter setting. The storm,
like the storm in *King Lear*, is described in such a way as to sug-
gest that a whole order of things is being dissolved in a dark chaos
of destruction and devouring monsters, and the action of the first
part ends in almost unrelieved gloom. The second part is a tragi-
comedy where, as in *Cymbeline* and *Measure for Measure*, there
is frightening rather than actual hurting. Some of the frightening
seems cruel and unnecessary, but the principle of 'all's well that
ends well' holds in comedy, however great nonsense it may be in
life.

The two parts form a diptych of parallel and contrasting actions,
one dealing with age, winter, and the jealousy of Leontes, the
other with youth, summer, and the love of Florizel. The first part
follows Greene's *Pandosto* closely; for the second part no major
source has been identified. A number of symmetrical details, which
are commonplaces of Shakespearian design, help to build up the
contrast: for instance, the action of each part begins with an
attempt to delay a return. The two parts are related in two ways,
by sequence and by contrast. The cycle of nature, turning through
the winter and summer of the year and through the age and youth
of human generations, is at the center of the play's imagery. The

107

opening scene sets the tone by speaking of Mamillius and of the desire of the older people in the country to live until he comes to reign. The next scene, where the action begins, refers to Leontes' own youth in a world of pastoral innocence and its present reflection in Mamillius. The same cycle is also symbolized, as in *Pericles*, by a mother-daughter relationship, and Perdita echoes Marina when she speaks of Hermione as having "ended when I but began." In the transition to the second part the clown watches the shipwreck and the devouring of Antigonus; the shepherd exhibits the birth tokens of Perdita and remarks, "Thou mettest with things dying, I with things new-born." Leontes, we are told, was to have returned Polixenes' visit "this coming summer," but instead of that sixteen years pass and we find ourselves in Bohemia with spring imagery bursting out of Autolycus's first song, "When daffodils begin to peer." If Leontes is an imaginary cuckold, Autolycus, the thieving harbinger of spring, is something of an imaginative cuckoo. Thence we go on to the sheep-shearing festival, where the imagery extends from early spring to winter evergreens, a vision of nature demonstrating its creative power throughout the entire year, which is perhaps what the dance of the twelve satyrs represents. The symbolic reason for the sixteen-year gap is clearly to have the cycle of the year reinforced by the slower cycle of human generations.

Dramatic contrast in Shakespeare normally includes a superficial resemblance in which one element is a parody of the other. Theseus remarks in *A Midsummer Night's Dream* that the lunatic, the lover, and the poet are of imagination all compact. Theseus, like Yeats, is a smiling public man past his first youth, but not, like Yeats, a poet and a critic. What critical ability there is in that family belongs entirely to Hippolyta, whose sharp comments are a most effective contrast to Theseus's amiable bumble. Hippolyta objects that the story of the lovers has a consistency to it that lunacy would lack, and everywhere in Shakespearian comedy the resemblance of love and lunacy is based on their opposition. Florizel's love for Perdita, which transcends his duty to his father and his social responsibilities as a prince, is a state of mind above reason. He is advised, he says, by his "fancy":

> If my reason
> Will thereto be obedient, I have reason;
> If not, my senses, better pleased with madness,
> Do bid it welcome.

FABLES OF IDENTITY

Leontes' jealousy is a fantasy below reason, and hence a parody of Florizel's state. Camillo, who represents a kind of middle level in the play, is opposed to both, calling one diseased and the other desperate. Both states of mind collide with reality in the middle, and one is annihilated and the other redeemed, like the two aspects of law in Christianity. As the Gentleman says in reporting the finding of Perdita, "They looked as they had heard of a world ransomed, or one destroyed." When Leontes has returned to his proper state of mind, he echoes Florizel when he says of watching the statue,

> No settled senses of the world can match
> The pleasure of that madness.

The play ends in a double recognition scene: the first, which is reported only through the conversation of three Gentlemen, is the recognition of Perdita's parentage; the second is the final scene of the awakening of Hermione and the presenting of Perdita to her. The machinery of the former scene is the ordinary *cognitio* of New Comedy, where the heroine is proved by birth tokens to be respectable enough for the hero to marry her. In many comedies, though never in Shakespeare, such a *cognitio* is brought about through the ingenuity of a tricky servant. Autolycus has this role in *The Winter's Tale*, for though "out of service" he still regards Florizel as his master, and he has also the rascality and the complacent soliloquies about his own cleverness that go with the role. He gains possession of the secret of Perdita's birth, but somehow or other the denouement takes place without him, and he remains superfluous to the plot, consoling himself with the reflection that doing so good a deed would be inconsistent with the rest of his character. In *The Winter's Tale* Shakespeare has combined the two traditions which descended from Menander, pastoral romance and New Comedy, and has consequently come very close to Menandrine formulas as we have them in such a play as *Epitripontes*. But the fact that this conventional recognition scene is only reported indicates that Shakespeare is less interested in it than in the statue scene, which is all his own.

In *Measure for Measure* and *The Tempest* the happy ending is brought about through the exertions of the central characters, whose successes are so remarkable that they seem to many critics to have something almost supernatural about them, as though they were the agents of a divine providence. The germ of truth in this conception is that in other comedies of the same general structure, where there is no such character, the corresponding dramatic role is filled by a supernatural being—Diana in *Pericles* and Jupiter in *Cymbeline*. *The Winter's Tale* belongs to the second group, for the return of Perdita proceeds from the invisible providence of Apollo.

In *Pericles* and *Cymbeline* there is, in addition to the recognition scene, a dream in which the controlling divinity appears with an announcement of what is to conclude the action. Such a scene forms an emblematic recognition scene, in which we are shown the power that brings about the comic resolution. In *The Tempest*, where the power is human, Prospero's magic presents three emblematic visions: a wedding masque of gods to Ferdinand, a disappearing banquet to the Court Party, and "trumpery" (4.1.186) to entice Stephano and Trinculo to steal. In *The Winter's Tale* Apollo does not enter the action, and the emblematic recognition scene is represented by the sheep-shearing festival. This is also on three levels. To Florizel it is a kind of betrothal masque and "a meeting of the petty gods"; to the Court Party, Polixenes and Camillo, it is an illusion which they snatch away; to Autolycus it is an opportunity to sell his "trumpery" (4.4.608) and steal purses.

An emblematic recognition scene of this kind is the distinguishing feature of the four late romances. As a convention, it develops from pastoral romance and the narrative or mythological poem. The sheep-shearing festival resembles the big bravura scenes of singing-matches and the like in Sidney's *Arcadia*, and *The Rape of Lucrece* comes to an emblematic focus in the tapestry depicting the fall of Troy, where Lucrece identifies herself with Hecuba and Tarquin with Sinon, and determines that the second Troy will not collapse around a rape like the first one. In the earlier comedies the emblematic recognition scene is usually in the form of burlesque. Thus in *Love's Labour's Lost* the pageant of Worthies elaborates on Don Armado's appeal to the precedents of Solomon, Samson, and Hercules when he falls in love; but his appeal has also burlesqued the main theme of the play. The allegorical garden episode in *Richard II* represents a similar device, but one rather different in its relation to the total dramatic structure.

In any case the controlling power in the dramatic action of *The Winter's Tale* is something identified both with the will of the gods, especially Apollo, and with the power of nature. We have to keep this association of nature and pagan gods in mind when we examine the imagery in the play that reminds us of religious, even explicitly Christian, conceptions. At the beginning Leontes' youth is referred to as a time of paradisal innocence; by the end of the scene he has tumbled into a completely illusory knowledge of good and evil. He says:

> How blest am I
> In my censure, in my true opinion!
> Alack, for lesser knowledge! How accurs'd
> In being so blest!

Or, as Ford says in *The Merry Wives*, "God be praised for my jealousy!" The irony of the scene in which Leontes is scolded by Paulina turns on the fact that Leontes tries to be a source of righteous wrath when he is actually an object of it. Hermione's trial is supposed to be an act of justice and the sword of justice is produced twice to have oaths sworn on it, but Leontes is under the wrath of Apollo and divine justice is his enemy. The opposite of wrath is grace, and Hermione is associated throughout the play with the word grace. During the uneasy and rather cloying friendliness at the beginning of the play Hermione pronounces the word "grace" conspicuously three times, after which the harsh dissonances of Leontes' jealousy begin. She also uses the word when she is ordered off to prison and in the only speech that she makes after Act 3. But such grace is not Christian or theological grace, which is superior to the order of nature, but a secular analogy of Christian grace which is identical with nature—the grace that Spenser celebrates in the sixth book of *The Faerie Queene*.

In the romances, and in some of the earlier comedies, we have a sense of an irresistible power, whether of divine or human agency, making for a providential resolution. Whenever we have a strong sense of such a power, the human beings on whom it operates seem greatly diminished in size. This is a feature of the romances which often disappoints those who wish that Shakespeare had simply kept on writing tragedies. Because of the heavy emphasis on reconciliation in *Cymbeline*, the jealousy of Posthumus is not titanic, as the jealousy of Othello is titanic; it expresses only a childish petulance about women in general: "I'll write against them, Detest them, curse them." Similarly Leontes (as he himself points out) falls far short of being a somber demonic tyrant on the scale of Macbeth, and can only alternate between bluster and an uneasy sense of having done wrong:

> Away with that audacious lady! Antigonus,
> I charg'd thee that she should not come about me.
> I knew she would.

This scaling down of the human perspective is in conformity with a dramatic structure that seems closely analogous to such Christian conceptions as wrath and grace. But the only one of the four romances in which I suspect any explicit—which means allegorical —references to Christianity is *Cymbeline*. Cymbeline was king of Britain at the birth of Christ, and in such scenes as the Jailer's speculations about death and his wistful "I would we were all of one mind, and that mind good," there are hints that some far-reaching change in the human situation is taking place off-stage. The play ends on the word "peace" and with Cymbeline's promise to pay tribute to Rome, almost as though, as soon as the story ended, another one were to begin with Augustus Caesar's decree that all the world should be taxed.

No such explicit links are appropriate to *The Winter's Tale*, though it is true that the story does tell of a mysterious disappearing child born in the winter who has four father-figures assigned to her: a real one, a putative one who later becomes her father-in-law, a fictional one, Smalus of Libya in Florizel's tale, and a shepherd foster-father. This makes up a group of a shepherd and three kings, of whom one is African. The first part of *The Winter's Tale* is, like *Cymbeline*, full of the imagery of superstitious sacrifice. Leontes, unable to sleep, wonders if having Hermione burnt alive would not give him rest. Antigonus offers to spay his three daughters if Hermione is guilty, though he would prefer to castrate himself. Mamillius, whom Leontes thinks of as a part of himself, becomes the victim necessary to save Leontes, and the exposing of Perdita is attended by a sacrificial holocaust. Not only is Antigonus devoured by a bear, but the ship and its crew were "Wrecked the same instant of their master's death and in the view of the shepherd; so that all the instruments which aided to expose the child were even then lost when it was found." In contrast, the restoring of Perdita to her mother is an act of sacramental communion, but it is a secular communion, and the "instruments" aiding in it are the human arts. The main characters repair to Paulina's house intending to "sup" there, and are taken into her chapel and presented with what is alleged to be a work of painting and sculpture. Hermione, like Thaisa in *Pericles*, is brought to life by the playing of music, and references to the art of magic follow. Art, therefore, seems part of the regenerating power of the play, and the imagination of the poet is to be allied with that of the lover as against that of the lunatic.

Apart from the final scene, at least three kinds of art are mentioned in the play. First, there is the art of the gardener who, according to Polixenes' famous speech, may help or change nature by marrying a gentler scion to the wildest stock but can do so only through nature's power, so that "the art itself is nature." This is a sound humanist view: it is the view of Sidney, who contrasts the brazen world of nature with the golden world of art but also speaks of art as a second nature. Sidney's view does not necessitate, but it is consistent with, his ridiculing of plays that show a character as an infant in one act and grown up in the next, and that mingle kings and clowns in the same scene. It is also the view of Ben Jonson who, recognizing a very different conception of nature in Shakespeare's romances, remarked good-humoredly that he was "loth to make nature afraid in his plays, like those that beget tales, tempests, and suchlike drolleries." We note that Polixenes' speech entirely fails to convince Perdita, who merely repeats that she will have nothing to do with bastard flowers:

> No more than, were I painted, I would wish
> This youth should say 'twere well, and only therefore
> Desire to breed by me. . . .

—a remark which oddly anticipates the disappearance of the painted statue of Hermione into the real Hermione. It also, as has often been pointed out, fails to convince Polixenes himself, for a few moments later we find him in a paroxysm of fury at the thought of his own gentle scion marrying the wild stock of a shepherd's daughter. Whatever its merits, Polixenes' view of art hardly seems to describe the kind of art that the play itself manifests.

Secondly, there is the kind of art represented by Julio Romano, said to be the painter and sculptor of Hermione's statue, a mimetic realist who "would beguile Nature of her custom, so perfectly is he her ape." But it turns out that in fact no statue has been made of Hermione, and the entire reference to Romano seems pointless. We do not need his kind of art when we have the real Hermione, and here again, whatever Romano's merits, neither he nor the kind of realism he represents seems to be very central to the play itself. The literary equivalent of realism is plausibility, the supplying of adequate causation for events. There is little plausibility in *The Winter's Tale*, and a great deal of what is repeatedly called "wonder." Things are presented to us, not explained. The jealousy of Leontes explodes without warning: an actor may rationalize it in various ways; a careful reader of the text may suspect that the references to his youth have touched off some kind of suppressed guilt; but the essential fact is that the jealousy suddenly appears where it had not been before, like a second subject in a piece of music. "How should this grow?" Polixenes asks of Camillo, but Camillo evades the question. At the end of the play Hermione is first a statue, then a living woman. The explanations given do not satisfy even Leontes, much less us. He says:

> But how, is to be question'd; for I saw her,
> As I thought, dead, and have in vain said many
> A prayer upon her grave.

As often in Shakespeare, further explanations are promised to the characters, but are not given to the audience: Paulina merely says, "it appears she lives."

Thirdly, though one blushes to mention it, there is the crude popular art of the ballads of Autolycus, of which one describes "how a usurer's wife was brought to bed of twenty money-bags at a burden." "Is it true, think you?" asks Mopsa, unconsciously using one of the most frequently echoed words in the play. We notice that Shakespeare seems to be calling our attention to the incredibility of his story and to its ridiculous and outmoded devices when he makes both Paulina and the Gentlemen who report the recognition of Perdita speak of what is happening as "like an old tale." The magic words pronounced by Paulina that draw speech from Hermione are "Our Perdita is found," and Paulina has previously said that the finding of Perdita is "monstrous to our human reason." And when one of the Gentlemen says "Such a deal of wonder is broken out within this hour that ballad-makers cannot be able to express it," we begin to suspect that the kind of art manifested by the play itself is in some respects closer to these "trumpery" ballads than to the sophisticated idealism and realism of Polixenes and Romano.

My late and much beloved colleague Professor Harold S. Wilson has called attention to the similarity between Polixenes' speech and a passage in Puttenham's *Arte of English Poesie* (1589), which in discussing the relation of art and nature uses the analogy of the gardener and the example of the "gillyvor." Puttenham also goes on to say that there is another context where art is "only a bare imitator of nature's works, following and counterfeiting her actions and effects, as the Marmoset doth many countenances and gestures of man; of which sort are the arts of painting and carving." We are reminded of Romano, the painter and carver who is the perfect "ape" of nature. The poet, says Puttenham, is to use all types of art in their proper place, but for his greatest moments he will work "even as nature her self working by her own peculiar virtue and proper instinct and not by example or meditation or exercise as all other artificers do." We feel that Puttenham, writing before Shakespeare had got properly started and two centuries earlier than Coleridge, has nonetheless well characterized the peculiar quality of Shakespeare's art.

The fact that Leontes' state of mind is a parody of the imagination of lover and poet links *The Winter's Tale* with Shakespeare's 'humor' comedies, which turn on the contrast between fantasy and reality. Katharina moves from shrew to obedient wife; Falstaff from the seducer to the gull of the merry wives; the King of Navarre and his followers from contemplative pedants seeking authority from books to helpless lovers performing the tasks imposed on them by their ladies. Similarly when Florizel says that his love for Perdita

> cannot fail but by
> The violation of my faith; and then
> Let nature crush the sides o' th' earth together
> And mar the seeds within! . . .

—he is supplying the genuine form of what Camillo describes in parallel cosmological terms:

> you may as well
> Forbid the sea for to obey the moon,
> As or by oath remove or counsel shake
> The fabric of his folly, whose foundation
> Is piled upon his faith.

Puttenham begins his treatise by comparing the poet, as a creator, to God, "who without any travail to his divine imagination made all the world of nought." Leontes' jealousy is a parody of a creation out of nothing, as the insistent repetition of the word "nothing" in the first act indicates, and as Leontes himself says in his mysterious mumbling half-soliloquy:

> Affection, thy intention stabs the centre!
> Thou dost make possible things not so held,
> Communicat'st with dream—how can this be?
> With what's unreal thou coactive art,
> And fellow'st nothing.

A humor is restored to a normal outlook by being confronted, not directly with reality, but with a reflection of its own illusion, as Katharina is tamed by being shown the reflection of her own shrewishness in Petruchio. Similarly Leontes, in the final scene, is "mocked with art," the realistic illusion of Romano's statue which gradually reveals itself to be the real Hermione.

In the artificial society of the Sicilian court there are Mamillius, the hopeful prince who dies, and the infant Perdita who vanishes. In the rural society of Bohemia there are the shepherdess Perdita who is "Flora Peering in April's front," and Florizel who, as his name suggests, is her masculine counterpart, and the Prince Charming who later reminds Leontes strongly of Mamillius and becomes Leontes' promised heir. Perdita says that she would like to strew Florizel with flowers:

> like a bank for love to lie and play on,
> Not like a corse; or if, not to be buried,
> But quick and in mine arms.

The antithesis between the two worlds is marked by Polixenes, who is handed "flowers of winter" and who proceeds to destroy the festival like a winter wind, repeating the *senex iratus* role of Leontes in the other kingdom. But though he can bully Perdita, he impresses her no more than Leontes had impressed Hermione. Perdita merely says:

> I was not much afeard; for once or twice
> I was about to speak and tell him plainly
> The selfsame sun that shines upon his court
> Hides not his visage from our cottage but
> Looks on alike.

There is a faint New Testament echo here, but of course to Perdita the god of the sun would be Apollo, who does see to it that Polixenes is outwitted, though only by the fact that Perdita is really a princess. As always in Shakespeare, the structure of society is unchanged by the comic action. What happens in *The Winter's Tale* is the opposite of the art of the gardener as Polixenes describes it. A society which is artificial in a limited sense at the beginning of the play becomes at the end still artificial, but natural as well. Nature provides the means for the regeneration of artifice. But still it is true that "The art itself is nature," and one wonders why a speech ending with those words should be assigned to Polixenes, the opponent of the festival.

The context of Polixenes' theory is the Renaissance framework in which there are two levels of the order of nature. Art belongs to human nature, and human nature is, properly speaking, the state that man lived in in Eden, or the Golden Age, before his fall into a lower world of physical nature to which he is not adapted. Man attempts to regain his original state through law, virtue, education, and such rational and conscious aids as art. Here nature is a superior order. In poetry this upper level of nature, uncontaminated by the sin and death of the fall, is usually symbolized by the starry spheres, which are now all that is left of it. The starry spheres produce the music of the spheres, and the harmony of music usually represents this upper level of nature in human life.

Most Shakespearian comedy is organized within this framework, and when it is, its imagery takes on the form outlined by G. Wilson Knight in *The Shakespearean Tempest* (1932). The tempest symbolizes the destructive elements in the order of nature, and music the permanently constructive elements in it. Music in its turn is regularly associated with the starry spheres, of which the one closest to us, the moon, is the normal focus. The control of the tempest by the harmony of the spheres appears in the image of the moon pulling the tides, an image used once or twice in *The Winter's Tale*. The action of *The Merchant of Venice*, too, extends from the cosmological harmonies of the fifth act, where the moon sleeps with Endymion, to the tempest that wrecked Antonio's ships. In *Pericles*, which employs this imagery of harmony and tempest most exhaustively, Pericles is said to be a master of music, Cerimon revives Thaisa by music, Diana announces her appearance to Pericles by music, and the final recognition scene unites the music and tempest symbols, since it takes place in the temple of Diana during the festival of Neptune. Music also accompanies the revival of Hermione in the final scene of *The Winter's Tale*. All the attention is absorbed in Hermione as she begins to move while music plays; and we are reminded of Autolycus and of his role as a kind of rascally Orpheus at the sheep-shearing festival: "My clown . . . would not stir his pettitoes till he had both tune and words; which so drew the rest of the herd to me that all their other senses stuck in ears. . . . No hearing, no feeling, but my sir's song, and admiring the nothing of it." Here again Autolycus seems to be used to indicate that something is being subordinated in the play, though by no means eliminated.

In another solstitial play, *A Midsummer Night's Dream*, the cosmology is of this more conventional Renaissance kind. In the middle, between the world of chaos symbolized by tempest and the world of starry spheres symbolized by music, comes the cycle of nature, the world of Eros and Adonis, Puck and Pyramus, the love-god and the dying god. To this middle world the fairies belong, for the fairies are spirits of the four natural elements, and their dissension causes disorder in nature. Above, the cold fruitless moon of Diana, whose nun Hermia would have to be, hangs over the action. While a mermaid is calming the sea by her song and attracting the stars by the power of harmony, Cupid shoots an arrow at the moon and its vestal: it falls in a parabola on a flower and turns it "purple with love's wound." The story of Pyramus is not very coherently told in Peter Quince's play, but in Ovid there is a curious image about the blood spurting out of Pyramus in an arc like water out of a burst pipe and falling on the white mulberry and turning it purple. Here nature as a cycle of birth and death, symbolized by the purple flower, revolves underneath nature as a settled and predictable order or harmony, as it does also in a third solstitial play, *Twelfth Night*, which begins with an image comparing music to a wind blowing on a bank of violets.

But in *The Winter's Tale* nature is associated, not with the credible, but with the incredible: nature as an order is subordinated to the nature that yearly confronts us with the impossible miracle of renewed life. In Ben Jonson's animadversions on Shakespeare's unnatural romances it is particularly the functional role of the dance, the "concupiscence of jigs," as he calls it, that he objects to. But it is the dance that most clearly expresses the pulsating energy of nature as it appears in *The Winter's Tale*, an energy which communicates itself to the dialogue. Such words as "push" and "wild" (meaning rash) are constantly echoed; the play ends with the words "Hastily lead away," and we are told that the repentant Leontes

> o'er and o'er divides him
> 'Twixt his unkindness and his kindness; th' one
> He chides to hell and bids the other grow
> Faster than thought of time.

Much is said about magic in the final scene, but there is no magician, no Prospero, only the sense of a participation in the redeeming and reviving power of a nature identified with art, grace, and love. Hence the final recognition is appropriately that of a frozen statue turning into a living presence, and the appropriate Chorus is Time, the destructive element which is also the only possible representative of the timeless.

❧ Literature as Context: Milton's *Lycidas*

I SHOULD LIKE TO BEGIN WITH A BRIEF DISCUSSION OF A FAMILIAR poem, Milton's *Lycidas*, in the hope that some of the inferences drawn from the analysis will be relevant to the theme of this conference. *Lycidas*, then, is an elegy in the pastoral convention, written to commemorate a young man named Edward King who was drowned at sea. The origins of the pastoral are partly classical, the tradition that runs through Theocritus and Virgil, and partly Biblical, the imagery of the twenty-third Psalm, of Christ as the Good Shepherd, of the metaphors of "pastor" and "flock" in the Church. The chief connecting link between the traditions in Milton's day was the Fourth or Messianic Eclogue of Virgil. Hence it is common enough to have pastoral images echoing both traditions at once, and not surprising to find that *Lycidas* is a Christian poem as well as a humanistic one.

In the classical pastoral elegy the subject of the elegy is not treated as an individual but as a representative of a dying spirit of nature. The pastoral elegy seems to have some relation to the ritual of the Adonis lament, and the dead poet Bion, in Moschus's poem, is celebrated with much the same kind of imagery as Bion himself uses in his lament for Adonis. The phrase "dying god," for such a figure in later pastoral, is not an anachronism: Virgil says of Daphnis, for example, in the Fifth Eclogue: "*deus, deus ille, Menalca.*" Besides, Milton and his learned contemporaries, Selden, for example, or Henry Reynolds, knew at least as much about the symbolism of the "dying god" as any modern student could get out of *The Golden Bough*, which depends mainly on the same classical sources that were available to them. The notion that twentieth-century poets differ from their predecessors in their understanding or use of myth will not bear much scrutiny. So King is given the pastoral name of Lycidas, which is equivalent to Adonis, and is associated with the cyclical rhythms of nature. Of these three are of particular importance: the daily cycle of the sun across the sky, the yearly cycle of the seasons, and the cycle of water, flowing from wells and fountains through rivers to the sea. Sunset, winter, and the sea are emblems of Lycidas' death; sunrise and spring, of his resurrection. The poem begins in the morning, "Under the opening eyelids of the morn," and ends with the sun, like Lycidas himself, dropping into the western ocean, yet due to rise again as Lycidas is to do. The imagery of the opening lines, "Shatter your leaves before the mellowing year," suggests the frosts of autumn killing the flowers, and in the great roll-call of flowers towards the end, most of them early blooming flowers like the "rathe primrose," the spring returns. Again, the opening invocation is to the "Sisters of the sacred well," and the water imagery carries through a great variety of Greek, Italian, and English rivers to the sea in which the dead body of Lycidas lies.

Lycidas, then, is the "archetype" of Edward King. By an archetype I mean a literary symbol, or cluster of symbols, which are used recurrently throughout literature, and thereby become conventional. A poetic use of a flower, by itself, is not necessarily an archetype. But in a poem about the death of a young man it is conventional to associate him with a red or purple flower, usually a spring flower like the hyacinth. The historical origin of the convention may be lost in ritual, but it is a constantly latent one, not only in literature but in life, as the symbolism of the scarlet poppies in World War I shows. Hence in *Lycidas* the "sanguine flower inscrib'd with woe" is an archetype, a symbol that recurs regularly in many poems of its kind. Similarly Lycidas himself is not only the literary form of Edward King, but a conventional or recurring form, of the same family as Shelley's Adonais, the Daphnis of Theocritus and Virgil, and Milton's own Damon. King was also a clergyman and, for Milton's purposes, a poet, so, having selected the conventional archetype of King as drowned young man, Milton has then to select the conventional archetypes of King as poet and of King as priest. These are, respectively, Orpheus and Peter.

Both Orpheus and Peter have attributes that link them in imagery with Lycidas. Orpheus was also an "enchanting son" or spirit of nature; he died young, in much the same role as Adonis, and was flung into the water. Peter would have drowned too without the help of Christ; hence Peter is not named directly, but only as "The Pilot of the Galilean Lake," just as Christ is not named directly, but only as "Him that walked the waves." When Orpheus was torn to pieces by the Maenads, his head went floating "Down the swift Hebrus to the Lesbian shore." The theme of salvation out of water is connected with the image of the dolphin, a conventional type of Christ, and dolphins are called upon to "waft the hapless youth" just before the peroration begins.

The body of the poem is arranged in the form ABACA, a main theme repeated twice with two intervening episodes, as in the musical rondo. The main theme is the drowning of Lycidas in the prime of his life; the two episodes, presided over by the figures of Orpheus and Peter, deal with the theme of premature death as it relates to poetry and to the priesthood respectively. In both the same type of image appears: the mechanical instrument of execution that brings about a sudden death, represented by the "abhorred shears" in the meditation on fame and the "grim two-handed engine" in the meditation on the corruption of the Church. The most difficult part of the construction is the managing of the transitions from these episodes back to the main theme. The poet does this by alluding to his great forerunners in the pastoral convention, Theocritus of Sicily, Virgil of Mantua, and the legendary Arcadians who preceded both:

> O fountain Arethuse, and thou honour'd flood,
> Smooth-sliding Mincius, crown'd with vocal reeds . . .

and later:

> Return, Alpheus, the dread voice is past
> That shrunk thy streams: return, Sicilian Muse.

The allusion has the effect of reminding the reader that this is, after all, a pastoral. But Milton also alludes to the myth of Arethusa and Alpheus, the Arcadian water-spirits who plunged underground and reappeared in Sicily, and this myth not only outlines the history of the pastoral convention, but unites the water imagery with the theme of disappearance and revival.

In pastoral elegy the poet who laments the death is often so closely associated with the dead man as to make him a kind of double or shadow of himself. Similarly Milton represents himself as intimately involved with the death of Lycidas. The theme of premature death is skilfully associated in the opening lines with the conventional apology for a "harsh and crude" poem; the poet hopes for a similar elegy when he dies, and at the end he accepts the responsibilities of survival and turns "Tomorrow to fresh woods, and pastures new," bringing the elegy to a full rich *tierce de Picardie* or major chord. By appearing himself at the beginning and end of the poem, Milton presents the poem as, in a sense, contained within the mind of the poet.

Apart from the historical convention of the pastoral, however, there is also the conventional framework of ideas or assumptions which forms the background of the poem. I call it a framework of ideas, and it may also be that, but in poetry it is rather a framework of images. It consists of four levels of existence. First is the order revealed by Christianity, the order of grace and salvation and of eternal life. Second is the order of human nature, the order represented by the Garden of Eden in the Bible and the Golden Age in classical myth, and which man in his fallen state can, up to a point, regain through education, obedience to law, and the habit of virtue. Third is the order of physical nature, the world of animals and plants which is morally neutral but theologically "fallen." Fourth is the disorder of the unnatural, the sin and death and corruption that entered the world with the Fall.

Lycidas has his connections with all of these orders. In the first place, all the images of death and resurrection are included in and identified with the body of Christ. Christ is the sun of righteousness, the tree of life, the water of life, the dying god who rose again, the saviour from the sea. On this level Lycidas enters the Christian heaven and is greeted by the "Saints above" "In solemn troops, and sweet societies," where the language echoes the Book of Revelation. But simultaneously Lycidas achieves another apotheosis as the Genius of the shore, corresponding to the Attendant Spirit in *Comus*, whose habitation is said to be a world above our own, identified, not with the Christian heaven, but with Spenser's Gardens of Adonis. The third level of physical nature is the world of ordinary experience, where death is simply a loss, and those who mourn the death have to turn to pick up their tasks again. On this level Lycidas is merely absent, "to our moist vows denied," represented only by the empty bier with its flowers. It is on this level too that the poem is contained within the mind of the surviving poet, as on the Christian level it is contained within the body of Christ. Finally, the world of death and corruption holds the drowned corpse of Lycidas, which will soon come to the surface and "welter to the parching wind." This last is an unpleasant and distressing image, and Milton touches it very lightly, picking it up again in an appropriate context:

> But swoln with wind and the rank mist they draw,
> Rot inwardly . . .

In the writing of *Lycidas* there are four creative principles of particular importance. To say that there are four does not mean, of course, that they are separable. One is convention, the reshaping of the poetic material which is appropriate to this subject. Another is genre, the choosing of the appropriate form. A third is archetype, the use of appropriate, and therefore recurrently employed, images and symbols. The fourth, for which there is no name, is the fact that the forms of literature are autonomous: that is, they do not exist outside literature. Milton is not writing an obituary: he does not start with Edward King and his life and times, but with the conventions and archetypes that poetry requires for such a theme.

Of the critical principles illustrated by this analysis, one will be no surprise to the present audience. *Lycidas* owes quite as much to Hebrew, Greek, Latin, and Italian traditions as it does to English. Even the diction, of which I have no space to speak, shows strong Italian influence. Milton was of course a learned poet, but there is no poet whose literary influences are entirely confined to his own language. Thus every problem in literary criticism is a problem in comparative literature, or simply of literature itself.

The next principle is that the provisional hypothesis which we must adopt for the study of every poem is that that poem is a unity. If, after careful and repeated testing, we are forced to conclude that it is not a unity, then we must abandon the hypothesis and look for the reasons why it is not. A good deal of bad criticism of *Lycidas* has resulted from not making enough initial effort to understand the unity of the poem. To talk of "digressions" in *Lycidas* is a typical consequence of a mistaken critical method, of backing into the poem the wrong way round. If, instead of starting with the poem, we start with a handful of peripheral facts about the poem, Milton's casual knowledge of King, his ambitions as a poet, his bitterness against the episcopacy, then of course the poem will break down into pieces corresponding precisely to those fragments of knowledge. *Lycidas* illustrates, on a small scale, what has happened on a much bigger scale in, for example, the criticism of Homer. Critics knowing something about the fragmentary nature of heroic lays and ballads approached the *Iliad* and the *Odyssey* with this knowledge in mind, and the poems obediently split up into the pieces that they wished to isolate. Other critics came along and treated the poems as imaginative unities, and today everyone knows that the second group were more convincing.

The same thing happens when our approach to "sources" becomes fragmentary or piecemeal. *Lycidas* is a dense mass of echoes from previous literature, chiefly pastoral literature. Reading through Virgil's Eclogues with *Lycidas* in mind, we can see that Milton had not simply read or studied these poems: he possessed them; they were part of the material he was shaping. The passage about the hungry sheep reminds us of at least three other passages: one in Dante's *Paradiso*, one in the Book of Ezekiel, and one near the beginning of Hesiod's *Theogony*. There are also echoes of Mantuan and Spenser, of the Gospel of John, and it is quite possible that there are even more striking parallels with poems that Milton had not read. In such cases there is not *a* source at all, no one place that the passage "comes from," or, as we say with such stupefying presumption, that the poet "had in mind." There are only archetypes, or recurring themes of literary expression, which *Lycidas* has recreated, and therefore re-echoed, yet once more.

The next principle is that the important problems of literary criticism lie within the study of literature. We notice that a law of diminishing returns sets in as soon as we move away from the poem itself. If we ask, who is Lycidas? the answer is that he is a member of the same family as Theocritus' Daphnis, Bion's Adonis, the Old Testament's Abel, and so on. The answer goes on building up a wider comprehension of literature and a deeper knowledge of its structural principles and recurring themes. But if we ask, who was Edward King? What was his relation to Milton? How good a poet was he? we find ourselves moving dimly in the intense inane. The same is true of minor points. If we ask, why is the image of the two-handed engine in *Lycidas?* we can give an answer, along the lines suggested above, that illustrates how carefully the poem has been constructed. If we ask, what is the two-handed engine? there are forty-odd answers, none of them completely satisfactory; yet the fact that they are not wholly satisfactory hardly seems to be important.

Another form of the same kind of fallacy is the confusion between personal sincerity and literary sincerity. If we start with the facts that *Lycidas* is highly conventional and that Milton knew King only slightly, we may see in *Lycidas* an "artificial" poem without "real feeling" in it. This red herring, though more common among third-rate romantics, was dragged across the study of *Lycidas* by Samuel Johnson. Johnson knew better, but he happened to feel perverse about this particular poem, and so deliberately raised false issues. It would not have occurred to him, for example, to question the conventional use of Horace in the satires of Pope, or of Juvenal in his own. Personal sincerity has no place in liter-

FABLES OF IDENTITY

ature, because personal sincerity as such is inarticulate. One may burst into tears at the news of a friend's death, but one can never spontaneously burst into song, however doleful a lay. *Lycidas* is a passionately sincere poem, because Milton was deeply interested in the structure and symbolism of funeral elegies, and had been practising since adolescence on every fresh corpse in sight, from the university beadle to the fair infant dying of a cough.

If we ask what inspires a poet, there are always two answers. An occasion, an experience, an event, may inspire the impulse to write. But the impulse to write can only come from previous contact with literature, and the formal inspiration, the poetic structure that crystallizes around the new event, can only be derived from other poems. Hence while every new poem is a new and unique creation, it is also a reshaping of familiar conventions of literature, otherwise it would not be recognizable as literature at all. Literature often gives us the illusion of turning from books to life, from second-hand to direct experience, and thereby discovering new literary principles in the world outside. But this is never quite what happens. No matter how tightly Wordsworth may close the barren leaves of art and let nature be his teacher, his literary forms will be as conventional as ever, although they may echo an unac-customed set of conventions, such as the ballad or the broadside. The pretence of personal sincerity is itself a literary convention, and Wordsworth makes many of the flat simple statements which represent, in literature, the inarticulateness of personal sincerity:

> No motion has she now, no force:
> She neither hears nor sees.

But as soon as a death becomes a poetic image, that image is assimilated to other poetic images of death in nature, and hence Lucy inevitably becomes a Proserpine figure, just as King becomes an Adonis:

> Rolled round in earth's diurnal course
> With rocks, and stones, and trees.

In Whitman we have an even more extreme example than Wordsworth of a cult of personal statement and an avoidance of learned conventions. It is therefore instructive to see what happens in *When Lilacs Last in Dooryard Bloomed*. The dead man is not called by a pastoral name, but neither is he called by his historical name. He is in a coffin which is carried the length and breadth of the land; he is identified with a "powerful western fallen star"; he is the beloved comrade of the poet, who throws the purple flower of the lilac on his coffin; a singing bird laments the death, just as the woods and caves do in *Lycidas*. Convention, genre, archetype, and the autonomy of forms are all illustrated as clearly in Whitman as they are in Milton.

Lycidas is an occasional poem, called forth by a specific event. It seems, therefore, to be a poem with a strong external reference. Critics who cannot approach a poem except as a personal statement of the poet's thus feel that if it says little about King, it must say a good deal about Milton. So, they reason, *Lycidas* is really autobiographical, concerned with Milton's own preoccupations, including his fear of death. There can be no objection to this unless Milton's conventional involving of himself with the poem is misinterpreted as a personal intrusion into it.

For Milton was even by seventeenth-century standards an unusually professional and impersonal poet. Of all Milton's poems, the one obvious failure is the poem called *The Passion,* and if we look at the imagery of that poem we can see why. It is the only poem of Milton's in which he is preoccupied with himself in the process of writing it. "My muse," "my song," "my harp," "my roving verse," "my Phoebus," and so on for eight stanzas until Milton abandons the poem in disgust. It is not a coincidence that Milton's one self-conscious poem should be the one that never gets off the ground. There is nothing like this in *Lycidas:* the "I" of that poem is a professional poet in his conventional shepherd disguise, and to think of him as a personal "I" is to bring *Lycidas* down to the level of *The Passion,* to make it a poem that has to be studied primarily as a biographical document rather than for its own sake. Such an approach to *Lycidas* is apt to look most plausible to those who dislike Milton, and want to see him cut down to size.

One more critical principle, and the one that I have written this paper to enunciate, seems to me to follow inevitably from the previous ones. Every poem must be examined as a unity, but no poem is an isolatable unity. Every poem is inherently connected with other poems of its kind, whether explicitly, as *Lycidas* is with Theocritus and Virgil, or implicitly, as Whitman is with the same tradition, or by anticipation, as *Lycidas* is with later pastoral elegies. And, of course, the kinds or genres of literature are not separable either, like the orders of pre-Darwinian biology. Everyone who has seriously studied literature knows that he is not simply moving from poem to poem, or from one aesthetic experience to another: he is also entering into a coherent and progressive discipline. For literature is not simply an aggregate of books and poems and plays: it is an order of words. And our total literary experience, at any given time, is not a discrete series of memories or impressions of what we have read, but an imaginatively coherent body of experience.

It is literature as an order of words, therefore, which forms the primary context of any given work of literary art. All other contexts—the place of *Lycidas* in Milton's development; its place in the history of English poetry; its place in seventeenth-century thought or history—are secondary and derivative contexts. Within the total literary order certain structural and generic principles, certain configurations of narrative and imagery, certain conventions and devices and *topoi*, occur over and over again. In every new work of literature some of these principles are reshaped.

Lycidas, we found, is informed by such a recurring structural principle. The short, simple, and accurate name for this principle is myth. The Adonis myth is what makes *Lycidas* both distinctive and traditional. Of course if we think of the Adonis myth as some kind of Platonic idea existing by itself, we shall not get far with it as a critical conception. But it is only incompetence that tries to reduce or assimilate a poem to a myth. The Adonis myth in *Lycidas* is the structure of *Lycidas*. It is in *Lycidas* in much the same way that the sonata form is in the first movement of a Mozart symphony. It is the connecting link between what makes *Lycidas* the poem it is and what unites it to other forms of poetic experience. If we attend only to the uniqueness of *Lycidas*, and analyze the ambiguities and subtleties of its diction, our method, however useful in itself, soon reaches a point of no return to the poem. If we attend only to the conventional element, our method will turn it into a scissors-and-paste collection of allusive tags. One method reduces the poem to a jangle of echoes of itself, the other to a jangle of echoes from other poets. If we have a unifying principle that holds these two tendencies together from the start, neither will get out of hand.

Myths, it is true, turn up in other disciplines, in anthropology, in psychology, in comparative religion. But the primary business of the critic is with myth as the shaping principle of a work of literature. Thus for him myth becomes much the same thing as Aristotle's *mythos*, narrative or plot, the moving formal cause which is what Aristotle called the "soul" of the work and assimilates all details in the realizing of its unity.

In its simplest English meaning a myth is a story about a god, and Lycidas is, poetically speaking, a god or spirit of nature, who eventually becomes a saint in heaven, which is as near as one can get to godhead in ordinary Christianity. The reason for treating Lycidas mythically, in this sense, is conventional, but the convention is not arbitrary or accidental. It arises from the metaphorical nature of poetic speech. We are not told simply that Lycidas has left the woods and caves, but that the woods and caves and all their echoes mourn his loss. This is the language of that curious identification of subject and object, of personality and thing, which the poet has in common with the lunatic and the lover. It is the language of metaphor, recognized by Aristotle as the distinctive language of poetry. And, as we can see in such phrases as sun-god and tree-god, the language of metaphor is interdependent with the language of myth.

I have said that all problems of criticism are problems of comparative literature. But where there is comparison there must be some standard by which we can distinguish what is actually comparable from what is merely analogous. The scientists discovered long ago that to make valid comparisons you have to know what your real categories are. If you're studying natural history, for instance, no matter how fascinated you may be by anything that has eight legs, you can't just lump together an octopus and a spider and a string quartet. In science the difference between a scientific and a pseudo-scientific procedure can usually be spotted fairly soon. I wonder if literary criticism has any standards of this kind. It seems to me that a critic practically has to maintain that the Earl of Oxford wrote the plays of Shakespeare before he can be clearly recognized as making pseudo-critical statements. I have read some critics on Milton who appeared to be confusing Milton with their phallic fathers, if that is the right phrase. I should call them pseudo-critics; others call them neo-classicists. How is one to know? There is such a variety of even legitimate critics. There are critics who can find things in the Public Records Office, and there are critics who, like myself, could not find the Public Records Office. Not all critical statements or procedures can be equally valid.

The first step, I think, is to recognize the dependence of value-judgments on scholarship. Scholarship, or the knowledge of literature, constantly expands and increases; value-judgments are produced by a skill based on the knowledge we already have. Thus scholarship has both priority to value-judgments and the power of veto over them. The second step is to recognize the dependence of

FABLES OF IDENTITY

scholarship on a coordinated view of literature. A good deal of critical taxonomy lies ahead of us. We need to know much more than we do about the structural principles of literature, about myth and metaphor, conventions and genres, before we can distinguish with any authority a real from an imaginary line of influence, an illuminating from a misleading analogy, a poet's original source from his last resource. The basis of this central critical activity that gives direction to scholarship is the simple fact that every poem is a member of the class of things called poems. Some poems, including *Lycidas*, proclaim that they are conventional, in other words that their primary context is in literature. Other poems leave this inference to the critic, with an appealing if often misplaced confidence.

❧ Towards Defining
an Age of Sensibility

THE PERIOD OF ENGLISH LITERATURE WHICH COVERS ROUGHLY THE second half of the eighteenth century is one which has always suffered from not having a clear historical or functional label applied to it. I call it here the age of sensibility, which is not intended to be anything but a label. This period has the "Augustan" age on one side of it and the "Romantic" movement on the other, and it is usually approached transitionally, as a period of reaction against Pope and anticipation of Wordsworth. The chaos that results from treating this period, or any other, in terms of reaction has been well described by Professor Crane in a recent article in the *University of Toronto Quarterly*. What we do is to set up, as the logical expression of Augustanism, some impossibly pedantic view of following rules and repressing feelings, which nobody could ever have held, and then treat any symptom of freedom or emotion as a departure from this. Our students are thus graduated with a vague notion that the age of sensibility was the time when poetry moved from a reptilian Classicism, all cold and dry reason, to a mammalian Romanticism, all warm and wet feeling.

As for the term "pre-romantic," that, as a term for the age itself, has the peculiar demerit of committing us to anachronism before we start, and imposing a false teleology on everything we study. Not only did the "pre-romantics" not know that the Romantic movement was going to succeed them, but there has probably never been a case on record of a poet's having regarded a later poet's work as the fulfillment of his own. However, I do not care about terminology, only about appreciation for an extraordinarily interesting period of English literature, and the first stage in renewing that appreciation seems to me the gaining of a clear sense of what it is in itself.

Some languages use verb-tenses to express, not time, but the difference between completed and continuous action. And in the history of literature we become aware, not only of periods, but of a recurrent opposition of two views of literature. These two views

130

are the Aristotelian and the Longinian, the aesthetic and the psychological, the view of literature as product and the view of literature as process. In our day we have acquired a good deal of respect for literature as process, notably in prose fiction. The stream of consciousness gets careful treatment in our criticism, and when we compare Arnold Bennett and Virginia Woolf on the subject of Mrs. Brown we generally take the side of Virginia Woolf. So it seems that our age ought to feel a close kinship with the prose fiction of the age of sensibility, when the sense of literature as process was brought to a peculiarly exquisite perfection by Sterne, and in lesser degree by Richardson and Boswell.

All the great story-tellers, including the Augustan ones, have a strong sense of literature as a finished product. The suspense is thrown forward until it reaches the end, and is based on our confidence that the author knows what is coming next. A story-teller does not break his illusion by talking to the reader as Fielding does, because we know from the start that we are listening to Fielding telling a story—that is, Johnson's arguments about illusion in drama apply equally well to prose fiction of Fielding's kind. But when we turn to *Tristram Shandy* we not only read the book but watch the author at work writing it: at any moment the house of Walter Shandy may vanish and be replaced by the author's study. This does break the illusion, or would if there were any illusion to break, but here we are not being led into a story, but into the process of writing a story: we wonder, not what is coming next, but what the author will think of next.

Sterne is, of course, an unusually pure example of a process-writer, but even in Richardson we find many of the same characteristics. Johnson's well-known remark that if you read Richardson for the story you would hang yourself indicates that Richardson is not interested in a plot with a quick-march rhythm. Richardson does not throw the suspense forward, but keeps the emotion at a continuous present. Readers of *Pamela* have become so fascinated by watching the sheets of Pamela's manuscript spawning and secreting all over her master's house, even into the recesses of her clothes, as she fends off assault with one hand and writes about it with the other, that they sometimes overlook the reason for an apparently clumsy device. The reason is, of course, to give the impression of literature as process, as created on the spot out of the events it describes. And in the very beginning of *Boswell in London* we can see the boy of twenty-one already practising the art of writing as a continuous process from experience. When he writes of his adventure with Louisa he may be writing several days after the event, but he does not use his later knowledge.

In poetry the sense of literature as a finished product normally expresses itself in some kind of regularly recurring metre, the general pattern of which is established as soon as possible. In listening to Pope's couplets we have a sense of continually fulfilled expectation which is the opposite of obviousness: a sense that eighteenth-century music also often gives us. Such a technique demands a clear statement of what sound-patterns we may expect. We hear at once the full ring of the rhyming couplet, and all other sound-patterns are kept to a minimum. In such a line as:

> And strains from hard-bound brains eight lines a year,

the extra assonance is a deliberate discord, expressing the difficulties of constipated genius. Similarly with the alliteration in:

> Great Cibber's brazen, brainless brothers stand,

and the fact that these are deliberate discords used for parody indicates that they are normally not present. Johnson's disapproval of such devices in serious contexts is written all over the *Lives of the Poets*.

When we turn from Pope to the age of sensibility, we get something of the same kind of shock that we get when we turn from Tennyson or Matthew Arnold to Hopkins. Our ears are assaulted by unpredictable assonances, alliterations, interrhymings and echolalia:

> Mie love ys dedde,
> Gon to hys death-bedde . . .

> With brede ethereal wove,
> O'erhang his wavy bed . . .

> The couthy cracks begin whan supper's o'er,
> The cheering bicker gars them glibly gash . . .

> But a pebble of the brook
> Warbled out these metres meet . . .

In many of the best-known poems of the period, in Smart's *Song to David*, in Chatterton's elegies, in Burns's songs and Blake's lyrics, even in some of the Wesley hymns, we find a delight in refrain for refrain's sake. Sometimes, naturally, we can see the appropriate literary influences helping to shape the form, such as the incremental repetition of the ballad, or Old Norse alliteration in *The Fatal Sisters*. And whatever may be thought of the poetic value of the Ossianic poems, most estimates of that value parrot Wordsworth, and Wordsworth's criticisms of Ossian's imagery are quite beside the point. The vague generalized imagery of Ossian, like the mysterious resonant names and the fixed epithets, are part of a deliberate and well unified scheme. *Fingal* and *Temora* are long poems for the same reason that *Clarissa* is a long novel: not because there is a complicated story to be told, as in *Tom Jones* or an epic of Southey, but because the emotion is being maintained at a continuous present by various devices of repetition.

The reason for these intensified sound-patterns is, once again, an interest in the poetic process as distinct from the product. In the composing of poetry, where rhyme is as important as reason, there is a primary stage in which words are linked by sound rather than sense. From the point of view of sense this stage is merely free or uncontrolled association, and in the way it operates it is very like the dream. Again like the dream, it has to meet a censor-principle, and shape itself into intelligible patterns. Where the emphasis is on the communicated product, the qualities of consciousness take the lead: a regular metre, clarity of syntax, epigram and wit, repetition of sense in antithesis and balance rather than of sound. Swift speaks with admiration of Pope's ability to get more "sense" into one couplet than he can into six: concentration of sense for him is clearly a major criterion of poetry. Where the emphasis is on the original process, the qualities of subconscious association take the lead, and the poetry becomes hypnotically repetitive, oracular, incantatory, dreamlike and in the original sense of the word charming. The response to it includes a subconscious factor, the surrendering to a spell. In Ossian, who carries this tendency further than anyone else, the aim is not concentration of sense but diffusion of sense, hence Johnson's remark that anybody could write like Ossian if he would abandon his mind to it. Literature as product may take a lyrical form, as it does in the sublime ode about which Professor Maclean has written so well, but it is also the conception of literature that makes the longer continuous poem possible. Literature as process, being based on an irregular and unpredictable coincidence of sound-patterns, tends to seek the brief or even the fragmentary utterance, in other words to centre itself on the lyric, which accounts for the feeling of a sudden emergence of a lyrical impulse in the age of sensibility.

The "pre-romantic" approach to this period sees it as developing a conception of the creative imagination, which became the basis of Romanticism. This is true, but the Romantics tended to see the poem as the *product* of the creative imagination, thus reverting in at least one respect to the Augustan attitude. For the Augustan, art is posterior to nature because nature is the art of God; for the Romantic, art is prior to nature because God is an artist; one deals in physical and the other in biological analogies, as Professor Abrams' *Mirror and the Lamp* has shown. But for the Romantic poet the poem is still an artefact: in Coleridge's terms, a secondary or productive imagination has been imposed on a primary imaginative process. So, different as it is from Augustan poetry, Romantic poetry is like it in being a conservative rhetoric, and in being founded on relatively regular metrical schemes. Poe's rejection of the continuous poem does not express anything very central in Romanticism itself, as nearly every major Romantic poet composed poems of considerable, sometimes immense, length. Poe's theory is closer to the practice of the age of sensibility before him and the *symbolistes* after him.

In the age of sensibility most of the long poems, of course, simply carry on with standard continuous metres, or exploit the greater degree of intensified recurrent sound afforded by stanzaic forms, notably the Spenserian. But sometimes the peculiar problems of making associative poetry continuous were faced in a more experimental way, experiments largely ignored by the Romantics. Oracular poetry in a long form often tends to become a series of utterances, irregular in rhythm but strongly marked off one from the other. We notice in Whitman, for instance, that the end of every line has a strong pause—for when the rhythm is variable there is no point in a run-on line. Sometimes this oracular rhythm takes on at least a typographical resemblance to prose, as it does in Rimbaud's *Saison en Enfer*, or, more frequently, to a discontinuous blend of prose and verse in which the sentence, the paragraph and the line are much the same unit. The chief literary influence for this rhythm has always been the translated Bible, which took on a new impetus in the age of sensibility; and if we study carefully the rhythm of Ossian, of Smart's *Jubilate Agno* and of the Blake Prophecies, we can see three very different but equally logical developments of this semi-Biblical rhythm.

Where there is a strong sense of literature as aesthetic product, there is also a sense of its detachment from the spectator. Aristotle's theory of catharsis describes how this works for tragedy: pity and fear are detached from the beholder by being directed towards objects. Where there is a sense of literature as process, pity and fear become states of mind without objects, moods which are common to the work of art and the reader, and which bind them together psychologically instead of separating them aesthetically.

Fear without an object, as a condition of mind prior to being afraid *of* anything, is called *Angst* or anxiety, a somewhat narrow term for what may be almost anything between pleasure and pain. In the general area of pleasure comes the eighteenth-century conception of the sublime, where qualities of austerity, gloom, grandeur, melancholy or even menace are a source of romantic or penseroso feelings. The appeal of Ossian to his time on this basis needs no comment. From here we move through the graveyard poets, the Gothic-horror novelists and the writers of tragic ballads to such *fleurs du mal* as Cowper's *Castaway* and Blake's Golden Chapel poem in the Rossetti MS.

Pity without an object has never to my knowledge been given a name, but it expresses itself as an imaginative animism, or treating everything in nature as though it had human feelings or qualities. At one end of its range is the apocalyptic exultation of all nature bursting into human life that we have in Smart's *Song to David* and the ninth Night of *The Four Zoas*. Next comes an imaginative sympathy with the kind of folklore that peoples the countryside with elemental spirits, such as we have in Collins, Fergusson, Burns and the Wartons. Next we have the curiously intense awareness of the animal world which (except for some poems of D. H. Lawrence) is unrivalled in this period, and is expressed in some of its best realized writing: in Burns's *To a Mouse*, in Cowper's exquisite snail poem, in Smart's superb lines on his cat Jeoffry, in the famous starling and ass episodes in Sterne, in the opening of Blake's *Auguries of Innocence*. Finally comes the sense of sympathy with man himself, the sense that no one can afford to be indifferent to the fate of anyone else, which underlies the protests against slavery and misery in Cowper, in Crabbe and in Blake's *Songs of Experience*.

This concentration on the primitive process of writing is projected in two directions, into nature and into history. The appropriate natural setting for much of the poetry of sensibility is nature at one of the two poles of process, creation and decay. The poet is attracted by the ruinous and the mephitic, or by the primeval and "unspoiled"—a picturesque subtly but perceptibly different from the Romantic picturesque. The projection into history assumes that the psychological progress of the poet from lyrical through epic to dramatic presentations, discussed by Stephen at the end of Joyce's *Portrait*, must be the historical progress of literature as well. Even as late as the preface to Victor Hugo's *Cromwell* this assumption persists. The Ossian and Rowley poems are not simple hoaxes: they are pseudepigrapha, like the Book of Enoch, and like it they take what is psychologically primitive, the oracular process of composition, and project it as something historically primitive.

The poetry of process is oracular, and the medium of the oracle is often in an ecstatic or trance-like state: autonomous voices seem to speak through him, and as he is concerned to utter rather than to address, he is turned away from his listener, so to speak, in a state of rapt self-communion. The free association of words, in which sound is prior to sense, is often a literary way of representing insanity. In Rimbaud's terrifyingly accurate phrase, poetry of the associative or oracular type requires a "dérèglement de tous les sens." Hence the qualities that make a man an oracular poet are often the qualities that work against, and sometimes destroy, his social personality. Far more than the time of Rimbaud and Verlaine is this period of literature a period of the *poète maudit*. The list of poets over whom the shadows of mental breakdown fell is far too long to be coincidence. The much publicized death of Chatterton is certainly one of the personal tragedies of the age, but an easier one to take than the kind of agony which is expressed with an almost definitive poignancy by Smart in *Jubilate Agno*:

For in my nature I quested for beauty, but God, God, hath sent me to sea for pearls.

It is characteristic of the age of sensibility that this personal or biographical aspect of it should be so closely connected with its central technical feature. The basis of poetic language is the metaphor, and the metaphor, in its radical form, is a statement of identity: "this is that." In all our ordinary experience the metaphor is non-literal: nobody but a savage or a lunatic can take metaphor literally. For Classical or Augustan critics the metaphor is a condensed simile: its real or common-sense basis is likeness, not identity, and when it obliterates the sense of likeness it becomes barbaric. In Johnson's strictures on the music and water metaphor of Gray's *Bard* we can see what intellectual abysses, for him, would open up if metaphors ever passed beyond the stage of resemblance. For the Romantic critic, the identification in the metaphor is ideal: two images are identified within the mind of the creating poet.

But where metaphor is conceived as part of an oracular and half-ecstatic process, there is a direct identification in which the poet himself is involved. To use another phrase of Rimbaud's, the poet feels not "je pense," but "on me pense." In the age of sensibility some of the identifications involving the poet seem manic, like Blake's with Druidic bards or Smart's with Hebrew prophets, or depressive, like Cowper's with a scapegoat figure, a stricken deer or castaway, or merely bizarre, like Macpherson's with Ossian or Chatterton's with Rowley. But it is in this psychological self-identification that the central "primitive" quality of this age really emerges. In Collins's *Ode on the Poetical Character*, in Smart's *Jubilate Agno*, and in Blake's *Four Zoas*, it attains its greatest intensity and completeness.

In these three poems, especially the last two, God, the poet's soul and nature are brought into a white-hot fusion of identity, an imaginative fiery furnace in which the reader may, if he chooses, make a fourth. All three poems are of the greatest complexity, yet the emotion on which they are founded is of a simplicity and directness that English literature has rarely attained again. With the 1800 edition of *Lyrical Ballads*, secondary imagination and recollection in tranquillity took over English poetry and dominated it until the end of the nineteenth century. The primitivism of Blake and Smart revived in France with Rimbaud and Gérard de Nerval, but even this development had become conservative by the time its influence reached England, and only in a few poems of Dylan Thomas, and those perhaps not his best, does the older tradition revive. But contemporary poetry is still deeply concerned with the problems and techniques of the age of sensibility, and while the latter's resemblance to our time is not a merit in it, it is a logical enough reason for re-examining it with fresh eyes.

❧ Blake After Two Centuries

THE VALUE OF CENTENARIES AND SIMILAR OBSERVANCES IS THAT they call attention, not simply to great men, but to what we do with our great men. The anniversary punctuates, so to speak, the scholarly and critical absorption of its subject into society. From this point of view, a centenary date might well be more impressive for those interested in William Blake than his birth on November 28, 1757. The year 1857 would bring us to a transitional point in the life of Alexander Gilchrist, who had recently got a life of Etty off his hands, married, moved to Chelsea to be near his idol Carlyle, was busy winding up some family business, and was preparing to start in earnest on *The Life of William Blake, Pictor Ignotus*. This last was no empty phrase. Scattered notices of Blake had appeared in collections of artists' biographies, but nothing like a full volume had been devoted to Blake in the thirty years since his death. Blake was fortunate in his first posthumous group of admirers. Gilchrist was a remarkable person, his wife Anne equally so, and Rossetti and Swinburne, if not exactly emancipated spirits, were at least sufficiently free of the more lethal Victorian virtues to admire Blake without undue inhibitions. They make an instructive contrast to whoever it was (apparently not Ruskin, who has been accused of it) that cut up one of the two coloured copies of *Jerusalem,* the anonymous worthy who apparently destroyed the great 'Vision of the Last Judgement,' and the member of the Linnell family who erased the genitalia from the drawings on the *Four Zoas* manuscript.

Gilchrist died in 1861 with his masterpiece unfinished: Anne Gilchrist brought it out in 1863 in two volumes. The first volume was Gilchrist's biography: no better biography has been written since, for all our advance in understanding. The main part of the second volume was Rossetti's edition of the lyrics, where Blake, however expurgated and improved in his metres, still did achieve something like a representative showing as a poet. Swinburne's critical essay appeared in 1868, and soon afterwards there began, a slow trickle at first, then a flood still in full spate, of critical studies, biographies, editions, illustrated editions, collections of paintings and engravings, handbooks, catalogues, appreciations, research articles, chapters in other books, and specialized studies pouring out of the presses of at least twenty countries. Max Beerbohm's Enoch Soames sold his soul to the devil in exchange for a glance at the future British Museum catalogue of critical work on him, only to discover that posterity took the same view of him that his contemporaries had done. Such irony is not for Blake, who in his lifetime was something of an Enoch Soames too, but an Enoch Soames who was right.

Much more than a Cinderella success story is involved here. In her little British Council bibliography, Miss Kathleen Raine remarks on the spontaneous personal affection shown in the public response to the recent discovery of a large and rather confused allegorical picture by Blake in a house in Devon. A new Michelangelo would have been more important, but it would not have aroused that specific reaction of affectionate pride. Blake's deep love of England is clearly not an unrequited love, nor is the sense that he is one of us confined to Englishmen. People get attracted to him through feeling that he is for them a personal discovery and something of a private possession. I constantly hear of doctors, housewives, clergymen, teachers, manual workers, shopkeepers, who are, in the most frequent phrase used, 'frightfully keen on Blake,' who have bought every book on him they could afford, and kept him around like an amiable household god. I have taught Blake to Jesuits and I have taught him to Communist organizers; I have taught him to deans of women and I have taught him to ferocious young poets of unpredictable rhythms and unprintable (or at least privately printed) diction. His admirers have nothing in common except the feeling that Blake says something to them that no one else can say: that whatever their standards and values may be, Blake has the charity to include them, not as part of a general principle of benevolence, which Blake himself would have despised, but uniquely as individuals.

Undergraduates, too, have fewer barriers against Blake than against most poets: besides the absence of unfamiliar conventions or a special poetic language, he lacks the two qualities that undergraduates are most afraid of, sentimentality and irony. Again, some poets travel better than others, and just as Byron and Poe in the nineteenth century proved to be more readily exportable than Wordsworth or Hawthorne, so in the twentieth century Blake seems the easiest of all our poets to export to India or Japan. He can hardly ever lack admirers among the fellow countrymen of Rouault and of Gérard de Nerval, or of Hölderlin and of Novalis. Within ninety years after the first critical study of him was published, Blake appears to be headed for what at one time seemed his least likely fate: a genuine, permanent, and international popularity.

This popularity has been achieved in spite of Blake's reputation for being difficult and esoteric, and someone not to be understood without preliminary study of a dozen occult systems of thought and several thousand pages of commentary. I have written one of the thickest of the commentaries myself, and I certainly meant all I said, but I quite realize how often the popular estimate of Blake is sounder in perspective than the scholarly one. Scholars will assert that the famous 'Jerusalem' hymn is crypto-Anglo-Israelitism or what not; but when it was sung in front of Transport House at the Labour victory of 1945 the singers showed that they understood it far better than such scholars did. Scholars will assert that the question in *The Tyger*, 'Did he who made the lamb make thee?' is to be answered with a confident yes or no: yes if Blake is believed to be a pantheist, no if he is believed to be a Gnostic. Most of those who love the poem are content to leave it a question, and they are right. 'You say,' wrote Blake to the Rev. Dr. Trusler, author of *The Way to be Rich and Respectable*, 'that I want somebody to Elucidate my Ideas. But you ought to know that What is Grand is necessarily obscure to Weak men. That which can be made Explicit to the Idiot is not worth my care.' Having thus brought his correspondent into focus, he goes on: 'But I am happy to find a Great Majority of Fellow Mortals who can Elucidate My Visions, & Particularly they have been Elucidated by Children, who have taken a greater delight in contemplating my Pictures than I even hoped.' Children have always found Blake easier than the Truslers have done.

II

Clearly, if Blake can be popular we need a new definition of popularity. Several very different things are included under the term popular, and the simple conception 'What the public wants' will not do. Best-seller popularity depends more on news value than on any aesthetic qualities, whether good or bad. But there is another sense in which the term popular may be used, as referring to the art which affords a key to imaginative experience for the untrained. The centre of gravity of popular fiction in this sense is the folk tale, and in American culture, for instance, it would be represented by *Huckleberry Finn, Rip van Winkle*, some tales of Poe, of Uncle Remus, and the various cycles of native humour like the Western tall tale. Much that is popular even in this context is still rubbish, and some of it may be quite unpopular in the best-seller meaning of the word. The popular in the second sense is the contemporary primitive, and it tends to become primitive with the passing of time. Such primitive and popular elements recur in great art, even very difficult and complex art. One thinks of Shakespeare's late romances, with their archaic nature myths and their improbable coincidences turning up 'like an old tale.' One thinks more particularly of the Bible, which is one long folk tale from beginning to end, and the most primitive and popular book in the world.

The two senses of popular seem to be, up to a point, connected with the distinction of content and form. 'What the public wants,' as the first word suggests, relates primarily to content: certain conventional choices of subject—domestic, sentimental, heroic, sexually provocative—come into vogue by turns. Certain story types, on the other hand, which remain fairly constant from ancient myth to contemporary comic strip, are isolated in the art which is popular in the second sense. Like the corresponding primitive and popular forms in the plastic arts, they are abstract and stylized, and have a curiously archaic look about them whenever they appear. The generic term for such story types is myth, because myths are stories about divine beings which are abstract and stylized stories in the sense that they are unaffected by canons of realism or probability.

Blake's only fictions are in his Prophetic Books, and although they are certainly mythical enough, there are other aspects of popular literature in its formal sense more obviously relevant to him. The conceptual element in poetry is also a part of its content, and conceptual thinking in poetry is more or less assimilated to another kind of thinking which organizes the poetic structure. The unit of this formally poetic thinking is the metaphor, and the metaphor is inherently illogical, an identification of two or more things which could never be identified except by a lunatic, a lover, or a poet—one may perhaps add an extremely primitive savage. We are educated in conceptual thinking, and so usually find poetry which comes to terms with it easier to read, like Wordsworth's. Poetry which is popular in the sense of having a vogue is popular by reason of having such a conceptual content: it talks about the Deity in the eighteenth century, or Duty in the nineteenth, or it speaks to the eternal bourgeois in the heart of man, like Kipling's *If*, Longfellow's *Psalm of Life*, or Burns's *A Man's a Man for a' that*. Poetry which concentrates on metaphor to the point of appearing to exclude conceptual thought altogether, like surrealist poetry, impresses most readers as wilfully crazy, or, if they are compelled to take it seriously, as incredibly difficult and esoteric.

Yet greater experience with literature soon shows that it is metaphor which is direct and primitive, and conceptual thought which is sophisticated. Hence there is a body of verse that can be called popular in the sense of providing the direct, primitive, metaphorical key to poetic experience for educated and uneducated alike. Most good teaching anthologies are largely composed of such verse, and in such anthologies the lyrics of Blake leap into the foreground with a vividness that almost exaggerates Blake's relative importance as a poet:

> O Rose, thou art sick!
> The invisible worm
> That flies in the night,
> In the howling storm,
>
> Has found out thy bed
> Of crimson joy,
> And his dark secret love
> Does thy life destroy.

I say exaggerates, because there are many fine poets who do not have this specific kind of directness. One may always meet a poem with a set of questions designed to avoid its impact: what does it mean; why is it considered a good poem; is it morally beneficial; does it say profound things about life, and so forth. But such a poem as *The Sick Rose* has a peculiar power of brushing them aside, of speaking with the unanswerable authority of poetry itself. Blake's lyrics, with many of those of Herrick, Burns, and Donne, the sonnets of Shakespeare, Wordsworth's Lucy poems, and a few of the great ballads, are popular poetry in the sense that they are a practically foolproof introduction to poetic experience.

Metaphor, then, is a formal principle of poetry, and myth of fiction. We begin to see how Blake hangs together: his prophecies are so intensely mythical because his lyrics are so intensely metaphorical. At present his prophecies seem to have little to do with popular literature in any sense of the word, but opinion will have changed on this point long before the tercentenary rolls around. It will then be generally understood that just as Blake's lyrics are among the best possible introductions to poetic experience, so his prophecies are among the best possible introductions to the grammar and structure of literary mythology. His practice again is consistent with his theory, which lays an almost exclusive emphasis on the imagination or forming power. However, there comes a point at which our distinction of form and content breaks down, and we have to raise the question of what kind of content formal art has.

'The Nature of my Work is Visionary or Imaginative,' said Blake: 'it is an Endeavour to Restore what the Ancients call'd the Golden Age.' By vision he meant the view of the world, not as it might be, still less as it ordinarily appears, but as it really is when it is seen by human consciousness at its greatest height and intensity. It is the artist's business to attain this heightened or transfigured view of things, and show us what kind of world is actually in front of us, with all its glowing splendours and horrifying evils. It is only the direct, metaphorical, and mythical perceptions, which work without compromise with unimaginative notions of reality, that can clearly render the forms of such a world. Such psychological experiments as those recorded in Mr. Aldous Huxley's *The Doors of Perception* (the title of which comes from Blake, although taking mescalin is not precisely what Blake meant by 'cleansing' the doors of perception) seem to show that the formal principles of this heightened vision are constantly latent in the mind, which perhaps explains the communicability of such visions. For Blake, however, the Bible provides the key to the relation between the two worlds. The ordinary world is 'fallen,' the manifestation of man's own sin and ignorance; the true world is the apocalypse presented at the end of the Bible and the paradise presented at the beginning of it: the true city and garden that is man's home, and which all existing cities and gardens struggle to make manifest in the lower world.

The apocalypse of the Bible is a world in which all human forms are identified, as Blake says at the end of his *Jerusalem*. That is, all forms are identified as human. Cities and gardens, sun moon and stars, rivers and stones, trees and human bodies—all are equally alive, equally parts of the same infinite body which is at once the body of God and of risen man. In this world 'Each Identity is Eternal,' for 'In Eternity one Thing never Changes into another Thing.' It is a world of forms like Plato's except that in Blake these forms are images of pure being seen by a spiritual body, not ideas of pure essence seen by a soul, a conception which would rule out the artist as a revealer of reality. To Blake this vision of apocalypse and resurrection was the grammar of poetry and painting alike, and it was also the source of the formal principles of art. He lived in a way that brought him into the most constant contact with this world, for we notice that isolation, solitude, and a certain amount of mental stress or disturbance have a tendency to light up this vision in the mind. When Christopher Smart is shut into a madhouse with no company except his cat Jeoffry, the cat leaps into the same apocalyptic limelight as Blake's tiger:

> For he keeps the Lord's watch in the night against the adversary.
> For he counteracts the powers of darkness by his electrical skin and glaring eyes. . .
> For he is of the tribe of Tiger.
> For the Cherub Cat is a term of the Angel Tiger . . .
> For by stroaking of him I have found out electricity.
> For I perceived God's light about him both wax and fire.
> For the electrical fire is the spiritual substance, which God sends from heaven to sustain the bodies both of man and beast.

Similarly when John Clare is confined to an asylum and is in the depths of schizophrenia, the luminous fragility of Blake's *Book of Thel*, along with the glowing lights and gemmed trees of Mr. Huxley's adventures in heaven and hell, appear in his vision:

> The birds sing on the clouds in that eternal land,
> Jewels and siller are they a', and gouden is the sand.
> The sun is one vast world of fire that burneth a' to-day,
> And nights wi' hells of darkness for ever keeps away.
> And dearly I love the queen o' that bright land,
> The lily flowers o' woman that meeteth no decay.

Blake's attitude to art makes no psychological distinctions among the arts, and the same imagination that the poet uses appears in Blake's theory of painting as 'outline,' which again is an intense concentration on the formal principles of the art. The abstract school of painting today assumes that the formal principles of painting are quasi-geometrical, but Blake, with the faded white ghosts of eighteenth-century classicism in front of him, warned sharply against the preference of 'mathematic form' to 'living form.' Blake despised everything that was amorphous or vague in art: the imagination for him could express itself only as rigorous and exactly ordered form. But by living form he meant a vitalized classicism, where the outline is held in the tight grip of imaginative intensity, a classicism that would have more in common with Van Gogh than with Flaxman or David. Blake's painting, though strongly formalized, is not abstract in tendency, but what one might call hieroglyphic in tendency. It presents the same world that his poetry presents; yet (except in lapses) it is not literary painting. The tense stylized figures of the Byzantines with their staring eyes and weightless bodies; mediaeval primitives with their glittering gold haloes and childlike sense of primary colour; Eastern 'mandalas' that communicate the sense of powerful spiritual discipline in repose; the calligraphic distortions of Klee: these all belong in different ways to the hieroglyphic tradition in painting, and are allied to the vision that Blake evolved from his study of Renaissance prints.

III

The conception of formally popular art which underlies the present argument is still an unexplored subject in criticism, and many aspects of it can be only suggested here. It has been neglected partly because the original proponents of it, notably Herder, confused it by mixing it up with a pseudo-historical myth of the Golden Age family. Formally popular art was supposed to have been derived from a 'folk' whose art was rural and spontaneous and communal and unspecialized and a number of other things that no art can be. When we remove this notion of a 'folk,' we are left with a third conception of popular art as the art which is central to a specific cultural tradition. There is no question here of looking for *the* centre or isolating an imaginary essence of a tradition, but only of seeing what some of its prevailing and recurrent rhythms have been. The sources of a cultural tradition are, of course, its religious and social context as well as its own earlier products. In English culture we notice at once a strong and constant affinity with art which is popular in the formal sense, in striking contrast to, say, French culture, which has much more the character of something deliberately imposed.

One characteristic of the English tradition has obviously been affected by Protestantism. This is the tendency to anchor the apocalyptic vision in a direct individual experience, as the product, not of sacramental discipline, but of imaginative experiment. The experience may be as forced as *Grace Abounding* or as relaxed as Keats's speculations about a vale of soul-making, but it tends to be autonomous, to make the experience its own authority. The 1611 Bible is not a 'monument of English prose,' but the exact opposite of what a monument is: it is a translation with a unique power of making the Bible a personal possession of its reader, and to this its enormous popularity as well as its importance in English culture is due. It has also fostered, of course, the kind of Biblical culture that has made *The Pilgrim's Progress* one of the most popular books in the language, that has given *Paradise Lost* its central place in English literature, and that has instigated some very inadequate performances of Handel's *Messiah* (a work with a unique power of catching this quality of direct vision in music) in Midland towns. Such Biblical culture, absorbed as part of a poet's own imaginative experience, was inspiring visions of revelation and resurrection at least as early as the *Pearl* poet, and had lost nothing of its intensity when Dylan Thomas was shattering the sedate trumpet of the BBC with the same tones:

> Though they be mad and dead as nails,
> Heads of the characters hammer through daisies;
> Break in the sun till the sun breaks down,
> And death shall have no dominion.

Blake, who was brought up on the Bible and on Milton, is unusually close to this simple and naïve Biblism even for an English poet. The occult and esoteric elements in his thought have been grossly exaggerated by critics who, as Johnson said of Hume, have not read the New Testament with attention. What is so obviously true of most of his paintings is true also of his poetry: it is the work of a man whose Bible was his textbook. The prophecies recreate the Bible in English symbolism, just as the 1611 translation recreates it in the English language, and, no less than *Paradise Lost* or *The Pilgrim's Progress*, they record a direct search for the New Jerusalem which exists here and now in England's green and pleasant land.

A second characteristic of the English tradition is of social origin, and is derived from an apparently permanent English tendency to political resistance. This tendency has taken different forms in different ages—Roundhead, Whig, radical, liberal, socialist—but is so constant that it may be actually a kind of anarchism, or what in a play of Bernard Shaw's is called an obstinate refusal to be governed at all. From Milton's defence of the liberty of prophesying to Mill's defence of the right to be eccentric, it is pervaded by a sense that the final cause of society is the free individual. This sense distinguishes it sharply from such revolutionary traditions as those of America or Russia, where a fundamental social pattern is established *a priori* by the revolution, and other patterns are rejected as un-American or counter-revolutionary.

In Blake's political outlook one finds a radicalism of a common English type, which includes a strong individual protest against all institutional radicalism. Blake was brought up in the centre of English social resistance, the city of London, in the period of Wilkes and the Gordon riots. His sympathy first with the American and then with the French revolution placed him as far to the left as he could go and still continue to function as an artist. Yet his denunciation of what he called the 'Deism' of the French revolutionaries, and of the ideology of Voltaire and Rousseau, is nearly as strong as Burke's. At the same time his poems point directly towards the English society of his time: even his most complex prophecies have far more in common with Dickens than they have with Plotinus. And though he said 'Houses of Commons & Houses of Lords appear to me to be fools; they seem to me to be something Else besides Human Life,' this expresses, not a withdrawal from society, but a sense of the inadequacy of everything that falls short of the apocalyptic vision itself. Blake's is the same impossible vision that caused Milton to break with four kinds of revolt in England, and which still earlier had inspired the dream of John Ball, a dream based, like *Areopagitica* and *The Marriage of Heaven and Hell*, on a sense of ironic contrast between the fallen and unfallen worlds:

> When Adam delved and Eve span,
> Who was then the gentleman?

In breaking with all forms of social organization, however, Blake is merely following the logic of art itself, whose myths and visions are at once the cause and the clarified form of social developments. Every society is the embodiment of a myth, and as the artist is the shaper of myth, there is a sense in which he holds in his hand the thunderbolts that destroy one society and create another. Another busy and versatile English radical, William Morris, not a mythopoeic poet himself but a mere collector of myths, nevertheless portrayed those myths in *The Earthly Paradise* as a group of old men who had outgrown the desire to be made kings or gods. In this cycle they are ineffectual exiles, but in Morris's later work they return as revolutionary dreams, though of a kind that, again, rejects all existing types of revolutionary organization.

The possibility is raised in passing that formally popular art has a perennially subversive quality about it, whereas art that has a vogue popularity remains subservient to society. We note that Russian Communism denounced 'formalism' as the essence of the bourgeois in art, and turned to vogue popularity instead, a vogue artificially sustained by political control, as part of its general policy of perverting revolutionary values. This tendency follows the example set by Tolstoy, who, though a greater artist than Morris, was also more confused about the nature of popular art.

Blake formed his creative habits in the age immediately preceding Romanticism: still, his characteristics are romantic in the expanded sense of giving a primary place to imagination and individual feeling. Like the Romantics, Blake thought of the 'Augustan' period from 1660 to 1760 as an interruption of the normal native tradition. This sense of belonging to and restoring the native tradition helps to distinguish Romanticism in England from Romanticism on the Continent, especially in France. It also enabled the English Romantic writers—in their fertile periods at any rate—to lean less heavily on religious and political conservatism in their search for a tradition.

The great achievement of English Romanticism was its grasp of the principle of creative autonomy, its declaration of artistic independence. The thing that is new in Wordsworth's *Prelude,* in Coleridge's criticism, in Keats's letters, is the sense, not that the poet is superior or inferior to others, but simply that he has an authority, as distinct from a social function, of his own. He does not need to claim any extraneous authority, and still less need he take refuge in any withdrawal from society. The creative process is an end in itself, not to be judged by its power to illustrate something else, however true or good. Some Romantics, especially Coleridge, wobble on this point, but Blake, like Keats and Shelley, is firm, and consistent when he says, 'I will not Reason & Compare: my business is to Create.' The difficulties revealed by such poems as Shelley's *Triumph of Life* or Keats's *Fall of Hyperion* are concerned with the content of the poetic vision, not with any doubts about the validity of that vision as a mean between subjective dream and objective action. 'The poet and the dreamer are distinct,' says Keats's Moneta, and Rousseau in Shelley's poem is typically the bastard poet whose work spilled over into action instead of remaining creative.

148

Hence the English Romantic tradition has close affinities with the individualism of the Protestant and the radical traditions. In all three the tendency is to take the individual as the primary field or area of operations instead of the interests of society, a tendency which is not necessarily egocentric, any more than its opposite is necessarily altruistic. English Romanticism is greatly aided in its feeling of being central to the tradition of English literature by the example of Shakespeare, who was in proportion to his abilities the most unpretentious poet who ever lived, a poet of whom one can predicate nothing except that he wrote plays, and stuck to his own business as a poet. He is the great poetic example of an inductive and practical approach to experience in English culture which is another aspect of its individualism.

I have no thought of trying to prefer one kind of English culture to another, and I regard all value-judgments that inhibit one's sympathies with anything outside a given tradition as dismally uncritical. I say only that this combination of Protestant, radical, and Romantic qualities is frequent enough in English culture to account for the popularity, in every sense, of the products of it described above. There has been no lack of Catholic, Tory, and Classical elements too, but the tradition dealt with here has been popular enough to give these latter elements something of the quality of a consciously intellectual reaction. During the twenties of the present century, after the shock of the First World War, this intellectual reaction gathered strength. Its most articulate supporters were cultural evangelists who came from places like Missouri and Idaho, and who had a clear sense of the shape of the true English tradition, from its beginnings in Provence and mediaeval Italy to its later developments in France. Mr. Eliot's version of this tradition was finally announced as Classical, royalist, and Anglo-Catholic, implying that whatever was Protestant, radical, and Romantic would have to go into the intellectual doghouse.

Many others who did not have the specific motivations of Mr. Eliot or of Mr. Pound joined in the chorus of denigration of Miltonic, Romantic, liberal, and allied values. Critics still know too little of the real principles of criticism to have any defence against such fashions, when well organized; hence although the fashion itself is on its way out, the prejudices set up by it still remain. Blake must of course be seen in the context of the tradition he belonged to, unless he is to be unnaturally isolated from it, and when the fashionable judgments on his tradition consist so largely of pseudo-critical hokum, one's understanding of Blake inevitably suffers. We come back again to the reason for anniversaries. There may be others in the English tradition as great as Blake, but there can hardly be many as urgently great, looming over the dither of our situation with a more inescapable clarity, full of answers to questions that we have hardly learned how to formulate. Whatever other qualities Blake may have had or lacked, he certainly had courage and simplicity. Whatever other qualities our own age may have or lack, it is certainly an age of fearfulness and complexity. And every age learns most from those who most directly confront it.

≥ The Imaginative and the Imaginary

I SHOULD LIKE TO BEGIN BY DISTINGUISHING TWO SOCIAL CONTEXTS OF the human mind. What I say in this connexion will be familiar enough to you, but I need to establish some common ground between an association of psychiatrists and a literary critic. Man lives in an environment that we call nature, and he also lives in a society or home, a human world that he is trying to build out of nature. There is the world he sees and the world he constructs, the world he lives in and the world he wants to live in. In relation to the world he sees, or the environment, the essential attitude of his mind is that of recognition, the ability to see things as they are, the clear understanding of what is, as distinct from what we should like it to be. This is an attitude often associated, sometimes correctly, with the reason. I should prefer to call it "sense," because it is a pragmatic and practical habit of mind, not theoretical, as reason is, and because it requires emotional as well as intellectual balance. It is the attitude with which the scientist initially faces nature, determined to see first of all what is there without allowing any other of his mental interests to cook the evidence. And it is, I should think, the attitude that psychiatry would take as the standard of the "normal," the condition of mental health from which mental illness deviates.

The other attitude is usually described as "creative," a somewhat hazy metaphor of religious origin, or as imaginative. This is the vision, not of what is, but of what otherwise might be done with a given situation. Along with the given world, there is or may be present an invisible model of something non-existent but possible and desirable. Imagination exists in all areas of human activity, but in three of particular importance, the arts, love and religion. Where we see a landscape, a painter also sees the possibility of a picture. He sees more than we see, and the picture itself is the proof that he really does see it. The standard of reality does not inhere in what is there, but in an unreal and subjective excess over what is there which then comes into being with its own kind of reality. In

151

love, we frequently hear the voice of sense in some such phrase as "I don't know what he sees in her," or vice versa. But it is generally admitted that here it is the subjective excess over reality which is appropriate. Similarly in religion. The New Testament defines faith as the evidence of things unseen: reality in religion is not "there": it is brought into being through a certain kind of experience. The religious life is, like the artist's picture, the manifestation of such experience in the world of sense, or what the gospel calls letting one's light shine.

The imaginative or creative force in the mind is what has produced everything that we call culture and civilization. It is the power of transforming a sub-human physical world into a world with a human shape and meaning, a world not of rocks and trees but of cities and gardens, not an environment but a home. The drive behind it we may call desire, a desire which has nothing to do with the biological needs and wants of psychological theory, but is rather the impulse toward what Aristotle calls *telos*, realizing the form that one potentially has. As desire, it works dialectically, separating what is wanted from what is not wanted. Planting a garden develops the conception "weed," a conception of vegetable value unintelligible except in the context of a garden.

The attitude we have just called sense can only distinguish itself from what is below itself. It can separate the real from the imaginary, sense from nonsense, what is there from what is not there, but it has no criteria for recognizing what is above itself. It is a fact of experience that the world we live in is a world largely created by the human imagination. It is a part of sense's own recognition of reality that there must be a standard above sense, and one that has the power of veto over it. But it is the resemblance between vision and hallucination, ecstasy and neurosis, the imaginative and the imaginary, that impresses itself on sense. These resemblances are, of course, obvious and remarkable. The creative and the neurotic reactions to experience are both dissatisfied with what they see; they both believe that something else should be "there"; they both attempt to remake the world of experience into something more responsive to their desire. There are equally important differences, but in themselves the visions of the artist, the lover and the saint can only be regarded by sense as illusions, and all that sense can say about them is that certain significant types of activity seem to be guided by illusion.

We may therefore see the creative imagination as polarized by two opposite and complementary forces. One is sense itself, which tells us what kind of reality the imagination must found itself on, what is possible for it, and what must remain on the level of wish or fantasy. The other pole I shall call vision, the pure uninhibited wish or desire to extend human power or perception (directly or by proxy in gods or angels) without regard to its possible realization. This polarizing of creative power between vision and sense is the basis of the distinction between the arts and the sciences. The sciences begin with sense, and work toward a mental construct founded on it. The arts begin with vision, and work toward a complementary mental construct founded on it. As sense is incorporated in science, and as science continually evolves and improves, what sense declares to be impossible in one age, such as aeroplanes, may become possible in the next. The arts do not evolve or improve, partly because vision, being pure wish, can reach its conceivable limits at once. The aeroplane is a recent invention, but the vision that produced it was already ancient in the arts when Daedalus flew out of the labyrinth and Jehovah rode the sky on the wings of a seraph.

But there may be considerable differences of emphasis within the arts themselves. Some cultures have a more uninhibited vision than other cultures: we find the most soaring imaginations, as a rule, in defeated or oppressed nations, like the Hebrews and the Celts. The attitude in the arts that we call "romantic," too, tends to stress vision rather than sense, and our ordinary use of the word indicates that a "romantic" approach to things may sometimes be in danger of a facile or rose-coloured idealization. On the other hand, a culture may be dominated by a feeling of proportion and limitation derived ultimately from what we have been calling sense, and a culture of this kind may achieve the clarity and simplicity that we associate with the word "classical." The most impressive example of such a culture is probably the Chinese, but in our Western tradition we tend naturally to think of the Greeks.

Greek culture was founded on the conception of *dike*, a contract entered into by gods, man and nature, where each accepted certain limitations. The working out of this contract was the process of *ananke* or *moira*, words that we translate, very loosely, as "fate." Zeus, in the Iliad, goes to bed with his consort Hera and nearly allows the Greeks to win the Trojan war, that being Hera's idea in getting him to bed, and scrambles out in time to help the Trojans, whom on the whole he prefers. But the contract says that the Greeks are to win in the end, and Zeus himself dares not ignore it. And if the contract binds even the king of gods and men, still more is man bound to avoid the proud and boastful spirit that the Greeks called *hybris* and saw as the main cause of tragedy; still more must he avoid excess and seek moderation and limits in all things. Know thyself, said the Delphic oracle, implying that self-knowledge was the final secret of wisdom. For man's mind is turned outward to nature, and his knowledge of himself is an inference from his knowledge of the much greater thing that is not himself.

The classical inheritance was incorporated into later Western culture: medieval philosophers described the attitude we call sense as *prudentia*, and gave it a central place in their moral hierarchy. Even so, the attitude of the age of Shakespeare to sense and imagination was very different from ours, and perhaps we can learn something about our own age by examining the differences.

When Shakespeare's Theseus, in *A Midsummer Night's Dream*, classified "The lunatic, the lover, and the poet," as being "of imagination all compact," he was expressing an Elizabethan commonplace, and one usually summed up in the word "melancholy." Melancholy was a physiological disturbance caused by the excess of one of the four humours, but this excess in its turn was the cause of emotional and mental illness. Body and mind were therefore treated as a unit: a collection of remarkably cheerful songs bears the title "Pills to Purge Melancholy." There were two kinds of melancholy. One was a disease; the other was a mood which was the prerequisite of certain important experiences in religion, love or poetry. Love and poetry were combined in the literary convention within which the bulk of poetry in that age was produced. A young man sees his destined mistress and instantly falls a prey to melancholy. He stays awake all night and keeps his house dark all day; he mopes, sighs, forsakes his friends, turns absent-minded and slovenly in his appearance. More to the point, he writes poetry incessantly, complaining of his lady's inflexibility, cruelty and disdain. It was understood that a poet could hardly get properly started as a poet without falling in love in this way, and that a lover was hardly doing his duty by his lady without leaving a stack of lyrical complaints at her door. In the background was the religious experience on which this conventional love was modelled, and of which it was to some extent a parody: the experience of becoming aware of sin and the wrath of God, of the necessity for supplicating grace and acceptance.

Melancholy of this kind was certainly an emotional disturbance:

it could become a mental disease, or at least there are many love poems threatening madness or suicide to impress an obdurate mistress. Normally, however, such disturbance was more in the nature of a calculated risk, undertaken for the sake of a certain intensity of experience. It was a kind of male pregnancy, a creative state with some analogies to illness. But melancholy as a disease was equally familiar, and Shakespeare's audience would have recognized its characteristic symptoms in Hamlet. The indecision, the inability to act through "thinking too precisely on th' event," the clairvoyant sense of the evil and corruption of human nature, the addiction to black clothes, the obsession with death both in others and in oneself, the deranged behavior that could easily modulate into actual madness with little outward change, were stock attributes of melancholy. So too was the fact that Hamlet, though not a poet, as he tells Ophelia, shows many similarities to the poetic temperament. Polonius, who has literary tastes, has a literary explanation for Hamlet's melancholy: he is in love with Ophelia; but the audience has already been given a more convincing reason. Of course a tendency to melancholy would be greatly increased if one had been born under either of the two melancholy planets, Saturn and the moon, which tended to make one saturnine or lunatic. Nations as well as individuals had their tutelary planets, and the fact that England's was the moon was responsible for many jokes, including some from Hamlet's grave-digger.

Not only the most fascinating play of the period, but its greatest prose work (in England), has melancholy for its theme. Burton's *Anatomy of Melancholy* is an exhaustive analysis of the causes, symptoms, treatment and cure of melancholy, with two enormous appendices on love melancholy and religious melancholy. Burton was an Oxford don, and his chief amusement is said to have been going down to the Isis river and listening to the bargemen swear. The story may be true, or it may have been invented by someone who noticed that the qualities of Burton's prose, with its vast catalogues, piled-up epithets, Latin tags, allusiveness and exhaustive knowledge of theology and personal hygiene, are essentially the qualities of good swearing. Burton assumes rather than discusses the connexion of melancholy with creative power: being a scholar himself, like Hamlet, he associates it rather with the scholarly temperament, and includes a long digression on the miseries of scholars. On religious melancholy his position is simple: one can best avoid it by sticking to the reasonable middle way of the

Church of England, avoiding the neurotic extremes of papist and puritan on either side. But in love there is no reasonable ground to take, for its very essence is illusion. On this point we had better let Burton speak for himself:

> Every lover admires his mistress, though she be very deformed of herself, ill-favoured, wrinkled, pimpled, pale, red, yellow, tanned, tallow-faced, having a swollen juggler's platter face, or a thin, lean, chitty face, have clouds in her face, be crooked, dry, bald, goggle-eyed, blear-eyed, or with staring eyes, she looks like a squis'd cat, hold her head still awry, heavy, dull, hollow-eyed, black or yellow about the eyes, or squint-eyed, sparrow-mouthed, Persian hook-nosed, have a sharp fox-nose, a red nose, China flat, great nose, *nare simo patuloque*, a nose like a promontory, gubber-tushed, rotten teeth, black, uneven, brown teeth, beetle-browed, a witch's beard, her breath stink all over the room, her nose drop winter and summer, with a Bavarian poke under her chin, a sharp chin, lave-eared, with a long crane's neck, which stands awry too, *pendulis mammis*, "her dugs like two double jugs," or else no dugs, in that other extreme, bloody-fallen fingers, she have filthy, long unpared nails, scabbed hands or wrists, a tanned skin, a rotten carcass, crooked back, she stoops, is lame, splay-footed, "as slender in the middle as a cow in the waist," gouty legs, her ankles hang over her shoes, her feet stink, she breed lice, a mere changeling, a very monster, an oaf imperfect, her whole complexion savours, an harsh voice, incondite gesture, vile gait, a vast virago, or an ugly tit, a slug, a fat fustilugs, a truss, a long lean rawbone, a skeleton, a sneaker (*si qua latent meliora puta*), and to thy judgment looks like a mard in a lanthorn, whom thou couldst not fancy for a world, but hatest, loathest, and wouldest have spit in her face, or blow thy nose in her bosom, *remedium amoris* to another man, a dowdy, a slut, a scold, a nasty, rank, rammy, filthy, beastly quean, dishonest peradventure, obscene, base, beggarly, rude, foolish, untaught, peevish, Irus' daughter, Thersites' sister, Grobian's scholar; if he love her once, he admires her for all this, he takes no notice of any such errors or imperfections of body or mind, *Ipsa haec Delectant, veluti Balbinum polypus Agnae;* he had rather have her than any woman in the world.

Renaissance writers, when they speak of the imagination, are interested chiefly in its pathology, in hysteria and hallucination and the influence of the mind on the body. This is true of Montaigne's essay on the force of imagination, where an example of what may be called psychological vampirism comes from his own experience:

> *Simon Thomas* was a great Physitian in his daies. I remember upon a time comming by chance to visit a rich old man that dwelt in *Tholouse,* and who was troubled with the cough of the lungs, who discoursing with the said *Simon Thomas* of the meanes of his recoverie, he told him, that one of the best was, to give me occasion to be delighted in his companie, and that fixing his eyes upon the livelines and freshness of my face, and setting his thoughts upon the jolitie and vigor, wherewith my youthfull age did then flourish, and filling all his senses with my florishing estate, his habitude might thereby be amended, and his health recovered. But he forgot to say, that mine might also be empaired and infected.

At that stage of scientific development, scientific and occult explanations could be given of the same phenomena, and hysteria and hallucination might be explained either as mental disorders or as caused by witchcraft or diabolical suggestion. Burton gives a good deal of attention to such matters, though with a detachment toward them unusual in his age. He has read all the books about devils and witches, and has gathered from them that there is more theorizing than solid knowledge of the subject. He drops a hint that belief in their existence is convenient for an organized priestcraft, and continues:

> Many such stories I find amongst pontifical writers, to prove their assertions; let them free their own credits; some few I will recite in this kind out of most approved physicians. Cornelius Gemma, *lib. 2 de nat. mirac. cap.* 4, related of a young maid, called Katherine Gualter, a cooper's daughter, *anno* 1571, that had such strange passions and convulsions, three men could not sometimes hold her; she purged a live eel, which he saw, a foot and a half long, and touched himself; but the eel afterwards vanished; she vomited some twenty-four pounds of fulsome stuff of all colours, twice a day for fourteen days; and after that she voided great balls of hair,

pieces of wood, pigeon's dung, parchment, goose dung, coals; and after them two pound of pure blood, and then again coals and stones, of which some had inscriptions, bigger than a walnut, some of them pieces of glass, brass, etc., besides paroxysms of laughing, weeping and ecstasies, etc. *Et hoc* (*inquit*) *cum horrore vidi,* "this I saw with horror." They could do no good on her by physic, but left her to the clergy.

Burton is aware that he is describing a case of hysteria; what he is not sure of is whether it was the doctor or the patient who had it, and the reader is left with the feeling that Burton regards hysteria as a highly contagious illness.

We notice that the association of poetry, love and melancholy extends only so far. The lover's melancholy was of no more lasting importance in his life than a contemporary teen-ager's crush on a movie star: it was understood to be normal, even expected, of youth, and it had nothing to do with the serious business of marriage which was being arranged for him by his parents. Religious melancholy would turn instantly to the church, and be restored to normality by the sacraments and disciplines of that church. The kind of lyrical poetry produced by the lover's melancholy, too, was regarded as relatively minor poetry, appropriate to young poets learning their trade or to well-born amateurs who were merely using poetry as a status symbol. The major poet, who had advanced to the major or heroic genres of epic and tragedy, was no longer inspired by melancholy but was working in the same general educational area as the philosopher, the jurist or the theologian. Thus the difference between the creative imagination of the professional artist and the practical skill of other professional men was minimized as far as possible. The great epic poet of Shakespeare's age, Edmund Spenser, includes in the second book of his *Faerie Queene* an allegory of the human body and mind, which he calls the House of Alma, and compares to a building. He explores the brain, and finds it divided into three parts. At the back of the brain is an old man called Eumnestes, good memory, who is concerned with the past. In the middle is the judgement, which is concerned with the present. In front is a melancholy figure named Phantastes, born under Saturn, concerned not so much with the future as with the possible, or rather with that uncritical kind of perception which cannot clearly distinguish the real from the fanciful:

158

His chamber was dispainted all within,
With sundry colours, in the which were **writ**
Infinite shapes of things dispersed thin;
Some such as in the world were neuer yit,
Ne can deuized be of mortall wit;
Some daily scene, and knowen by their names,
Such as in idle fantasies doe flit:
Infernall Hags, *Centaurs*, feendes, *Hippodames*,
Apes, Lions, Aegles, Owles, fooles, louers, children, Dames.

The poetic faculty, it is important to notice, does not belong to this aspect of the brain: it belongs to the judgement in the middle, which also produces philosophy and law:

Of Magistrates, of courts, of tribunals,
Of commen wealthes, of states, of policy,
Of Lawes, of iudgements, and of decretals;
All artes, all science, all Philosophy,
And all that in the world was aye thought wittily.

Spenser had a disciple in the next generation, Phineas Fletcher, who produced a long didactic poem called *The Purple Island* (*i.e.*, the body of man, traditionally formed of red clay). Half of it consists of an expansion of Spenser's House of Alma, an exhaustive survey of anatomy under the allegory of a building. Fletcher finds the same three divisions in the brain that Spenser found: he seems in fact to be merely cribbing from Spenser, but when he comes to Phantastes he makes a significant change:

The next that in the Castles front is plac't,
Phantastes hight; his yeares are fresh and green,
His visage old, his face too much defac't
With ashes pale, his eyes deep sunken been
    With often thoughts, and never slackt intention:
    Yet he the fount of speedy apprehension,
Father of wit, the well of arts, and quick invention.

Here, we see, Phantastes is the source of the arts, and of the creative aspect of the mind generally. The change may be sheer inadvertence, or it may mean that an actual change of emphasis is beginning to make itself felt on the level of informed but unspecialized opinion represented by such a poem. If so, it was not for another century that the change becomes generally perceptible.

The refusal of Renaissance thinkers to carry through the association of the creative and the neurotic temperaments is the result of a certain view of the world that was ultimately religious in origin.

They thought of human culture and civilization as an order of nature or reality separable from, and superior to, the ordinary physical environment. This latter world is theologically "fallen"; man entered it with Adam's sin, and is now in it but not of it. He does not belong in physical nature like the animals and plants; he is confronted with a moral choice, and must either rise above nature into his own proper human home, or sink below it into sin, the latter a degradation that the animals cannot reach. The crux of the argument, however, is that the higher human order was not created by man: it was created by God and designed for man. Adam awoke in a garden not of his planting, a human world pre-established and ordered by a divine mind. In Milton's *Paradise Lost* Adam and Eve are suburbanites in the nude, and angels on a brief outing from the City of God drop in for lunch. But the City of God was there, along with another city in hell, long before the descendants of Cain started imitating them on earth. The corollary of this view was that the divine intention in regard to man was revealed in law and in the institutions of society, not in the dreams of poets. All ancient societies tend to ascribe their laws and customs to the gods, and, as the name of Moses reminds us, the Judaeo-Christian tradition is no exception.

We said at the beginning that the order of human existence represented by such words as culture and civilization has been established by man. This statement may seem obviously true now, but it is only within the last two centuries that it has been generally accepted. In earlier centuries, when man was not regarded as the creator of the human order, it could even be disputed whether the arts themselves, poetry, painting, architecture, were genuinely educational agencies or not. Naturally the poets insisted that poetry at least was; for most, however, obedience to law, the habit of virtue, and the disciplines of religion were far safer guides than the arts.

Even those who were sympathetic to poetry, in fact even the poets themselves, placed strict limits on human creative power. The poet was urged to follow nature, and the nature he was to follow was conceived, not as the physical world, which could only be copied at second hand, but as an order of reality, a structure or system of divine ordinance. If one believes, as Sir Thomas Browne says in his *Religio Medici,* that "nature is the art of God," the art of man which follows nature does not transform the world but merely comes to terms with it. The social results of such a view are, of course, intensely conservative. Whatever is of serious importance, in the arts or elsewhere, serves the interests of the community of church and state; whatever is immature is also divisive and anarchic, and exalts the individual at the expense of society. The imaginary belongs to the melancholy individual and his whims; the imaginative is incorporated into a natural and human order established by divine decree.

The eighteenth century was the period in which this view of the imagination struggled with, and was finally defeated by, an opposed conception which came to power in the Romantic movement. At the beginning of the century, we have Swift, for whom established authority in church and state was the only thing in human life strong enough to restrain the desperately irrational soul of man. In his day the conception of "melancholy" was out of fashion, but another ancient medical notion of "spirits" or "vapors" rising from the loins into the head was still going strong. For Swift, or at least for the purposes of Swift's satire, all behavior that breaks down society is caused by an uprush either of digestive disturbances or of sexual excitement into the head. Swift's chief target is the left-wing Protestantism which in the seventeenth century had carried religious melancholy to the point of replacing the authority of the Church with private judgement and had made a virtue even of political rebellion. But he finds the same phenomena in the political tyrant who substitutes his own will for the social contract, or the poet who allows his emotions to take precedence over communication. "The very same principle," he says, "that influences a bully to break the windows of a whore who has jilted him, naturally stirs up a great prince to raise mighty armies, and dream of nothing but sieges, battles and victories." In his *Discourse of the Mechanical Operation of Spirit* Swift says that three sources of abnormal behavior have been generally recognized. One is of divine origin, or revelation, one of demonic origin, or possession, and one of natural origin, which produces such emotions as grief and anger. To these he proposes to add a fourth, which is artificial or mechanical, and is essentially a transfer of sexual energy to the brain, where it produces lofty rationalizations of erotic drives. Or, as Swift says with a nice calculation of *doubles entendres:*

. . . . however Spiritual Intrigues begin, they generally conclude like all others; they may branch upwards toward Heaven, but the Root is in the Earth. Too intense a Contemplation is not the Business of Flesh and Blood; it must by the necessary Course of Things in a little Time, let go its Hold, and fall into *Matter*. Lovers, for the sake of Celestial Converse, are but another sort of *Platonicks*, who pretend to see Stars and Heaven in Ladies Eyes, and to look or think no lower; but the same *Pit* is provided for both; and they seem a perfect Moral to the Story of that Philosopher, who, while his Thoughts and Eyes were fixed upon the *Constellations*, found himself seduced by his *lower Parts* into a *Ditch*.

Swift is a satirist, and the attitude he takes is congenial to satire. For satire usually takes the point of view of sense: it requires a standard of the normal against which the absurd is to be measured, and, like sense, does not distinguish what is above it from what is below it. Such satire speaks with the voice of the consensus of society, and society can protect itself but cannot surpass itself. Hence a great age of satire like the early eighteenth century is likely to represent a culture which has clearly defined views about madness, but feels fairly confident about its own sanity.

But even as Swift was writing there was beginning one of those great changes in cultural attitude, where we cannot see any origin or clear development of the change, but realize after a certain time that we are looking at a different world. As this different world, which came in with Romanticism, is essentially our world, we may take a moment to characterize some of the changes. Slowly but steadily the doctrine of the divine creation of the human order fades out, not perhaps as a religious conception, but as a historical and literal fact taking place at a specific point in past time. Man thus comes to be thought of as the architect of his own order, a conception which instantly puts the creative arts in the very centre of human culture. This new emphasis on the primacy of the arts in social life is clear in the statements and assumptions of the Romantic poets. The conception of nature as a divine artefact also fades out, and nature is thought of, not so much as a structure or system presented objectively to man, but rather as a total creative process in which man, the creation of man, and the creation of man's art, are all involved. For the Romantics, the poet no longer follows nature: nature works through the poet, and poems are natural as well as human creations. But if man has created his own order, he is in a position to judge of his own achievement, and to measure that achievement against the kind of ideals his imagination suggests. In Rousseau we meet the doctrine that much of human culture and civilization has in fact been perverse in direction, full of inequalities caused by aggression which have blotted out the true form of human community. This latter Rousseau saw as a society made up of a "general will" of free and equal individuals. And as society can speak only with the middle voice of sense, and cannot by itself distinguish the creative from the neurotic, we thus arrive at two typically Romantic, and therefore modern, conceptions.

First, any genuinely creative individual is likely to be regarded by society as antisocial or even mad, merely because he is creative. The association of the creative and the neurotic, being largely imposed on the artist by society, places creative abilities under a curse, a capacity of misunderstanding that may blight or destroy the artist's social personality. Baudelaire symbolizes the creative spirit by an albatross, so superbly beautiful in its lonely flight, so grotesquely awkward and comic when captured and brought into the view of a human society. If we compare the target of Swift's satire, the melancholy individual creating his own poetry and religion out of a powerful erotic stimulus, with the figure of Byron a century later, we can see how completely cultural standards have reversed themselves. Byron like Swift was a satirist, but his satire does not speak with the voice of society against the erratic individual: it speaks with the voice of the individual against society, and assumes the individual's possession of a set of standards superior to those of society. This leads us at once to the second new conception: a society may judge an individual to be mad because that society is actually mad itself.

The notion that the whole of mankind has been injured in its wits as the result of Adam's fall was familiar enough, and is the basis for a great deal of satire, including that of Burton's *Anatomy*. In the seventeenth century the poet and dramatist Nathaniel Lee, a contemporary of Dryden, remarked when confined to a madhouse: "They said I was mad, and I said they were mad, and, damn them, they outvoted me." Fifty years later Hogarth, depicting the last stage of the rake's progress in the madhouse of Bedlam, sticks an enormous penny on the wall, indicating that the whole of Britannia is as mad as the rake. But the notion that madness can be a social disease affecting a specific society· at a specific time is, I think, not older than the French Revolution. At that time those on one side of politics saw a whole society gone mad in revolutionary France; those on the opposite side saw an equally dangerous delusion in accepting the status quo. This social dimension of madness is, to put it mildly, still with us in the century of Fascism, Communism, and the parasites in the democracies who devote themselves to spreading hysteria.

Of all the great artists of the Romantic movement, the most interesting for our present purposes is William Blake. Blake had practically no influence in his own day, and his reputation during his life and for long after his death was that of a lunatic. Gradually it was realized that he was a great creative genius, and that if the normal attitude regards him as a lunatic, so much the worse for the normal attitude. Blake himself had very clear notions of what constituted mental health and mental disease. For him, mental health consisted in the practice of the imagination, a practice exemplified by the artist, but manifested in every act of mankind that proceeds from a vision of a better world. Madness, for Blake, was essentially the attitude of mind that we have been calling sense, when regarded as an end in itself. The world outside us, or physical nature, is a blind and mechanical order, hence if we merely accept its conditions we find ourselves setting up blind and mechanistic patterns of behaviour. The world outside is also a fiercely competitive world, and living under its conditions involves us in unending war and misery. Blake's lyrics contrast the vision of experience, the stupefied adult view that the evils of nature are built into human life and cannot be changed, with the vision of innocence in the child, who assumes that the world is a pleasant place made for his benefit. The adult tends to think of the child's vision as ignorant and undeveloped, but actually it is a clearer and more civilized vision than his own.

Blake interpreted the ancient myths of titans, giants and universal deluges to mean that man had in the past very nearly succeeded in exterminating himself. He warns us that this danger will return unless we stop accepting experience and shift our energies to remaking the world on the model of a more desirable vision. This model Blake found in the Bible, but in his reading of the Bible he identifies God with the imaginative or creative part of the human mind. Thus his vision is quixotic in the strict sense, seeing the world about him as having fallen away from the vision of the Word of God, just as Don Quixote saw the world of his day as having fallen away from a vision of chivalry which he found in his library.

Don Quixote is of course another great Renaissance masterpiece in which imagination is treated primarily as diseased vision. It would be easy to see in Quixote a relatively harmless example of a very sinister type, one of the line of paranoiacs culminating in Hitler who have attempted to destroy the present on the pretext of restoring the past. But we soon realize that there is something better than this in Quixote, something that gives him a dignity and pathos which he never loses in his wildest escapades. He is followed by Sancho Panza, who is so completely an incarnation of sense that only one thing about him is mysterious: the source of his loyalty to Quixote. We get a clue to this near the beginning of the book. Quixote and Sancho meet a group of peasants who invite them to share their lunch of goat's milk and acorns. Acorns were traditionally the food of those who lived in the golden age, that legendary time of simplicity and equality which has haunted so many discussions of human culture from Plato's *Laws* to Rousseau's *Social Contract*. Don Quixote is prompted by the sight of acorns to make a long speech about the golden age, first inviting Sancho to sit beside him, quoting from the Bible the verse about the exalting of the humble. He says that it is his mission to restore the golden age, which is, incidentally, exactly what Blake said the purpose of his art was. True, elsewhere he tells Sancho that the golden age would soon return if people would only see things as they really are, and not allow themselves to be deluded by enchanters who make giants look like windmills. But we can see that Quixote's obsession about chivalry is not so much what he believes in as what he thinks he believes in, a childish world where dreams of conquered giants and rescued damsels keep coming true, and which has thrust itself in front of his real social vision. This latter is a vision of simplicity and innocence, not childish but childlike, the element in Quixote that makes him courteous, chaste, generous (except that he has no money), intelligent and cultured within the limits of his obsession, and, of course, courageous. It is the solid core of moral reality in the middle of his fantasy that holds the loyalty not only of Sancho but of the readers of his adventures. For this wistful sense of a golden age, lost but still possible, the child's vision which the Gospel tells us is so dangerous to lose, is something that makes Quixotes of us all, and gives our minds, too, whatever dignity they may possess.

In Part Two of the book, Quixote and Sancho come into the dominions of a duke who has read Part One, and who, to amuse himself, makes Sancho the governor of an island. We are perhaps less surprised than he to learn that Sancho rules his island so honestly and efficiently that he has to be pulled out of office in a hurry before he starts to disintegrate the Spanish aristocracy. We are even less surprised to find that Quixote's advice to him is full of gentle and shrewd good sense. The world is still looking for that lost island, and it still asks for nothing better than to have Sancho Panza for its ruler and Don Quixote for his honoured counsellor.

In the fifth book of Wordsworth's *Prelude*, the great epic poem in which he describes the growth and formation of his own very modern mind, Wordsworth deals with the influence that his reading has had on him. As a student he was interested in mathematics and literature, and the literary works he particularly mentions are the Arabian Nights and *Don Quixote*. He tells us that he (at least we may assume it was he) fell asleep while reading *Don Quixote*, and had a strange dream. He saw an Arab horseman, who was also Don Quixote, riding over the sands of a desert carrying a stone and a shell, which were also books. The books were Euclid and an unnamed book of poetry: in other words they were the keys to the worlds of words and numbers, the two great instruments that man has invented for transforming reality. The Arab, or "Semi-Quixote" as Wordsworth calls him, is fleeing from some unimaginable catastrophe, which the poet calls a deluge, and is going to bury these two books to keep them safe until the disaster is past. Wordsworth says that he often reverts to this dream, and that he has felt

> A reverence for a Being thus employ'd;
> And thought that in the blind and awful lair
> Of such a madness, reason did lie couch'd.
> Enow there are on earth to take in charge
> Their Wives, their Children, and their virgin Loves,
> Or whatsoever else the heart holds dear;
> Enow to think of these; yea, will I say,
> In sober contemplation of the approach
> Of such great overthrow, made manifest
> By certain evidence, that I, methinks,
> Could share that Maniac's anxiousness, could go
> Upon like errand.

Perhaps in the age of the useless bomb-shelter it may be easier for us than it was even for Wordsworth to understand that if the

FABLES OF IDENTITY

human race is to have any future at all, it can only obtain it through a concern for preserving its powers of creation which it will be difficult, if not impossible, to distinguish clearly from a "Maniac's anxiousness."

≱ Lord Byron

IT IS HARDLY POSSIBLE TO DISCUSS BYRON'S POETRY WITHOUT TELLING
the story of his life in some detail. His father was Captain Jack
Byron, a nephew of the fifth Baron Byron, and a psychopathic
spendthrift and sponger on women who had run through the
fortunes of two heiresses. The first, a marchioness, he had acquired
by divorce from her husband, and by her he had a daughter,
Augusta Byron, later Augusta Leigh, the poet's half-sister. The
second was a Scotswoman, Catherine Gordon of Gight, an explo-
sive, unbalanced, ill-educated but affectionate woman whose only
child was the poet. Byron was born in London on January 22,
1788, in great poverty and distress as his mother was returning
from France to Scotland to get some relief from her rapacious
spouse. He was handicapped at birth with a lameness that em-
bittered his life (what was wrong, and which leg was affected, are
still uncertain points), and he also had some glandular imbalance
that forced him to a starvation diet in order to avoid grotesque
corpulence. The mother brought up her boy in Aberdeen, where
his religious training was naturally Presbyterian, giving many a
later critic a somewhat dubious cliché about the "persisting Cal-
vinism" in Byron's mind. When Byron was three his father died;
when he was six his cousin, the heir to the Byron title, was killed;
and when he was ten his great-uncle, who held the title, died and
the poet became the sixth Lord Byron. The fact that Byron made
so professional a job of being a lord is perhaps the result of his
entering on that state when he was old enough to notice the
difference his title made in the attitude that society took toward
him.

He was then educated at Harrow and at Trinity College, Cam-
bridge. The most important of the friendships he formed there was
with John Cam Hobhouse, in later life Lord Broughton, who
founded a "Whig Club" at Cambridge, and whose influence had
much to do with Byron's left-of-center political views. Byron's
chief athletic interests were swimming and pistol-shooting, the
latter a useful accomplishment in the days when gentlemen were
expected to fight the odd duel, and he got around a regulation

against keeping a dog at Cambridge by keeping a bear instead. What with his extravagance, his lack of discipline, and the liberties he took with his rank, he was anything but a model student. He announced more than once that he wished he had gone to Oxford instead, and the Cambridge authorities must often have wished so too. However, he acquired the usual gentleman's classical education, and while still an undergraduate he produced a slim volume of melodious if not very arresting lyrics. This volume was, after some vicissitudes, published in 1807 under the title given it by the publisher, *Hours of Idleness*. *Hours of Idleness* got roughly handled in the *Edinburgh Review*, and the result was Byron's first major satire, *English Bards and Scotch Reviewers* (1809). Although the motivation for this poem was revenge on the Edinburgh reviewer, Byron took the opportunity to satirize most of his poetic contemporaries, including Scott, Southey, Wordsworth and Coleridge.

Meanwhile Byron had been planning a variant of the "Grand Tour" that it was fashionable for young well-to-do Englishmen to take. Instead of the usual journey to France and Italy, he decided to go first to Portugal and Spain, bypass Italy by way of Malta, and then travel in what were at that time Turkish dominions: Greece, Asia Minor, and the practically unknown Albania. He set out with Hobhouse on July 2, 1809, on the "Lisbon Packet." The Peninsular War was in progress, but life was made easy for people in Byron's social position, and one would never dream from his letters that this was the time and place of Goya's *Disasters of War*. The travelers passed through Malta, where a Mrs. Spencer Smith became the "Florence" of some of Byron's love poems, and on to Albania. Byron and his party were hospitably received by a local ruler, Ali Pasha, who found Byron as attractive as most people did, besides having political reasons for welcoming English visitors. Once, on suspicion that was no more than gossip, he had had fifteen women kidnapped and flung into the sea. Another woman narrowly escaped the same fate on a charge of infidelity: this incident was used by Byron as the basis for his tale *The Giaour*, and rumor maintained that Byron himself had been her lover. Next came Greece and Asia Minor, where Byron duplicated Leander's famous swim across the Hellespont, pondered over the sites of Marathon and Troy, and deplored the activities of Lord Elgin, who was engaged in hacking off the sculptures now called the Elgin Marbles from the ruined Parthenon and transporting them to England. Byron's satire on Lord Elgin's enterprise, "The Curse of Minerva" (i.e., Athene, the patron of Athens), was not published until 1815. Meanwhile he had begun to write a poem about his travels, *Childe Harold,* the first two cantos of the poem we now have.

On his return to England in July, 1811, he went back to Newstead, the estate of the Byrons, where he had established himself before he left, a rambling "Gothic" mansion he was later forced to sell. His mother died suddenly soon after his arrival, and the deaths of three close friends occurred about the same time. The relations between Byron and his mother had always been tense, especially after she had begun to see some of his father's extravagance reappearing in him, but they were fond enough of each other when they were not living together. Byron now entered upon a phenomenally successful literary and social career. *Childe Harold,* as he said, made him famous overnight, and it was followed by a series of Oriental tales, *The Giaour, The Bride of Abydos, The Corsair,* and *Lara,* which appeared in 1813 and 1814. He wrote with great speed, completing the thousand-odd lines of *The Bride of Abydos* in four days, and he seldom revised. "I am like the tyger," he said: "If I miss my first Spring, I go growling back to my Jungle. There is no second. I can't correct; I can't, and I won't."

When Byron said in *Beppo:*

> I've half a mind to tumble down to prose,
> But verse is more in fashion—so here goes.

the last statement, incredible as it may seem now, was true when he wrote. Nobody would turn to poetry for stories nowadays, but in Byron's day there was a popular demand for verse tales that Byron did not create, though he did much to expand it. The melancholy misanthropy, so full of romantic *frisson,* the pirates and the harems, the exotic Orientalism, the easy and pleasant versification, swept London as they were later to sweep the Continent. As a celebrity Byron could hold his own even in the most absorbing period of the Napoleonic War. *The Corsair* sold 10,000 copies on the day of its publication by John Murray, and ran through seven editions in a month. Byron probably made more money from his poetry than any other English poet, though being a lord who derived his income from rents, he often gave his royalties away to friends. The first money he accepted on his own account was £700 for the copyright of *Lara.*

Apart from literature Byron had many other activities, both serious and scandalous. Before he had left England he had taken the seat in the House of Lords that his title gave him, and he now became active in Whig circles. His first speech was made in defence of the "framebreakers," or workers who had destroyed some textile machines through fear of unemployment. He also supported a number of other liberal causes, including the relief of Catholics in Ireland. When Napoleon was banished to Elba, Byron wrote an ode on him in which he contrasted him unfavorably with Washington as a fighter for liberty. (There is an impressive musical setting of this ode, for orchestra and *Sprechgesang* solo, by Arnold Schönberg.) But his hatred of the reactionary English government, especially Lord Castlereagh, was strong enough to give him a considerable admiration for Napoleon, even to the point of regretting the outcome of Waterloo: he had hoped, he said, to see Castlereagh's head on a pole. In fact his attitude to Napoleon always retained a good deal of self-identification.

Meanwhile Byron was carrying on some highly publicized affairs with several women of fashion. Lady Caroline Lamb, always something of an emotional exhibitionist, kept London, which on Byron's social level was still a small town, buzzing with gossip over her pursuit of Byron, her visits to him disguised, her tantrums, and her public scenes. Lady Oxford, whose children, in an erudite contemporary joke, were known as the Harleian Miscellany, was another mistress of his, and there were briefer encounters with others. Despite his crowded schedule, Byron began seriously to consider marriage, making a trusted confidante of Lady Melbourne, Caroline Lamb's mother-in-law, to whom he wrote many frank and unaffected letters. Given Byron's temperament, he could only marry some kind of *femme fatale;* and the only really fatal type of woman for him would be an earnest, humorless, rather inhibited female who would represent everything that was insular and respectable in English society. His choice fell on Annabella Milbanke, heiress to a title in her own right and niece of Lady Melbourne, and who otherwise reminds one a little of Mary Bennett in *Pride and Prejudice.* She was highly intelligent and had many interests, including mathematics (Byron called her the "Princess of Parallelograms," as in those days any woman with such an interest could expect to be teased about it), but her mind ran to rather vague maxims of general conduct, and to an interest in the moral reformation of other people which boded ill for marriage to an unreformed poet with an unusually concrete view of life.

The marriage lasted a year (January, 1815, to January, 1816) and then fell apart. A separation (they were never divorced) was agreed upon, and Lady Byron obtained custody of their daughter, Augusta Ada. Byron appears to have gone somewhat berserk in his matrimonial bonds, and his wife's doubts about his sanity were probably genuine. The situation was aggravated by financial difficulties and by the fact that gossip had begun to whisper about Byron and his half-sister Augusta. That there were sexual relations between them seems obvious enough, though the matter is hotly disputed, and the relevant documents have been carefully removed from the prying eyes of scholars. The combination of this exceptionally delicious scandal with the matrimonial one, along with his expression of some perverse pro-French political views, made things unpleasant for Byron, and although social disapproval was perhaps not as intense as he pretended or thought, he felt forced to leave England once more. He set out for the Continent on April 25, 1816, never to return to England.

He made his way to Geneva, where he met, by prearrangement, Shelley and his wife Mary Godwin, along with her stepsister, Claire (or Jane) Clairmont. The last named had visited Byron before his departure from England and had thrown herself, as biographers say, at his head, the result of this accurate if morally unguided missile being a daughter, Allegra, whom Byron eventually placed in an Italian convent to be brought up as a Roman Catholic, and who died there at the age of eight. The association with Shelley, one of Byron's few intellectual friends, is marked in the new poetry that Byron now began writing—the third canto of *Childe Harold; Manfred;* the two remarkable poems "Darkness" and "The Dream"; and the most poignant of his tales, "The Prisoner of Chillon." Shelley's reaction to Byron may be found in his poem "Julian and Maddalo," but for all the skepticism he ascribes to Byron, he was unable to convince him that Christianity was less reasonable than his own brand of Platonism.

In the fall of 1817 Byron went over the Alps and settled in Venice. His "Ode to Venice," *Beppo*, the opening of the fourth canto of *Childe Harold*, and two of his dramas, *Marino Faliero* and *The Two Foscari*, are some of the evidence for the fascination that this dreamlike World's Fair of a city had for him. At Venice he plunged into an extraordinary sexual debauch, but he also wrote some of his best poetry, including the fourth canto of *Childe Harold* and the beginning of his greatest work, *Don Juan*. In the spring of 1819 he met Teresa Guiccioli, the wife of an elderly Count, who was both attractive enough to hold Byron and astute enough to keep other women away from him. Byron moved into the Guiccioli household in Ravenna, and settled down with Teresa into what by Byronic standards was practically an old-fashioned marriage. Ravenna saw the composition of *Sardanapalus* and *Cain*, as well as *The Vision of Judgment*, but his poetic energies were increasingly absorbed by *Don Juan*.

At that time the two great centers of classical civilization, Greece and Italy, were under foreign occupation: Greece was a Turkish dependency, and most of northern Italy was controlled by Austria. Byron and Shelley were passionate supporters of the efforts of Italian and Greek nationalists to get free of their foreign yokes. Teresa's family, the Gambas, were also Italian nationalists in sympathy, and hence were, as was Byron, closely watched and reported on by the Austrian police. The Gambas were forced to move from Ravenna to Pisa, and Byron followed them. At Pisa Byron rejoined the Shelleys, and here Shelley, on July 8, 1822, was drowned at sea and cremated on the shore. The cremation was carried out by Byron and their friend Edward Trelawny, an extraordinarily circumstantial liar who had reconstructed his past life along the general lines of a Byronic hero. Meanwhile Byron had broken with his publisher John Murray, and had formed an alliance through Shelley with Leigh Hunt, whom he brought to Pisa. The plan was to found a literary and left-wing political maga-zine, and this magazine, called *The Liberal*, printed a good deal of Byron's poetry, including *The Vision of Judgment*, in its four numbers. Hunt, however, was somewhat irresponsible (he is the original of Harold Skimpole in Dickens' *Bleak House*), and his absurd and even more Dickensian wife and their demonic children helped to keep relations strained.

Eventually the Gamba-Byron menage was forced to move on to Genoa, where Byron wrote some unimportant poems and finished what we have of *Don Juan*—sixteen cantos and a fragment of a seventeenth. Meanwhile a group of revolutionaries in Greece had been planning an insurrection against the Turkish authority, and knowing of Byron's sympathy with their cause, they offered him membership in their Committee. Byron had been meditating the possibility of going to Greece for some time, and on July 23, 1823, he left in the company of Trelawny and Pietro Gamba, Teresa's brother. He established connection at Missolonghi on January 5, 1824, with Prince Alexander Mavrocordato, the leader of the Western Greek revolutionaries, and put his money and his very real qualities of leadership at the service of the Greek cause. His health, which had been precarious for some time, broke down in a series of fevers, and he died at Missolonghi on April 19, 1824, three months after he had passed the thirty-sixth birthday which his valedictory poem records.

II

The main appeal of Byron's poetry is in the fact that it is Byron's. To read Byron's poetry is to hear all about Byron's marital difficulties, flirtations, love for Augusta, friendships, travels, and political and social views. And Byron is a consistently interesting person to hear about, this being why Byron, even at his worst of self-pity and egotism and blither and doggerel, is still so incredibly readable. He proves what many critics declare to be impossible, that a poem can make its primary impact as a historical and biographical document. The critical problem involved here is crucial to our understanding of not only Byron but literature as a whole. Even when Byron's poetry is not objectively very good, it is still important, because it is Byron's. But who was Byron to be so important? certainly not an exceptionally good or wise man. Byron is, strictly, neither a great poet nor a great man who wrote poetry, but something in between: a tremendous cultural force that was life and literature at once. How he came to be this is what we must try to explain as we review the four chief genres of his work: the lyrics, the tales (including *Childe Harold*), the dramas, and the later satires.

Byron's lyrical poetry affords a good exercise in critical catholicity, because it contains nothing that "modern" critics look for: no texture, no ambiguities, no intellectualized ironies, no intensity, no vividness of phrasing, the words and images being vague to the point of abstraction. The poetry seems to be a plain man's poetry, making poetic emotion out of the worn and blunted words of ordinary speech. Yet it is not written by a plain man: it is written, as Arnold said, with the careless ease of a man of quality, and its most striking and obvious feature is its gentlemanly amateurism. It is, to be sure, in an amateur tradition, being a romantic, subjective, personal development of the kind of Courtly Love poetry that was written by Tudor and Cavalier noblemen in earlier ages. Byron's frequent statements in prefaces that this would be his last work to trouble the public with, his offhand deprecating comments on his work, his refusal to revise, all give a studious impression of a writer who can take poetry or leave it alone. Byron held the view that lyrical poetry was an expression of passion, and that passion was essentially fitful, and he distrusted professional poets, who pretended to be able to summon passion at will and sustain it indefinitely. Poe was later to hold much the same view of poetry, but more consistently, for he drew the inference that a continuous long poem was impossible, whereas *Childe Harold* has the stretches of perfunctory, even slapdash writing that one would expect with such a theory.

In Byron's later lyrics, especially the *Hebrew Melodies* of 1815, where he was able to add some of his Oriental technicolor to the Old Testament, more positive qualities emerge, particularly in the rhythm. "The Destruction of Sennacherib" is a good reciter's piece (though not without its difficulties, as Tom Sawyer discovered), and anticipates some of the later experiments in verbal jazz by Poe and Swinburne. Some of the best of his poems bear the title "Stanzas for Music," and they have the flat conventional diction appropriate to poems that depend partly on another art for their sound:

> One shade the more, one ray the less,
>   Had half impaired the nameless grace
> Which waves in every raven tress,
>   Or softly lightens o'er her face;
> Where thoughts serenely sweet express
>   How pure, how dear their dwelling-place.

(If the reader would like a clue to the caressing rhythm of this stanza, he should read the iambic meters so as to give the stresses twice the length of the unstressed syllables. Then the lines will fall into four bars of three-four time, beginning on the third beat, and the rhythm of a nineteenth-century waltz will emerge.) We notice that while Byron's amateur predecessors wrote in a convention and Byron from personal experience, Byron was equally conventional, because his personal experience conformed to a literary pattern. Byron's life imitated literature: this is where his unique combination of the poetic and the personal begins.

Byron was naturally an extroverted person, fond of company, of travel, of exploring new scenes, making new friends, falling in love with new women. Like Keats, in a much more direct way, he wanted a life of sensations rather than of thoughts. As he said: "I can not repent me (I try very often) so much of any thing I have done, as of anything I have left undone. Alas! I have been but idle, and have the prospect of an early decay, without having seized every available instant of our pleasurable years." In the records of his journeys in his letters and Hobhouse's diaries, it is the more introverted Hobhouse who dwells on the dirt and the fleas, and it is Hobhouse too who does the serious studying and takes an interest in archaeology. It is Byron who swims across the Hellespont, learns the songs of Albanian mountaineers, makes friends with a Moslem vizier, amuses himself with the boys in a monastery school, flirts with Greek girls, and picks up a smattering of Armenian. He was continually speculating about unknown sensations, such as how it would feel to have committed a murder, and he had the nervous dread of growing older that goes with the fear of slowing down in the rhythm of experience. His writing depends heavily on experience; he seldom describes any country that he has not seen, and for all his solitary role he shows, especially in *Don Juan*, a novelist's sense of established society.

It was an essential part of his strongly extroverted and empirical bent that he should not be a systematic thinker, nor much interested in people who were. He used his intelligence to make common-sense judgements on specific situations, and found himself unable to believe anything that he did not find confirmed in his own experience. In his numerous amours, for example, the absence of any sense of sin was as unanswerable a fact of his experience as the presence of it would have been to St. Augustine. He thought of sexual love as a product of reflex and mechanical habit, not of inner emotional drives. When he said: "I do not believe in the existence of what is called love," we are probably to take him quite literally. Nevertheless, his extroversion made him easily confused by efforts at self-analysis, and he flew into rages when he was accused of any lack of feeling. One reason why his marriage demoralized him so was that it forced such efforts on him.

Now if we look into Byron's tales and *Childe Harold* we usually find as the central character an inscrutable figure with hollow cheeks and blazing eyes, wrapped in a cloud of gloom, full of mysterious and undefined remorse, an outcast from society, a wanderer of the race of Cain. At times he suggests something demonic rather than human, a Miltonic Satan or fallen angel. He may be a sinister brigand like the Corsair, or an aloof and icily polite aristocrat like the Lucifer of *The Vision of Judgment,* but he is always haughty and somber of demeanor; his glance is difficult to meet; he will not brook questioning, though he himself questions all established social standards, and he is associated with lonely and colorful predatory animals, as ordinary society is with gregarious ones like sheep and domestic fowl. "The lion is alone, and so am

I," says Manfred. The name of the Corsair is "linked with one virtue, and a thousand crimes": the virtue is manifested when he refuses, as a prisoner, to assassinate his captor to escape being impaled. Fortunately his mistress Gulnare was less scrupulous. As for Lara, who is the Corsair returned from exile to his estates:

> He stood a stranger in this breathing world,
> An erring spirit from another hurled.

This type of character is now known as the "Byronic hero," and wherever he has appeared since in literature there has been the influence, direct or indirect, of Byron. And if we ask how a witty, sociable, extroverted poet came to create such a character, we can see that it must have arisen as what psychologists call a projection of his inner self, that inner self that was so mysterious and inscrutable even to its owner.

It happened that this type of character had already been popularized in the "Gothic" thrillers or "horrid stories" of Mrs. Radcliffe, M. G. Lewis (a friend of Byron's, known as "Monk" Lewis from his violent and sadistic tale *The Monk*), John Moore, whose *Zeluco*, a much more serious work, Byron greatly admired, and lesser writers. The period of their greatest popularity was the last decade of the eighteenth century, but they survived through Byron's lifetime. Jane Austen's *Northanger Abbey* was written as a parody of them in 1798, but it still had a point when it was published in 1818. These thrillers were intended for an English Protestant middle-class reading public: consequently their horrid surroundings were normally Continental, Catholic and upper class, though Oriental settings also had a vogue. Into such settings stalked a character type, sometimes a villain, sometimes presented in a more sympathetic, or more-sinned-against-than-sinning, role, but in either case misanthropic, misunderstood, and solitary, with strong diabolical overtones. The devil is a powerfully erotic figure, his horns and hoofs descending from the ancient satyrs, and the various forms of sadism and masochism glanced at in these thrillers helped to make them extremely popular, not least with the female part of the reading public.

Childe Harold and the other lowering heroes of Byron's tales not only popularized a conventional type of hero, but popularized Byron himself in that role. For Byron was a dark and melancholy-looking lord with a reputation for wickedness and free thought; he seemed to prefer the Continent to England, and took a detached view of middle-class and even Christian morality. He owned a gloomy Gothic castle and spent evenings with revelers in it; he was pale and thin with his ferocious dieting; he even had a lame foot. No wonder he said that strangers whom he met at dinner "looked as if his Satanic Majesty had been among them." The prince of darkness is a gentleman, and so was Byron. Again, when a "nameless vice" was introduced into a Gothic thriller, as part of the villain's or hero's background, it generally turned out, when named, to be incest. This theme recurs all through Romantic literature, being almost obsessive in Shelley as well as Byron, and here again a literary convention turns up in Byron's life. Even a smaller detail, like the disguising of the ex-Corsair's mistress in *Lara* as the pageboy Kaled, recurs in Byron's liaison with Caroline Lamb, who looked well in a page's costume.

Byron did not find the Byronic hero as enthralling as his public did, and he made several efforts to detach his own character from Childe Harold and his other heroes, with limited success. He says of Childe Harold that he wanted to make him an objective study of gloomy misanthropy, hence he deliberately cut humor out of the poem in order to preserve a unity of tone. But Byron's most distinctive talents did not have full scope in this part of his work. Most of the Gothic thriller writers were simple-minded popular novelists, but the same convention had also been practised on a much higher level of literary intelligence. Apart from Goethe's early *Sorrows of Werther*, an extraordinarily popular tale of a solemn suicide, Addison in *The Vision of Mirza* and Johnson in *Rasselas* had used the Oriental tale for serious literary purposes. Also, Horace Walpole in *The Castle of Otranto* (1764) and William Beckford in *Vathek* (1786) had written respectively a Gothic and an Oriental romance in which melodrama and fantasy were shot through with flickering lights of irony. They were addressed to a reading public capable, to use modern phraseology, of taking their corn with a pinch of salt. It was this higher level of sophistication that Byron naturally wanted to reach, and he was oppressed by the humorless solemnity of his own creations. His sardonic and ribald wit, his sense of the concrete, his almost infallible feeling for the common-sense perspective on every situation, crackles all through his letters and journals, even through his footnotes. But it seems to be locked out of his serious poetry, and only in the very last canto of *Don Juan* did he succeed in uniting fantasy and humor.

Byron's tales are, on the whole, well-told and well-shaped stories. Perhaps he learned something from his own ridicule of Southey, who was also a popular writer of verse tales, sometimes of mammoth proportions. In any case he is well able to exploit the capacity of verse for dramatizing one or two central situations, leaving all the cumbersome apparatus of plot to be ignored or taken for granted. But he seemed unable to bring his various projections of his inner ghost to life: his heroes, like the characters of a detective story, are thin, bloodless, abstract, and popular. Nor could he seem to vary the tone, from romance to irony, from fantasy to humor, as Beckford does in *Vathek*. Byron was strongly attracted by Beckford, and is thinking of him at the very opening of *Childe Harold*, as Beckford had lived for two years in Portugal. When Byron writes:

> Deep in yon cave Honorius long did dwell,
> In hope to merit Heaven by making earth a Hell.

he obviously has in mind the demure remark in the opening of *Vathek:* "He did not think . . . that it was necessary to make a hell of this world to enjoy paradise in the next." But though Byron is the wittiest of writers, the Byronic hero cannot manage much more than a gloomy smile. Here, for instance, is Childe Harold on the "Lisbon Packet":

> The sails were filled, and fair the light winds
>   blew,
> As glad to waft him from his native home . . .
> And then, it may be, of his wish to roam
> Repented he, but in his bosom slept
> The silent thought, nor from his lips did come
> One word of wail, whilst others sate and wept,
> And to the reckless gales unmanly moaning kept.

and here is Byron himself in the same situation:

> Hobhouse muttering fearful curses,
>   As the hatchway down he rolls,
> Now his breakfast, now his verses,
>   Vomits forth—and damns our souls . . .
> "Zounds! my liver's coming up:
> I shall not survive the racket
> Of this brutal Lisbon Packet."

The same inability to combine seriousness and humor is also to be found in the plays, where one would expect more variety of tone. The central character is usually the Byronic hero again, and again he seems to cast a spell over the whole action. Byron recognīzed this deficiency in his dramas, and to say that his plays were not intended for the stage would be an understatement. Byron had a positive phobia of stage production, and once tried to get an injunction issued to prevent a performance of *Marino Faliero*. "I never risk *rivalry* in anything," he wrote to Lady Melbourne, and being directly dependent on the applause or booing of a crowd (modern theaters give us no notion of what either form of demonstration was like in Byron's day) was something he could not face, even in absence. Besides, he had no professional sense, and nothing of the capacity to write for an occasion that the practising dramatist needs. Hence, with the exception of *Werner*, a lively and well-written melodrama based on a plot by somebody else, Byron's plays are so strictly closet dramas that they differ little in structure from the tales.

The establishing of the Byronic hero was a major feat of characterization, but Byron had little power of characterization apart from this figure. Like many brilliant talkers, he had not much ear for the rhythms and nuances of other people's speech. Here again we find a close affinity between Byron's personality and the conventions of his art. For instance, in his life Byron seemed to have curiously little sense of women as human beings. Except for Lady Melbourne, he addressed himself to the female in them, took a hearty-male view of their intellectual interests, and concentrated on the ritual of love-making with the devotion of what an earlier age would have called a clerk of Venus. This impersonal and ritualistic approach to women is reflected in his tales and plays, where again it fits the conventions of Byronic romance. It is difficult for a heroine of strong character to make much headway against a gloomy misanthropic hero, and Byron's heroines, like the heroines of Gothic romance in general, are insipid prodigies of neurotic devotion.

But if Byron's plays are not practicable stage plays, they are remarkable works. *Manfred,* based on what Byron had heard about Goethe's *Faust,* depicts the Byronic hero as a student of magic whose knowledge has carried him beyond the limits of human society and given him superhuman powers, but who is still held to human desire by his love for his sister (apparently) Astarte. At the moment of his death the demons he has controlled, with a sense of what is customary in stories about magicians, come to demand his soul, but Manfred, in a crisp incisive speech which retains its power to surprise through any number of rereadings, announces that he has made no bargain with them, that whatever he has done, they can go to hell, and he will not go with them. The key to this final scene is the presence of the Abbot. Manfred and the Abbot differ on all points of theory, but the Abbot is no coward and Manfred is no villain: they face the crisis together, linked in a common bond of humanity which enables Manfred to die and to triumph at the same time.

Two of Byron's plays, *Cain* and *Heaven and Earth*, are described by Byron as "mysteries," by which he meant Biblical plays like those of the Middle Ages. Wherever we turn in Byron's poetry, we meet the figure of Cain, the first man who never knew Paradise, and whose sexual love was necessarily incestuous. In Byron's "mystery" Cain is Adam's eldest son and heir, but what he really inherits is the memory of a greater dispossession. "Dost thou not live?" asks Adam helplessly. "Must I not die?" retorts Cain. Adam cannot comprehend the mentality of one who has been born with the consciousness of death. But Lucifer can, for he too has been disinherited. He comes to Cain and gives him what he gave Adam: fruit of the tree of knowledge, of a kind that Raphael, in the eighth book of *Paradise Lost*, warned Adam against: a knowledge of other worlds and other beings, a realization that the fortunes of humanity are of less account in the scheme of things than he had assumed. From such knowledge develops the resentment that leads to the murder of Abel and to Cain's exile. And just as Milton tries to show us that we in Adam's place would have committed Adam's sin, so Byron makes us feel that we all have something of Cain in us: everybody has killed something that he wishes he had kept alive, and the fullest of lives is wrapped around the taint of an inner death. As the princess says in *The Castle of Otranto:* "This can be no evil spirit: it is undoubtedly one of the family."

The other "mystery," *Heaven and Earth*, deals with the theme of the love of angels for human women recorded in some mysterious verses of Genesis, and ends with the coming of Noah's flood. Angels who fall through sexual love are obvious enough subjects for Byron, but *Heaven and Earth* lacks the clear dramatic outline of *Cain*. All Byron's plays are tragedies, and as Byron moved further away from the easy sentiment of his earlier tales he moved toward intellectual paradox rather than tragedy. It is particularly in the final scenes that we observe Byron becoming too self conscious for the full emotional resonance of tragedy. In *Sardanapalus*, for example, we see the downfall of a king who pursued pleasure because he was too intelligent to want to keep his people plunged into warfare. His intelligence is identified by his people with weakness, and his pursuit of pleasure is inseparably attached to selfishness. What we are left with, despite his final death on a funeral pyre, is less tragedy than an irony of a kind that is very close to satire. Byron's creative powers were clearly running in the direction of satire, and it was to satire that he turned in his last and greatest period.

In *English Bards and Scotch Reviewers* Byron spoke of Wordsworth as "that mild apostate from poetic rule." This poem is early, but Byron never altered his opinion of the Lake Poets as debasers of the currency of English poetry. His own poetic idol was Pope, whom he called "the moral poet of all civilization," and he thought of himself as continuing Pope's standards of clarity, craftsmanship and contact with real life against the introverted metaphysical mumblings of Coleridge and Wordsworth. Byron's early models were standard, even old-fashioned, later eighteenth-century models. *English Bards* is in the idiom of eighteenth-century satire, less of Pope than of Pope's successors, Churchill, Wolcot, and Gifford, and the first part of *Childe Harold*, with its pointless Spenserian stanza and its semi-facetious antique diction—fortunately soon dropped by Byron—is also an eighteenth-century stock pattern. Byron was friendly with Shelley, but owes little to him technically, and in his letters he expressed a vociferous dislike for the poetry of Keats (considerably toned down in the eleventh canto of *Don Juan*). His literary friends, Sheridan, Rogers, Gifford, were of the older generation, and even Tom Moore, his biographer and by far his closest friend among his poetic contemporaries, preserved, like so many Irish writers, something of the eighteenth-century manner.

It was also an eighteenth-century model that gave him the lead for the phase of poetry that began with *Beppo* in September, 1817, and exploited the possibilities of the eight-line (*ottava rima*) stanza used there and in *Don Juan* and *The Vision of Judgment*. Byron seems to have derived this stanza from a heroi-comical poem, *Whistlecraft*, by John Hookham Frere, whom Byron had met in Spain, and which in its turn had owed something to the Italian romantic epics of the early Renaissance. Byron went on to study the Italian poems, and translated the first canto of one of the best of them, Pulci's tale of a good-natured giant, *Morgante Maggiore*. But there was one feature in Frere that he could not have found in the Italians, and that was the burlesque rhyme. In Italian the double rhyme is normal, but it is a peculiarity of English that even double rhymes have to be used with great caution in serious poetry, and that all obtrusive or ingenious rhymes belong to comic verse. This is a major principle of the wit of *Hudibras* before Byron's time, as of W. S. Gilbert and Ogden Nash since, and without it the wit of *Don Juan* is hardly conceivable:

> But—Oh! ye lords of ladies intellectual,
> Inform us truly, have they not hen-pecked you all?

Armed with this new technique, Byron was ready to tackle a narrative satire, and in narrative satire he found not only a means of exploiting all his best qualities, but of turning his very faults as a poet into virtues. He could digress to his heart's content, for digression is part of the fun in satire—one thinks of *Tristram Shandy* and the "Digression in Praise of Digressions" in *A Tale of a Tub*. He could write doggerel, but doggerel in satire is a sign of wit rather than incompetence. He could be serious if he liked, for sudden changes of mood belong to the form, and he could swing back to burlesque again as soon as he was bored with seriousness, or thought the reader might be. It is particularly the final couplet that he uses to undercut his own romantic Byronism, as in the description of Daniel Boone in Canto VIII:

> Crime came not near him—she is not the child
>   Of solitude; Health shrank not from him—for
> Her home is in the rarely trodden wild,
>   Where if men seek her not, and death be more
> Their choice than life, forgive them, as beguiled
>   By habit to what their own hearts abhor—
> In cities caged. The present case in point I
> Cite is, that Boon lived hunting up to ninety.

In the new flush of discovery, Byron wrote exultantly to his friend Douglas Kinnaird: "[*Don Juan*] is the sublime of *that there* sort of writing—it may be bawdy, but is it not good English? It may be profligate but is it not *life*, is it not *the thing*? Could any man have written it who has not lived in the world?" But even Byron was soon made aware that he was not as popular as he had been. The women who loved *The Corsair* hated *Don Juan*, for the reason that Byron gives with his usual conciseness on such subjects: "the wish of all women to exalt the *sentiment* of the passions, and to keep up the illusion which is their empire." Teresa, as soon as she understood anything of the poem, boycotted it, and forced Byron to promise not to go on with it, a promise he was able to evade only with great difficulty. His friend Harriet Wilson, significantly enough a courtesan who lived partly by blackmail, wrote him:

"Dear *Adorable* Lord Byron, *don't* make a mere *coarse* old libertine of yourself."

Don Juan is traditionally the incautious amorist, the counterpart in love to Faust in knowledge, whose pursuit of women is so ruthless that he is eventually damned, as in the last scene of Mozart's opera *Don Giovanni*. Consequently he is a logical choice as a mask for Byron, but he is a mask that reveals the whole Byronic personality, instead of concealing the essence of it as Childe Harold does. The extroversion of Byron's temperament has full scope in *Don Juan*. There is hardly any characterization in the poem: even Don Juan never emerges clearly as a character. We see only what happens to him, and the other characters, even Haidée, float past as phantasmagoria of romance and adventure. What one misses in the poem is the sense of engagement or participation. Everything happens to Don Juan, but he is never an active agent, and seems to take no responsibility for his life. He drifts from one thing to the next, appears to find one kind of experience as good as another, makes no judgements and no commitments. As a result the gloom and misanthropy, the secret past sins, the gnawing remorse of the earlier heroes is finally identified as a shoddier but more terrifying evil—boredom, the sense of the inner emptiness of life that is one of Byron's most powerfully compelling moods, and has haunted literature ever since, from the *ennui* of Baudelaire to the *Angst* and *nausée* of our own day.

The episodes of the poem are all stock Byronic scenes: Spain, the pirates of the Levant, the odalisques of Turkish harems, battlefields, and finally English high society. But there is as little plot as characterization: the poem exists for the sake of its author's comment. As Byron says:

> This narrative is not meant for narration,
> But a mere airy and fantastic basis,
> To build up common things with common places.

Its wit is constantly if not continuously brilliant, and Byron's contempt of cant and prudery, his very real hatred of cruelty, his detached view of all social icons, whether conservative or popular, are well worth having. Not many poets give us as much common sense as Byron does. On the other hand the opposition to the poem made him increasingly self-conscious as he went on, and his technique of calculated bathos and his deliberate refusal to "grow metaphysical"—that is, pursue any idea beyond the stage of initial reaction—keep the poem too resolutely on one level. The larger imaginative vistas that we are promised ("a panoramic view of hell's in training") do not materialize, and by the end of the sixteenth canto we have a sense of a rich but not inexhaustible vein rapidly thinning out. As *Don Juan* is not Don Juan's poem but Byron's poem, it could hardly have been ended, but only abandoned or cut short by its author's death. The Mozartian ending of the story Byron had already handled, in his own way, in *Manfred.*

The Vision of Judgment is Byron's most original poem, and therefore his most conventional one; it is his wittiest poem, and therefore his most serious one. Southey, Byron's favorite target among the Lake poets, had become poet laureate, and his political views, like those of Coleridge and Wordsworth, had shifted from an early liberalism to a remarkably complacent Toryism. On the death of George III in 1820 he was ill-advised enough to compose, in his laureate capacity, a "Vision of Judgment" describing the apotheosis and entry into heaven of the stammering, stupid, obstinate, and finally lunatic and blind monarch whose sixty-year reign had lost America, alienated Ireland, plunged the country into the longest and bloodiest war in its history, and ended in a desolate scene of domestic misery and repression. George III was not personally responsible for all the evils of his reign, but in those days royalty was not the projection of middle-class virtue that it is now, and was consequently less popular and more open to attack. The apotheosis of a dead monarch, as a literary form, is of classical origin, and so is its parody, Byron's poem being in the tradition of Seneca's brilliant mockery of the entry into heaven of the Emperor Claudius.

Byron's religious views were certainly unusual in his day, but if we had to express them in a formula, it would be something like this: the best that we can imagine man doing is where our conception of God ought to start. Religions that foment cruelty and induce smugness, or ascribe cruelty and smugness to God, are superstitions. In *Heaven and Earth,* for example, the offstage deity who decrees the deluge at the end is clearly the moral inferior of every human creature he drowns. In *The Vision of Judgment* the sycophantic Southey is contrasted with John Wilkes, who fought King George hard all his life, but who, when encouraged to go on persecuting him after death, merely says:

> I don't like ripping up old stories, since
> His conduct was but natural in a prince.

This is a decent human attitude, consequently it must be the least we can expect from heaven, and so the poet takes leave of the poor old king "practising the hundredth Psalm."

III

Byron has probably had more influence outside England than any other English poet except Shakespeare. In English literature, though he is always classified with the Romantic poets, he is Romantic only because the Byronic hero is a Romantic figure: as we have seen, he has little technically in common with other English Romantics. But on the Continent Byron has been the arch-romantic of modern literature, and European nineteenth-century culture is as unthinkable without Byron as its history would be without Napoleon. From the painting of Delacroix to the music of Berlioz, from the poetry of Pushkin to the philosophy of Nietzsche, the spell of Byron is everywhere. Modern fiction would be miserably impoverished without the Byronic hero: Balzac, Stendhal, Dostoevsky, have all used him in crucial roles. In the more advanced political atmosphere of England, Byron was only a Whig intellectual, whereas in Greece and Italy he was a revolutionary fighter for freedom, a poetic Mazzini or Bolivar, though, like them, not a class leveler. As he said:

> I wish men to be free
> As much from mobs as kings—from you as me.

Among English readers the reputation of the Romantic and sentimental Byron has not kept pace with his reputation as a satirist, but it would be wrong to accept the assertion, so often made today, that Byron is of little importance apart from his satires and letters. An immense amount of imitation and use of Byron, conscious or unconscious, direct or indirect, has taken place in English literature, too, and nearly all of it is of the Romantic Byron. Melville (whose Ishmael is in the line of Cain), Conrad, Hemingway, A. E. Housman, Thomas Wolfe, D. H. Lawrence, W. H. Auden—these writers have little in common except that they all Byronize.

The most important reason for Byron's great influence is that he was a portent of a new kind of sensibility. For many centuries poets had assumed a hierarchy of nature with a moral principle built into it. For Dante, for Shakespeare, for Milton, there was a top level of divine providence; a level of distinctively human nature which included education, reason and law; a level of physical nature, which was morally neutral and which man could not, like the animals, adjust to; and a bottom level of sin and corruption. This hierarchy corresponded to the teachings of religion and science alike. But from Rousseau's time on a profound change in the cultural framework of the arts takes place. Man is now thought of as a product of the energy of physical nature, and as this nature is subhuman in morality and intelligence and capacity for pleasure, the origin of art is morally ambivalent, and may even be demonic. The Byronic hero, for whom, as for Manfred, pride, lack of sympathy with humanity and a destructive influence even in love are inseparable from genius, dramatizes this new conception of art and life alike more vividly than anything else in the culture of the time. Hence it is no exaggeration to say that Byron released a mainspring of creative energy in modern culture.

Byron's immediate influence in his own country, on the other hand, though certainly very great, was qualified in many ways, by queasiness about his morality, by a refusal to separate him from his posing heroes, by a feeling that he lacked the sterner virtues and wrote with too much pleasure and too few pains. The first canto of *Don Juan* centers on the nervous prudery of Donna Inez, who is, not surprisingly, modeled on Byron's wife. But Donna Inez was Britannia as well. The sands of the Regency aristocracy were running out, the tide of middle-class morality had already set in, and the age that we think of as Victorian, with its circulating libraries, its custom of reading aloud to large family circles, and its tendency not to be amused, at any rate by anything approaching the ribald, was on the way. As Byron admitted ruefully of the opening cantos:

> . . . the publisher declares, in sooth,
> Through needles' eyes it easier for the camel is
> To pass, than those two cantos into families.

A more important barrier was raised by the lack of any sense of moral involvement in *Don Juan*, already mentioned. With the British Empire developing, and a greater number of poets and intellectuals issuing stentorian calls to duty, such detachment seemed inadequate, except for the fact that Byron himself took matters out of Don Juan's hands and died for a cause in Greece. In *Sartor Resartus* Carlyle summed up the later view of Byron as a poet who had gone through a gloomy stage of denial and defiance, an "Everlasting No," had then moved into a "Centre of Indifference," but had never gone on to the final "Everlasting

Yea." For this final stage, Carlyle recommended: "Close thy Byron; open thy Goethe."

However, Carlyle himself hardly succeeded in closing his Byron, as when he went on to work out his conception of the Great Man what he actually produced was a vulgarization of the Byronic hero. The author of *The Corsair* would have raised a quizzical eyebrow at Carlyle's hero journeying forward "escorted by the Terrors and the Splendours, the Archdemons and Archangels." This tendency to underestimate Byron without surpassing him has recurred more than once. Bernard Shaw, in the preface to his Don Juan play, *Man and Superman*, dismissed Byron's Don Juan as a mere "libertine vagabond." Yet Byron had certainly anticipated Shaw's central idea, that woman takes the lead in sexual relations and that Don Juan is consequently as much a victim as a pursuer. No, Byron will not stay closed. It is a better idea to open Goethe, and when we do we find a more liberal view of Byron. Goethe in fact was fascinated by Byron, who dedicated *Sardanapalus* to him, and he referred to him in the second part of *Faust* as Euphorion, a kind of Eros-figure whose passion for liberty, if self-destructive, is also an acceptance of life simply because it is there, and has nothing of the compulsion to justify existence that is often close to a distrust of its worth.

We have not yet shaken off our nineteenth-century inhibitions about Byron. A frequent twentieth-century jargon term for him is "immature," which endorses the Carlyle view that Byron is a poet to be outgrown. One thinks of Yeats's penetrating remark that we are never satisfied with the maturity of those whom we have admired in boyhood. Even those who have not admired Byron in boyhood have gone through a good deal of Byronism at that stage. There is certainly something youthful about the Byronic hero, and for some reason we feel more defensive about youth than about childhood, and more shamefaced about liking a poet who has captured a youthful imagination. If we replace "youthful" with the loaded term "adolescent" we can see how deeply ingrained this feeling is.

Among intellectuals the Southey type, who makes a few liberal gestures in youth to quiet his conscience and then plunges into a rapturous authoritarianism for the rest of his life, is much more common than the Byron type, who continues to be baffled by unanswered questions and simple anomalies, to make irresponsible jokes, to set his face against society, to respect the authority of his own mood—in short, to retain the rebellious or irreverent qualities of youth. Perhaps it is as dangerous to eliminate the adolescent in us as it is to eliminate the child. In any case the kind of poetic experience that Byronism represents should be obtained young, and in Byron. It may later be absorbed into more complex experiences, but to miss or renounce it is to impoverish whatever else we may attain.

❧ Emily Dickinson

EMILY DICKINSON WAS BORN IN AMHERST, MASSACHUSETTS, IN THE Connecticut River Valley, in 1830. She died in the house she was born in, and her travels out of the region consisted of one trip to Washington and Philadelphia and two or three to Boston and Cambridge. Amherst had recently acquired, largely through the energy of her grandfather, an academy, which she attended, and a college. Her father, Edward Dickinson, was a leading citizen of the town, a lawyer, active and successful in state politics, and treasurer of the college. Such a town illustrated, more effectively than any Oneida or Brook Farm, the Utopian pattern in nineteenth-century American society. It was a little world in itself, so well balanced economically as to be nearly self-sufficient, with a provincial but intense religious and intellectual culture, the latter growing as the college grew. Throughout her life Emily Dickinson·was able to say what she had said at sixteen: "I dont know anything more about affairs in the world, than if I was in a trance," and her ability to shut all distractions out of her life owed much to the social coherence of her surroundings.

There was a strong family feeling among the Dickinsons, and neither Emily nor her younger sister Lavinia married or left home. The older brother, Austin, went to Harvard Law School, where Emily pelted him with affectionate letters telling him how much he was missed, then returned to Amherst to practice law. Gossip said that the father's possessiveness kept his daughters beside him ministering to his domestic comforts, but this may not be true. The image of awful integrity he inspired, which made his daughter say at his death: "His Heart was pure and terrible, and I think no other like it exists," may have grown on her gradually, as her youthful remarks in letters to Austin sound normally bratty. Thus: "Father and mother sit in state in the sitting room perusing such papers only, as they are well assured have nothing carnal in them." Her mother she was never close to until later years. Austin's wife, Susan Gilbert, was another person whom Emily Dickinson seems always to have loved passionately, in spite of a good deal of tension and occasional open ruptures. To Sue, across the fence,

Emily sent nearly three hundred poems, besides messages, epigrams, gifts, and other symbols of affection.

At seventeen, Emily left the Amherst Academy and went to Mount Holyoke College, or Seminary, as it was then called, a few miles away in South Hadley. The discipline there was strict but humane, and she seems to have enjoyed herself in spite of the religious instruction, but her father withdrew her after a year. Emily thus had, for a poet, relatively little formal education. It is unlikely that she read any language except her own. She knew the Bible (involuntarily), she knew Shakespeare, she knew the classical myths, and she took a good deal of interest in contemporary women writers, especially Elizabeth Browning, George Eliot, and the Brontës. The Brontë references in earlier letters are to Charlotte, but "gigantic Emily Brontë" haunts the later ones. Dickens and Robert Browning appear in her rare literary allusions; there are one or two echoes of Tennyson; and, of the more serious American writers, she knew Emerson and something of Thoreau and Hawthorne. Her main literary instructors, however, were her dictionary and her hymnbook. She has a large vocabulary for a poet so limited in subject matter, and most of her stanzas, as has often been pointed out, are the ordinary hymn stanzas, the eight-six-eight-six "common meter" and the six-six-eight-six "short meter" being especially frequent.

Creative people often seem to need certain types of love or friendship that make manifest for them the human relations or conflicts with which their work is concerned. A poet of Shakespeare's day could hardly set up in business without a "mistress" to whom he vowed eternal devotion, though this mistress might have little if any part to play in his actual life, and very seldom had anything to do with his marriage. Emily Dickinson seemed to need in her life an older man to act as her "preceptor" or "master," to use her own terms, who could keep her in touch with qualities she did not profess to have: intellectual consistency, sociability, knowledge of the world, firm and settled convictions. Benjamin F. Newton, a lawyer who had articled with her father, was apparently her first "preceptor." Her letters to him have not been preserved, but he seems to have awakened her literary tastes, expanded her cultural horizons, and perhaps given her a more liberal idea of her religion—at any rate she refers to him as "a friend, who taught me Immortality." He died in 1853, before Emily had started to write poetry in earnest.

Then came Charles Wadsworth, a Presbyterian clergyman whom

Emily may have heard on her trip to Philadelphia, and who, for all his married and middle-aged respectability, seems to have been the one great love of the poet's life. It is unlikely that the kind of love she offered him would have interfered with his marriage or social position, but some pathetic drafts of letters addressed to a "Master," if they were intended for Wadsworth, indicate something of the tumult of her feelings. In 1862 Wadsworth accepted a call to a church in San Francisco, a removal which seems to have been a profound shock to the poet, for reasons we can only guess at—again the correspondence has not survived. The name of the church he went to—Calvary—became the center of a drama of loss and renunciation in which the poet becomes "Empress of Calvary," and the bride of an invisible marriage followed immediately by separation instead of union.

But Wadsworth, whatever her feeling for him, could hardly have had more than a perfunctory interest in the poetry that was now becoming the central activity of her life. In her early years she seems to have written little except letters and the occasional valentine, of which two most elaborate and ingenious efforts have been preserved. In the later 1850's she began writing poetry consistently, binding her completed poems up into packets, and sometimes sending copies to Sue or enclosing them in letters to other correspondents. In addition to her fair copies, there are many work-sheet drafts scribbled on anything within reach—once on the back of an invitation to a "candy pulling" sent her twenty-six years earlier. Her impetus to write seems to have come on her in a flood, as the poems written or copied out in the year 1862 alone average one a day. With Wadsworth gone, another "preceptor" was urgently needed, this time a literary critic. Having liked an article by Thomas Wentworth Higginson she had read in the *Atlantic Monthly*, Emily sent the author a letter (No. 260), enclosing her card and four poems, and asking if in his opinion her poetry was "alive" and "breathed." Higginson had been a Unitarian clergyman but had resigned his pastorate to devote himself to writing, and was then on the point of organizing a Negro regiment to fight in the Civil War (hence his later title of Colonel Higginson).

Higginson was an influential critic, and as such a natural target for amateur poets pretending that they wanted his frank opinion of their work when what they really wanted was advice on how to get published. He saw at once that Emily Dickinson was more serious business than this. She said explicitly that she wanted her work criticized by the literary standards that he knew about, and he was bound to be misled by that. But he realized, perhaps more quickly than she did, that she did not want specific criticisms of her poems, which she had no intention of altering for anyone's views. Nor was she interested in publication, as she made clear. All she wanted was contact with a sympathetic reader of informed taste and knowledge of the world of thought and action. Higginson had the sense to be flattered by her confidence, and seems to have responded with unfailing courtesy to her gentle but persistent nudgings to write her. She may have been exaggerating when she told him that he had saved her life, but she was not underestimating the service he did her, nor should we. At the same time, she was never in love with Higginson, and her attitude toward him was one of devotion tempered by an ironic detachment.

After 1862, the poet became increasingly a recluse, dressing in white, apparently with reference to her inner "Calvary" drama of renunciation. For the last decade of her life she did not leave her house and refused to see any strangers, her experience bounded by her house and garden, her social life completely absorbed in the brief letters she constantly sent to friends and neighbors, which sometimes contained poems and often accompanied small gifts of flowers or fruit. She expected her friends to be cultivated and tolerant people, and most of them were, prizing her enigmatic notes and respecting her privacy. There was no mistaking the good will and affection in her letters, however oblique in expression. One feels something Oriental in her manner of existence: the seclusion, the need for a "preceptor," the use of brief poems as a form of social communication, would have seemed normal enough in the high cultures of the Far East, however unusual in her own. And even her culture was one in which the telephone had not yet destroyed the traditional balance between the spoken and the written word.

Of her friends, some were well-known writers in their day, apart from Higginson. She was much attached to Samuel Bowles, editor of the Springfield *Republican,* one of the liveliest of the New England local papers, and representing a type of highly articulate journalism now practically extinct. Helen Hunt Jackson, born in Amherst in the same year as Emily Dickinson and a childhood playmate, came back into her life in later years. Mrs. Jackson was also a disciple of Higginson, and was the author of the Indian romance *Ramona* and the Saxe Holm stories. Whatever this may mean to the contemporary reader, it meant in her day that she was at the top of the literary tree. Another novel, *Mercy Philbrick's Choice,* and a short story, seem to have made some use of Emily Dickinson's smothered love affair for copy. She told Emily that she was a great poet and was defrauding her public by not publishing, and finally, after strenuous efforts, got one poem, "Success is counted sweetest," into a collection of anonymous verse called *A Masque of Poets,* many readers taking it to be Emerson's.

In the last decade of Emily Dickinson's life her father's friend Judge Otis P. Lord became a widower, and his friendship with the poet quickly ripened into love. Though, as usual, the letters themselves have disappeared, we do have a few drafts of letters to him among her papers which put the fact beyond doubt. After living as she had, the adjustment needed for marriage would have been formidable, probably impossible. But she was deeply in love, which indicates that her retired life was the choice of her temperament, not a dedication. She was not a nun *manquée,* even if she does call herself a "Wayward Nun." Conscious human perception is, we are told, highly selective, and very efficient about excluding whatever threatens its balance. "Strong" people and men of action are those for whom such perception functions predictably: they are made strong by habit, by continually meeting the expected response. Creative abilities normally go with more delicate and mysterious nuances of awareness, hence they are often accompanied by some kind of physical or psychic weakness. Emily Dickinson's perceptions were so immediate that they absorbed her whole energy, or as she says, "The mere sense of living is joy enough":

> To be alive–is Power–
> Existence–in itself–
> Without a further function–

But she realized that there was danger as well as ecstasy in so sensitive a response. "Had we the first intimation of the Definition of Life," she says, "the calmest of us would be Lunatics!" To reverse a well-known phrase from Lewis Carroll, it took all the staying in the same place she could do to keep running. The intensity of her ordinary consciousness left her with few reserves to spend on a social life.

In a life so retired it was inevitable that the main events should be the deaths of friends, and Emily Dickinson became a prolific writer of notes of condolence. Her father, her mother, Sue's little boy Gilbert (struck down by typhoid fever at the age of eight),

Bowles, Wadsworth, Lord, Helen Jackson, all died in the last few years of her life. As early as 1883 she had a nervous collapse, and observed: "The Crisis of the sorrow of so many years is all that tires me." Two years later a more serious illness began. In the second week of May, 1886, she wrote to her cousins Louisa and Fanny Norcross:

> Little Cousins,
> Called back.
> Emily.

A few days later she was dead.

A life in which such things as the death of her dog or an unexpected call by Wadsworth are prominent incidents is not simply a quiet life but a carefully obliterated one. There are poets—and they include Shakespeare—who seem to have pursued a policy of keeping their lives away from their readers. Human nature being what it is, it is precisely such poets who are most eagerly read for biographical allusions. We shall find Emily Dickinson most rewarding if we look in her poems for what her imagination has created, not for what event may have suggested it. When, under the spell of Ik Marvel's *Reveries of a Bachelor* (1850), a favorite book of hers, she writes:

> Many cross the Rhine
> In this cup of mine.
> Sip old Frankfort air
> From my brown Cigar

it would be a literal-minded reader who would infer that she had actually taken up cigar-smoking, yet this would be no more farfetched than many other biographical inferences. A poet is entitled to speak in many voices, male, female, or childlike, to express many different moods and to develop an experience in reading or life into an imaginative form that has no resemblance whatever to the original experience. Just as she made the whole of her conception of nature out of the bees and bobolinks and roses of her garden, so she constructed her drama of life, death and immortality, of love and renunciation, ecstasy and suffering, out of tiny incidents in her life. But to read biographical allegory where we ought to be reading poetry is precisely the kind of vulgarity that made her dread publication and describe it as a foul thing. Higginson's comment on her "Wild Nights!", that "the malignant" might "read into it more than that virgin recluse ever dreamed of putting there," indicates that glib speculations about the sexual feelings of virgins are much older than the popularizing of Freud. But whenever they are made they are incompetent as literary criticism.

It would be hard to name another poet in the history of the English language with so little interest in social or political events. The Civil War seemed to her "oblique," outside her orbit, and her only really peevish letter describes her reaction to a woman who told her that she ought to use her gifts for the good of humanity. There are one or two patriotic poems, but they show no freshness of insight. "My business is Circumference," she told Higginson. She concerned herself only with what she felt she could surround. It is characteristic of lyrical poetry to turn its back on the reader: the lyrical poet regularly pretends to be addressing his mistress or friend or God, or else he is soliloquizing or apostrophizing something in nature. But lyrical poetry also tends to create its own highly selected and intimate audience, like the sonnets and love poems of Shakespeare's day that circulated in manuscript among friends long before they reached print. For Emily Dickinson poetry was a form of private correspondence: "This is my letter to the World," is what she says of her poetry, and she describes the Gospel as "The Savior's . . . Letter he wrote to all mankind." Such a correspondence forms what, for Emily Dickinson, was the only genuine kind of human community, the small body of friends united in love and understanding. "Please to need me," as she wrote to Bowles.

> By a flower–By a letter–
> By a nimble love–
> If I weld the Rivet faster–
> Final fast–above–
>
> Never mind my breathless Anvil!
> Never mind Repose!
> Never mind the sooty faces
> Tugging at the Forge!

II

At her death Emily Dickinson was the author of seven published poems, all anonymous, some issued without her authorization, six of them at least in what she would have considered garbled versions, altered by editors to make them more conventional. Her friends knew that she wrote poetry, but nobody, not even her sister Lavinia who had lived with her all her life, had any notion that she had written close to eighteen hundred poems. She left instructions to Lavinia that her "papers" were to be destroyed, as was customary at that time, but no instructions were given about the piled-up packets of verse that Lavinia, to her astonishment, discovered in her sister's room. Lavinia took the packets to Sue, with a demand that they be transcribed and published immediately, meeting all complaints about the length and difficulty of the task with: "But they are Emily's poems!" Sue proved to be indolent, and perhaps jealous, and after a long wait Lavinia took them to Mrs. Mabel Loomis Todd, wife of an Amherst professor of astronomy, an attractive and highly accomplished young woman, who knew Emily, so to speak, by ear, having played the piano in the Dickinson house while the poet sat invisibly in the dark hall outside and commented on the music.

Higginson's help was enlisted. At first he felt that it would be a mistake to publish Emily Dickinson, perhaps thinking of an appeal she had made to him to talk Helen Jackson out of publishing "Success." But he gradually became, first interested, then fascinated, by what he found, and helped publicize her by writing articles about her. The two editors, Mrs. Todd and Higginson, produced *Poems by Emily Dickinson* in 1890, where a selection of her poems was distributed in various categories labeled "Life," "Love," "Nature" and the like, with titles for individual poems supplied by Higginson. A second and a third selection appeared in 1891 and 1896, respectively. Although Mrs. Todd's original transcripts were accurate, the poems were systematically smoothed out in punctuation, meter, grammar, and rhymes. Higginson took the lead in this at first, but as he went on he began to realize that the poet's liberties were not those of carelessness or incompetence. When the second selection was being prepared, he wrote to Mrs. Todd: "Let us alter as little as possible, now that the public ear is opened," including his own ear; but by that time Mrs. Todd had caught the improving fever. Mrs. Todd also went through the laborious task of collecting and publishing two volumes of Emily Dickinson's letters, where she had to engage in a long tactful struggle with the owners, and prevented a good many of them from being irreparably lost. Through no fault of hers, some of them, notably those to the Norcross sisters, survive only in mutilated versions.

Some highly unedifying family squabbles stopped further publication. Sue had been alienated by the giving of the manuscripts to Mrs. Todd; then Lavinia, for reasons too complicated to go into here, turned against Mrs. Todd after Austin Dickinson's death and brought suit to recover a strip of land willed to Mrs. Todd by Austin. Nothing further was done until the next generation grew up, in the form of Sue's daughter, Martha Dickinson Bianchi, and Mrs. Todd's daughter, Millicent Todd Bingham, who produced a series of editions of both poems and letters between 1914 and 1950. Finally, the bulk of the manuscripts came into the possession of Harvard. With Thomas H. Johnson's definitive edition of the poems (1955) and letters (1958), Emily Dickinson achieved publication on her own uncompromising terms.

When Mrs. Todd's volumes appeared, there were, despite her editorial efforts, some hostile reviews and some complaints about the poet's lack of "technique," by which was meant smooth rhymes and meters. The complaints came mainly from such minor poets as Andrew Lang in England and Thomas Bailey Aldrich in America, who naturally ascribed the greatest importance and difficulty to the only poetic quality they themselves had. Against this, we may set the fact that the first volume alone went through sixteen editions in eight years, and was constantly reprinted thereafter. Mrs. Todd gave dozens of lectures on the poet, and could have given far more. It is inconceivable that the first volume of an unknown poet today could achieve such a success, unless fortified by pornography. *Somebody* wanted Emily Dickinson's poetry, and we cannot avoid the inference that in the 1890's she was a genuinely popular poet who found her own public in spite of what the highbrows said. When she reappeared in the 1920's, her reputation was curiously reversed. Then the highbrows took her up, hailed her as a precursor of whatever happened to be fashionable at the time, such as imagism or free verse or metaphysical poetry, and emphasized everything in her work that was unconventional, difficult, or quaint. Both conceptions have some truth in them.

The good popular poet is usually one who does well what a great many have tried to do with less success. For the thousands of people, most of them women, who make verse out of a limited range of imaginative experience in life, love, nature, and religion, who live without fame and without much knowledge of literature beyond their schoolbooks, Emily Dickinson is the literary spokesman. She is popular too in her conceptual use of language, for popular expression tends to the proverbial, and the unsophisticated poet is usually one who tries to put prose statements into verse. The Sibyl of Amherst is no Lorelei: she has no Keatsian faery lands forlorn or Tennysonian low-lying Claribels; she does not charm and she seldom sings. Mrs. Todd often spoke of encountering poems in Emily Dickinson that took her breath away, but what surprises in her work is almost always some kind of direct statement, sharpened into wit or epigram. When she describes a hummingbird as "A route of evanescence," or says of the bluebird:

> Her conscientious Voice will soar unmoved
> Above ostensible Vicissitude.

she is using what medieval poets called "aureate diction," big soft bumbling abstract words that absorb images into categories and ideas. She does not—like, for example, D. H. Lawrence—try to get inside the bird's skin and identify herself with it; she identifies the bird with the human consciousness in herself. Many of her poems start out by making some kind of definition of an abstract noun:

> Presentiment—is that long Shadow—on the Lawn—

> Renunciation—is a piercing Virtue—

> Publication—is the Auction
> Of the Mind of Man—

and most of her best-loved poems are in one of the oldest and most primitive forms of poetry, the riddle or oblique description of some object. In "A route of evanescence" there is no explicit mention of a hummingbird, because the poem tries to catch the essence of the feeling of the bird without mentioning it. Similarly with the snow in "It sifts from leaden sieves," and with the railway train in "I like to see it lap the miles."

Such popular features in her work have their own difficulties, and there are others inherent in her peculiar style. She has for the most part no punctuation, except a point represented in the Johnson edition by a dash, which, as the editor points out, is really a rhythmical beat, and is of little use in unraveling the syntax. She also shows a curious preference for an indirect subjunctive form of expression that appears in such phrases as "Beauty be not caused," and she has what seems a most unreasonable dislike of adding the *s* to the third person singular of verbs. The effect of such sidelong grammar is twofold: it increases the sense of epigrammatic wit, and it makes her poetry sound oracular, as though the explicit statements of which her poetry is so largely made up were coming to us shrouded in mystery. As she says:

> Tell all the Truth but tell it slant—
> Success in Circuit lies

The result is not invariably success: sometimes we may agree with enthusiasm:

> How powerful the Stimulus
> Of an Hermetic Mind—

at other times we can only say, with the captain in *Pinafore* confronted with a similar type of gnomic utterance: "I don't see at what you're driving, mystic lady":

> Endanger it, and the Demand
> Of tickets for a sigh
> Amazes the Humility
> Of Credibility—
>
> Recover it to Nature
> And that dejected Fleet
> Find Consternation's Carnival
> Divested of it's Meat

Every age has its conventional notions of what poetry ought to be like, and the conventional notions of Emily Dickinson's day were that poetry should be close to prose in its grammar and syntax, and that its vocabulary should be more refined than that of ordinary speech. Thus Robert Louis Stevenson was outraged by the word "hatter" in a poem of Whitman's, and asserted that using such a word was not "literary tact." Emily Dickinson deliberately flouts both conventions. Her beat punctuation and offbeat syntax go with an abrupt and colloquial diction. The tang of her local speech comes out in such spellings as "Febuary" and "boquet," in such locutions as "it don't" and "it is him," and in such words as "heft" for "weight." Speaking of heaven, she writes:

> Yet certain am I of the spot
> As if the Checks were given—

meaning railway checks, the guarantee the conductor gives that one is proceeding to the right destination. Her editors altered this to "chart," which was a more conventionally poetic word, being slightly antique. Emily Dickinson could easily have provided such a word herself, but preferred to form her diction at a humorously twisted angle to the conventional expectations of the reader.

There is little in Emily Dickinson, then, of the feeling that a writer must come to terms with conventional language at all costs. When she meets an inadequacy in the English language she simply walks through it, as a child might do. If the dictionary does not

provide an abstract noun for "giant," the poet will coin "gianture";
if the ordinary "diminution" does not give her enough sense of
movement, she will substitute "diminuet." Similarly the fact that
there is no singular form for "grass" or "hay" does not stop her
from speaking of "every Grass," or from writing, to Higginson's
horror:

> The Grass so little has to do
> I wish I were a Hay-

A similar teasing of the conventional reader's ear comes out in her
slanting rhymes, which often have the effect of disappointing or
letting down one's sense of an expected sound. At the same time
even a conventional reader can see that her commonplace stanza
forms could hardly achieve any variety of nuance without some
irregularities. This is particularly true of the sinewy rhythm that
syncopates against her rigid hymnbook meters and keeps them so
far out of reach of monotony or doggerel:

> Those not live yet
> Who doubt to live again-
> "Again" is of a twice
> But this-is one-
> The Ship beneath the Draw
> Aground-is he?
> Death-so-the Hyphen of the Sea-
> Deep is the Schedule
> Of the Disk to be-
> Costumeless Consciousness-
> That is he-

In sophisticated poetry close attention is paid to the sounds of
words: vowels and consonants are carefully balanced for assonance
and variety, and we feel, when such poetry is successful, that we
have the inevitably right words in their inevitably right order. In
popular poetry there is a clearly marked rhythm and the words
chosen to fill it up give approximately the intended meaning, but
there is no sense of any *mot juste* or uniquely appropriate word.
In the ballad, for example, we may have a great number of verbal
variants of the same poem. Here again Emily Dickinson's practice
is the popular, not the sophisticated one. For a great many of her
poems she has provided alternative words, phrases, even whole
lines, as though the rhythm, like a figured bass in music, allowed
the editor or reader to establish his own text. Thus in the last line
of one poem, "To meet so enabled a Man," we have "religious,"

"accomplished," "discerning," "accoutred," "established," and "conclusive" all suggested as alternates for "enabled." Another poem ends:

> And Kinsmen as divulgeless
> As throngs of Down—

with "Kindred as responsive," "Clans of Down," "And Pageants as impassive As Porcelain"—or, presumably, any combination of these —as possible variants. It is rather more disconcerting to find "New" suggested as an alternate for "Old" in a poem ending with a reference to "Our Old Neighbor–God."

What we find in Emily Dickinson's poetry, then, is a diffused vitality in rhythm and the free play of a lively and exhilarating mind, crackling with wit and sharp perception. These were clearly the qualities that she herself knew were there and especially prized. She asked Higginson simply whether her verse was "alive." As a poet, she is popular in the sense of being able, like Burns or Kipling or the early Wordsworth, to introduce poetry to readers who have had no previous experience of it. She has, on the other hand, a withdrawn consciousness and an intense intellectual energy that makes her almost esoteric, certainly often difficult.

In any case she seems, after her early valentines, to have reached her mature style almost in a single bound. It is otherwise with her prose, no doubt because we have so much more of it from her early years. Her schoolgirl letters, with their engaging mixture of child's prattle and adolescent's self-consciousness, show a Lamb-like gift for fantasy and a detached and humorous shrewdness. She speaks of other girls who "are perfect models of propriety," and remarks: "There 'most always are a few, whom the teachers look up to and regard as their satellites"—which is sharp observation for a fourteen-year-old. After her writing of poetry begins, her prose rhythm moves very close to verse. The first letter to Higginson is really a free verse poem; some of her earlier poems were originally written as prose, and she often falls into her favorite metrical rhythms, as in the opening of a letter to Bowles: "I am so far from Land—To offer *you* the cup–it might some Sabbath come *my* turn–Of wine how solemn–full!", which is a short meter stanza. Her later letters show a remarkable command of the techniques of discontinuous prose: they were most carefully composed, and the appearance of random jottings is highly deceptive. Continuous or expository prose assumes an equality between writer and reader: the writer is putting all he has in front of us. Discontinuous prose, with gaps in the sense that only intuition can cross, assumes an aloofness on the writer's part, a sense of reserves of connection that we must make special efforts to reach. The aphoristic style of her later letters is, if slightly more frequent in Continental literatures, extremely rare in England or America, yet she seems to have developed it without models or influences.

> Her Grace is all she has–
> And that, so least displays–
> One Art to recognize, must be,
> Another Art, to praise.

III

The most cursory glance at Emily Dickinson will reveal that she is a deeply religious poet, preoccupied, to the verge of obsession, with the themes of death and of immortality—the latter being, as she called it, the "Flood subject." Even in her use of the Bible, her most frequent references are to the passages in Corinthians and Revelation usually read at funeral services; and Paul's remark, that we now see in a riddle, translated as "through a glass darkly," is echoed in her recurrent use of the words "Riddle" and "Disc":

> Further than Guess can gallop
> Further than Riddle ride–
> Oh for a Disc to the Distance
> Between Ourselves and the Dead!

Yet another glance at her letters will also show that in her evangelical surroundings she steadily resisted all revivals, all spiritual exhortations, all the solicitous and charitable heat that, at home, at school and at church, was steadily turned on the uncommitted. Like Huckleberry Finn, whom she resembles in more ways than one, Emily Dickinson had a great respect for orthodox religion and morality, did not question the sincerity of those who practiced it, and even turned to it for help. But she never felt that the path of social conformity and assent to doctrine was her path. Her resistance gave her no feeling of superiority: even her schoolgirl letters are full of a wistful regret that she could not feel what her friends all asserted that they felt. As she recalled later: "When a Child and fleeing from Sacrament I could hear the Clergyman saying 'All who loved the Lord Jesus Christ–were asked to remain–.' My flight kept time to the Words." She belonged in the congregation but not in the Church.

206

Her elders referred her to the Bible: she read the Bible and took an immediate dislike to the deity that she calls "Burglar! Banker—Father!"—that is, the legal providential God who seems to ratify everything that is meaningless and cruel in life. She remarked to Higginson that her family were all religious except her, "and address an Eclipse, every morning—whom they call their 'Father'." She read with distaste the stories of Elisha and the bears ("I believe the love of God may be taught not to seem like bears"), of the sacrifice of Isaac, of the drowning of the world in a divine tantrum and the corresponding threat to burn it later:

> No vacillating God
> Created this Abode
> To put it out.

of Adam who was asserted to be alone responsible for his fall:

> Of Heaven above the firmest proof
> We fundamental know
> Except for it's marauding Hand
> It had been Heaven below.

The whole "punishing" aspect of religious doctrine struck her as "a doubtful solace finding tart response in the lower Mind," and she asks: "Why should we censure Othello, when the Criterion Lover says, 'Thou shalt have no other Gods before Me'?" That is, why blame Othello for being jealous when God tells us that he is himself? She concluded that "I do not respect 'doctrines,'" and added, with a touch of snobbery: "I wish the 'faith of the fathers' didn't wear brogans, and carry blue umbrellas." In short, she took no care to distinguish the Father of Christianity from the cloud-whiskered scarecrow that Blake called Nobodaddy and Bernard Shaw an old man in the sky looking like the headmaster of an inferior public school.

The Son of God for her was also caught in this Father's legal machinery. "When Jesus tells us about his Father, we distrust him." She has a poem in which she compares the doctrine of the revelation of the Father in the Son to the courtship of Miles Standish, and another in which she speaks with contempt of the "some day we'll understand" rationalizings of suffering:

> I shall know why—when Time is over—
> And I have ceased to wonder why—
> Christ will explain each separate anguish
> In the fair schoolroom of the sky—

At other times, she seems to accept Jesus as everything that Christianity says he is. Thus: "That the Divine has been human is at first an unheeded solace, but it shelters without our consent." It seems clear that her relation to the Nonconformist faith in which she was brought up was itself nonconformist, and that it would have violated her conscience ever to have made either a final acceptance or a final rejection of that faith. Her method, the reverse of Tennyson's in *In Memoriam*, was to prove where she could not believe. She did not want to repudiate her faith but to struggle with it. She was fascinated by the story of the "bewildered Gymnast" Jacob, wrestling with and finally defeating an angel who—according to a literal reading of the text which the poet promptly adopted —turned out to be God, and to this story she reverts more than once in her letters. When she compares the Bible unfavorably with Orpheus, whose sermon captivated and did not condemn; when she speaks of Cupid as an authentic deity and asks if God is Love's adversary, she is saying that there is another kind of religious experience that counterbalances, but does not necessarily contradict, the legal and doctrinal Christianity which she had been taught. As she says with a calculated ambivalence: " 'We thank thee Oh Father' for these strange Minds, that enamor us against thee."

This other kind of religious experience is a state of heightened consciousness often called "Transport" and associated with the word "Circumference," when the poet feels directly in communion with nature and in a state of "identity"–another frequent term– with it. Nature is then surrounded by the circumference of human consciousness, and such a world is Paradise, the Biblical Eden, a nature with a human shape and meaning, a garden for man. "Home is the definition of God," and home is what is inside the circumference of one's being. In this state the mind feels immortal: "To include, is to be touchless, for Ourself cannot cease." It also enters into a condition of unity or oneness which is partly what the word identity means. "*One* is a dainty sum! One bird, one cage, one flight; one song in those far woods, as yet suspected by faith only!" Similarly the poet can speak, without any violation of grammar, of a "Myriad Daisy" (compare Wordsworth's "tree, of many, one"[1]), and, with Emerson, of the single Man who is all men:

> What News will do when every Man
> Shall comprehend as one

[1] See Wordsworth, "Ode: Intimations of Immortality from Recollections of Early Childhood," l. 52.

And not in all the Universe
A thing to tell remain?

Such an experience is based, not on the compelling argument, but on the infinitely suggestive image, or "emblem" as she calls it. "Emblem is immeasurable," she says, and speaks of human beings as the "trembling Emblems" of love. The language of emblems is as rational as the language of doctrine, but its logic is the poetic logic of metaphor, not the abstract logic of syllogism.

Circumference in its turn is the "Bride of Awe," and "Awe" is her most frequent name for the God that is reached by this experience. The human circumference is surrounded by a greater consciousness, to which the poet is related as bride to bridegroom, as sea to moon, as daisy to sun, as brook to ocean—all recurring images. Sometimes the poet uses the word "peninsula" to describe an individual consciousness projecting into experience and attached to an invisible mainland. Invisible, because "No man saw awe," any more than we can see our own backbones. Awe is a lover, incarnate in the bee who loves the rose and the harebell, and a divine lover for whom a feminine poet may make the response of a bacchante or of a vestal virgin with equal appropriateness. Thus Emily Dickinson may say both:

> Circumference thou Bride of Awe
> Possessing thou shalt be
> Possessed by every hallowed Knight
> That dares to covet thee

and (where "their" means the world of her bodily impulses):

> To their apartment deep
> No ribaldry may creep
> Untumbled this abode
> By any man but God—

Awe is not a dogmatic God, and is tolerant enough to satisfy not only the poet's Christian longings but the paganism that makes her feel that there ought to be a god for every mood of the soul and every department of nature:

> If "All is possible with" him
> As he besides concedes
> He will refund us finally
> Our confiscated Gods—

In fact he may even be female, a sheltering mother. "I always ran Home to Awe when a child . . . He was an awful Mother, but I liked him better than none."

In Christian terms, this divine Awe, as she well understood, is the third person of the Trinity, the Holy Spirit, symbolized in the Bible by two of her favorite images, the bird and the wind, the giver of life to nature and of inspiration to humanity, the creative force that makes the poet's verses "breathe," and the "Conscious Ear" that imagination hears with. The conventional Biblical image for the Holy Spirit is the dove, and the poet, picturing herself as Noah sailing the flood of experience, associates the dove who brought him news of land with the fact that the name of another well-known navigator, Christopher Columbus, also means dove:

> Thrice to the floating casement
> The Patriarch's bird returned,
> Courage! My brave Columba!
> There may yet be *Land!*

To this person of God, Emily Dickinson continually turned when other things in Christianity puzzled her imagination or were rejected by her reason. She seems to associate him with the power which "stands in the Bible between the Kingdom and the Glory, because it is wilder than either of them." In the detached comment on the Atonement which she superimposes on the famous proverb, "God tempers the wind to the shorn lamb," the "Wind" is the power that escapes from the breakdown of doctrinal machinery:

> How ruthless are the gentle–
> How cruel are the kind–
> God broke his contract to his Lamb
> To qualify the Wind–

In a congratulatory message on the occasion of a wedding, the divine power of making one flesh out of two bodies is associated, not with the Father or the Son, but with the wind that bloweth where it listeth:

> The Clock strikes one that just struck two–
> Some schism in the Sum–
> A Vagabond from Genesis
> Has wrecked the Pendulum–

The confusion with a female principle, as when she says that "the Little Boy in the Trinity had no Grandmama, only a Holy Ghost," is at least as old as the apocryphal Gospels, where Jesus speaks of the Holy Spirit as his mother. When she says, "The Bible dealt with the Centre, not with the Circumference," she means apparently that the Bible considers man in his ordinary state of isolation, separated from God by a gulf that only God can cross. Such a God is thought of as coming from the outside; but while God is known "By his intrusion," his movement in the human soul is to be compared rather to the tides moving in the sea. "They say that God is everywhere, and yet we always think of Him as somewhat of a recluse." If so, it takes a recluse to find him, and to discover him as the inmost secret of consciousness.

The first fact of Emily Dickinson's experience, then, was that whatever the Bible may mean by Paradise or Eden, the world of lost innocence and happiness symbolized by the unfallen Adam and Eve, it is something that is already given in experience. It is attainable; the poet has attained it; it is not, therefore, a "superhuman site," nor could it survive the extinction of the human mind. Earth is heaven, whether heaven is heaven or not: the supernatural is only the natural disclosed: the charms of the heaven in the bush are superseded by the heaven in the hand—to paraphrase almost at random. To her the essence of the Gospel was the proclamation of the Paradisal vision in such passages as "consider the lilies." But the Bible also speaks of regaining this Paradise and living in it eternally after death. If so, then the experience of Paradise in life is identical with the experience of eternity.

The people we ordinarily call mystics are the people for whom this is true. Eternity to them is not endless time, but a real present, a "now" which absorbs all possible hereafters. Emily Dickinson also often speaks with the mystics of death as a rejoining of heaven, of "Forever" as "composed of Nows," of an eternal state of consciousness symbolized by a continuous summer and noon, of a coming "Aurora," a dawn that will have no night. But in her background there were two powerful antimystical tendencies at work. One was the rationalism of her generation; the other was the Puritanism in which she had been reared, with its insistence that the divine will was inscrutable, that it made sense only to itself, not to man, and that no human experience could transcend the limits of fallen humanity. For Emily Dickinson, therefore, the identity between the experience of circumference she had had and the postmortal eternity taught in the Bible remained a matter of "inference." It could be held by faith or hope but not by direct knowledge. This "inference" became the central issue in her struggle with her faith, a fact which she expresses most poignantly when she says: "Consciousness is the only home of which we *now* know. That sunny adverb had been enough, were it not foreclosed."

Paradoxically, the experience of unity with God and nature also produces a sense of division, or "bisection" as the poet often calls it, in the mind. Part of oneself is certainly mortal; part may not be, though even it must also go through death. In a poem beginning "Conscious am I in my Chamber" she speaks of the indwelling Spirit as the immortal part of herself; sometimes the distinction is between the poet herself and her soul; sometimes, and more commonly, it is between the soul and the mind or consciousness. "We know that the mind of the Heart must live," she says, and a letter to her seems like immortality because "it is the mind alone without corporeal friend." She also speaks of the body as a "trinket" which is worn but not owned, and in one striking poem the soul is attended by a "single Hound" which is its own identity. But she never seemed to accept the Platonic view that the soul is immortal by nature. If the first fact of her experience is a vision of earth as heaven, the second fact is that this vision is "evanescent," comes and goes unpredictably, and, so far as experience itself goes, ceases entirely at death. It is significant, therefore, that Emily Dickinson should so often symbolize her vision as a temporary and abnormal state of drunkenness:

> Inebriate of Air–am I–
> And Debauchee of Dew–
> Reeling–thro endless summer days–
> From inns of Molten Blue–

The liquor responsible for this state is usually called rum, or some synonym like "Domingo," "Manzanilla," or "Jamaica." When it is the more traditional wine, the word "sacrament," as in the poem "Exhiliration–is within," is seldom far away, for such imaginative drunkenness is a genuine communion. Still, it can lead to hangovers, "With a to-morrow knocking," and, whatever it is or means, it goes and is replaced by ordinary experience.

Ordinary experience is the sacramental or ecstatic experience turned inside out. Here the mind is not a circumference at all, but a center, and the only circumference is an indifferent and unresponsive Nature–"Nature–in Her monstrous House." We may still realize that such "Vastness–is but the Shadow of the Brain which casts it," but in this state the brain cannot cast any other shadow. Where the mind is a center and nature the circumference, there is no place for any divinity: that has vanished somewhere beyond the sky or beyond life. This is the state of "Those Evenings of the Brain," in which the body, so far from being a circumference incorporating its experience, is a "magic Prison," sealed against all intimations of immortality:

> The Rumor's Gate was shut so tight
> Before my Mind was sown,
> Not even a Prognostic's Push
> Could make a Dent thereon—

Like Blake, with whom she has been compared ever since Higginson's preface to the 1890 volume, Emily Dickinson shows us two contrary states of the human soul, a vision of innocence and a vision of "experience," or ordinary life. One is a vision of "Presence," the other of "Place"; in one the primary fact of life is partnership, in the other it is parting. Thus she may say, depending on the context, both "Were Departure Separation, there would be neither Nature nor Art, for there would be no World" and

> Parting is all we know of heaven,
> And all we need of hell.

But she has nothing of Blake's social vision, and the state that he associates with child labor, Negro slavery, prostitution, and war she associates only with loneliness.

Her two states are often associated with summer and winter, or, less frequently, with day and night. Often, especially in poems addressed to Sue, she speaks of a "Summer–Sister–Seraph!" who inhabits the paradisal world, in contrast to herself as a "dark sister," a "Druid" spirit of winter, frost and the north, waiting for the birds to come back, like Noah's dove, to tell her of a sunnier world beyond. Hence the times of year that have the greatest significance for her are the equinoxes, the March when the birds return and the white dress of winter breaks into color, and the moment in late summer when the invisible presence of autumn enters the year and makes "a Druidic Difference" in nature. The association of this latter period with the moment at which human life faces death makes it particularly the point at which the two lines of her imagination converge:

> God made a little Gentian—
> It tried–to be a Rose—
> And failed–and all the Summer laughed—
> But just before the Snows

There rose a Purple Creature–
That ravished all the Hill–
And Summer hid her Forehead–
And Mockery–was still–

The Frosts were her condition–
The Tyrian would not come
Until the North–invoke it–
Creator–Shall I–bloom?

Emily Dickinson is an impressionist in the sense that she tends to organize her visual experience by color rather than outline, and purple, the color of mourning and of triumph, is the central symbol for her of the junction between life and death. Various synonyms of it such as "Iodine," "Amethyst" and the "Tyrian" above run through her writings.

At times the poet speaks of the paradisal vision as being, not only a "stimulant" given in cases of despair or stupor, but a light by which all the rest of life can be lived, as providing a final answer to the question raised by its passing:

Why Bliss so scantily disburse–
Why Paradise defer–
Why Floods be served to Us–in Bowls–
I speculate no more–

At other times, in such poems as those beginning "Why–do they shut Me out of Heaven?" and "If I'm lost–now," she laments over a lost vision that hints at a still greater loss. Such sudden changes of mood would be inconsistent if she were arguing a thesis, but, being a poet, what she is doing is expressing a variety of possible imaginative reactions to a central unsolved riddle. The fact that her vision is transient sharpens the intensity of her relation to it, for

In Insecurity to lie
Is Joy's insuring quality.

Two recurring words in her poems are "suspense" and "expanse." The former refers to the shadow that falls between an experience and the realization that it has happened, the shadow that adumbrates death; the latter to the possession of the spiritual body which, for us, brings vision but not peace. "These sudden intimacies with Immortality, are expanse–not Peace–as Lightning at our feet, instills a foreign Landscape." She deals mainly with the virtues of faith, hope, and love, but her life had shown her that love, which

normally tends to union, may incorporate a great deal of its oppo-
site, which is renunciation. Similarly with faith and hope: "Faith
is *Doubt*," she says, and hope is the thinnest crust of ice over
despair:

> Could Hope inspect her Basis
> Her Craft were done—
> Has a fictitious Charter
> Or it has none—

Like the Puritans before her, who refused to believe that their
own righteousness would necessarily impress God into recognizing
them, Emily Dickinson refused to believe that her own vision of
Paradise guaranteed the existence of Paradise, even though she had
nothing else to go on. And—Puritan to the last—she even faced the
possibility that the Spirit of life within her might turn out to be
Death, hence the ambiguous tone of such poems as "Doubt Me! My
Dim Companion!" and "Struck, was I, nor yet by Lightning." She
told Sue that if Jesus did not recognize her at the last day, "there
is a darker spirit will not disown it's child." She means death, not
the devil, though her pose recalls the demonic figures in Haw-
thorne. There are many poems about the physical experience of
dying, some tranquil, some agonizing, some dealing with death by
execution, by warfare, by drowning—in at least two poems the
poet is an Andromeda swallowed by a sea monster. The region of
death to be entered, or traversed, is usually a sea, sometimes a
forest, or a "Maelstrom—in the Sky," or simply "a wild Night and
a new Road," and in "I never told the buried gold," it is an under-
world guarded by a dragon.

The world of death is not one that we have to die to explore: it
is there all the time, the end and final cause of the vision of the
center, just as Awe is the end and final cause of the vision of
circumference. "I suppose there are depths in every Conscious-
ness," she says, "from which we cannot rescue ourselves—to which
none can go with us—which represent to us Mortally—the Adven-
ture of Death." Some of her psychological poems take us into this
buried jungle of the mind. There are a few about ghosts, where
the two aspects of the self are treated in the vein of Henry James's
The Jolly Corner. But Emily Dickinson's sharp inquiring mind has
little in common with the ectoplasmic, and these poems impress
us as made rather than born. A more genuine fear comes out at the
end of this:

Remembrance has a Rear and Front—
'Tis something like a House—
It has a Garret also
For Refuse and the Mouse.

Besides the deepest Cellar
That ever Mason laid—
Look to it by it's Fathoms
Ourselves be not pursued—

This is as near to hell as she ever brings us, as the original version of the last two lines indicates:

Leave me not ever there alone
Oh thou Almighty God!

Yet even such a hell as this has a place and a function. Its presence is in an odd way the basis of vision itself, for "the unknown is the largest need of the intellect," and "could we see all we hope—there would be madness near." Emily Dickinson has a poem about Enoch and Elijah, the two Biblical prophets who were taken directly to heaven, but the figure she identifies herself with is Moses, standing on the mountain top with the wilderness of death on one side and the Promised Land on the other, able to see his Paradise if not to enter it:

Such are the inlets of the mind—
His outlets—would you see
Ascend with me the Table Land
Of immortality—

Many, perhaps most, of Emily Dickinson's readers will simply take their favorite poems from her and leave the rest, with little curiosity about the larger structure of her imagination. For many, too, the whole bent of her mind will seem irresponsible or morbid. It is perhaps as well that this should be so. "It is essential to the sanity of mankind," the poet remarks, "that each one should think the other crazy." There are more serious reasons: a certain perversity, an instinct for looking in the opposite direction from the rest of society, is frequent among creative minds. When the United States was beginning to develop an entrepreneur capitalism on a scale unprecedented in history, Thoreau retired to Walden to discover the meaning of the word "property," and found that it meant only what was proper or essential to unfettered human life. When the Civil War was beginning to force on America the troubled vision of its revolutionary destiny, Emily Dickinson retired to her garden to remain, like Wordsworth's skylark, within the kindred points of heaven and home. She will always have readers who will know what she means when she says: "Each of us gives or takes heaven in corporeal person, for each of us has the skill of life." More restless minds will not relax from taking thought for the morrow to spend much time with her. But even some of them may still admire the energy and humor with which she fought her angel until she had forced out of him the crippling blessing of genius.

ᴥ Yeats and the Language of Symbolism

IN READING ANY POEM WE HAVE TO KNOW AT LEAST TWO LANGUAGES: the language the poet is writing and the language of poetry itself. The former exists in the words the poet uses, the latter in the images and ideas which those words express. And just as the words of a language are a set of verbal conventions, so the imagery of poetry is a set of symbolic conventions. This set of symbolic conventions differs from a symbolic system, such as a religion or a metaphysic, in being concerned, not with a content, but with a mode of apprehension. Religions, philosophies, and other symbolic systems are as a rule presented as doctrines; poetic symbolism is a language. Sometimes a symbolic system, such as classical mythology, may lose its doctrinal content and so become purely linguistic, but this does not affect the distinction. So while poetry can be made of any account of spiritual reality because it is itself the language of spiritual reality, it does not follow that poetry represents something truer, because broader, than religion or philosophy. The French language is a much broader thing than the philosophy of Montaigne or Pascal, and we can learn French without being converted to any Frenchman's views; but the French language itself represents no truth.

Just as the teacher of a language is a grammarian, so one of the functions of the literary critic is to be a grammarian of imagery, interpreting the symbolic systems of religion and philosophy in terms of poetic language. Yeats provides a fine example of such criticism in his essay on the philosophy of Shelley's poetry, though the use of the word philosophy here is, as just said, misleading. I imagine that the greatest creative periods in art are also those in which criticism is most aware of the importance of this particular task. In Elizabethan criticism, for instance, the importance attached to symbolic grammar comes out in the mythological hand-books, the elaborate allegorical commentaries on Virgil and Ovid, and the textbooks of rhetoric, in which every conceivable mode of utterance is studied and classified with what seems to us now the mere exuberance of pedantry. It may be true that as Samuel Butler said:

> . . . all a rhetorician's rules
> Teach nothing but to name his tools.

But if a critic, or for that matter a poet, cannot name his tools, the world is not likely to concede much authority to his craft. We should not entrust our cars to a mechanic who lived entirely in a world of gadgets and doohickeys. In any case the Elizabethan critical tradition, which, whatever one thinks of it, is certainly essential to the age of Spenserian allegory and court masque, eventually broke down. Augustan criticism had a grammatical interest in form, but its scope was far narrower, and by the Romantic period, in spite of the gigantic efforts of Coleridge, criticism was rapidly heading for a limbo of "appreciation," reflective *belles lettres*, and cogent comments.

The axioms and postulates of criticism cannot be taken over ready-made from theology, philosophy, or science. They have to grow out of the art which the criticism is dealing with. Hence each art has its own criticism, and whether aesthetics is a legitimate branch of philosophy or not, I do not see that a theory of beauty in general can have a direct application to any branch of criticism. When Lessing in the *Laokoön* protested against confusing the canons of the different arts, this was really the question he was raising. The importance of the question is not overthrown by historical criticism, which is a different subject altogether, and which deals with such conceptions as Baroque, Renaissance, Rococo, Gothic, Romantic, where all cultural products of a period are seen as symbols of that period. Beauty, the icon of aesthetics, is as big a stumbling-block to criticism as happiness is to morals, and it is significant that in our ordinary language about art the word is practically obsolete, having been long replaced simply by "good." For one thing, it has become sentimentalized in meaning until it is now synonymous with the particular quality of beauty more exactly described as loveliness. The reason for this is that ideas of beauty tend insensibly to become ideas of propriety and decorum. When we speak of the human body as beautiful we mean a body of someone in good physical condition between about eighteen and thirty, and when Dégas expresses interest in thick-bottomed matrons squatting in hip-baths, we confuse the shock to our sense of propriety with a shock to our sense of beauty. The same thing happens when Ibsen claims venereal disease as a subject for tragedy. The cult of beauty, then, is reactionary: it is continually setting up barriers to the conquest of experience by art, and limits the variety of expression in art wherever it can.

But with the breakdown of a tradition of grammatical criticism, ideas of general beauty become the critic's chief subject-matter; hence the nineteenth century was the golden age of aesthetic criticism. Criticism reacted on art, and when critics forgot how to teach the language of poetic imagery the poets forgot how to use it, the creative counterpart of aesthetic criticism being, of course, aestheticism. This fact affected both the content and the form of late romantic poetry. The content illustrates what may be called a Berlitz approach to symbolic language, apprehending it by means of evocation and sympathetic intuition, in which the first rule of criticism is never to push the meaning of an image too far, which means never giving it a grammatical or systematic meaning. The form similarly illustrates a deliberate fragmentation of poetic experience, in which the lack of explicit grammatical pattern is less noticeable. In the larger picture the different arts, having lost their particular critiques, tend to become one another's metaphors, as music becomes a metaphor for poetry in Mallarmé. In the age we are dealing with, Ruskin alone had any real sense of a critical workshop, and yet, as he was deeply involved with an aesthetic which continually relapses into propriety, and moral propriety at that, most of his direct influence on art was pernicious.

We shall never fully understand the nineteenth century until we realize how hampered its poets were by the lack of a coherent tradition of criticism which would have organized the language of poetic symbolism for them. This lack compelled many of them to turn to the symbolic systems available in their time to develop a poetic language out of them as best they might. Many conversions of poets to the Roman Catholic Church were obviously connected with the possibility of finding their language in the iconography of that Church. Other poets turned like Swinburne to a pagan mythology, still others, like Wagner and the early Yeats, to a national one; some worked out mythologies or metaphysics of their own, Poe's *Eureka* being an example only slightly less bizarre than Yeats' *Vision*. Connected with the same situation was the growing influence of occult systems in poetic thought, especially in France and Germany. The occult tradition, stemming as it did partly from Swedenborg and St. Martin in the West and partly from an increasing flow of information about Hindu and Buddhist philosophies, was especially attractive because it seemed to hint more clearly at a universal language of symbolism. This tradition comes to its climax near the end of the century with Madame Blavatsky's huge *Secret Doctrine,* after which the growth of the scientific study of comparative religion and psychoanalysis took the whole question out of the palsied hands of literary critics. Madame Blavatsky may well have been, like Paracelsus, a good deal of a charlatan. Henley said of her: "Of course she gets up fraudulent miracles, but a woman of genius has to do something." Yet *The Secret Doctrine,* whatever else it is, is a very remarkable essay on the morphology of symbols, and the charlatanism of its author is less a reflection on her than on the age that compelled her to express herself in such devious ways.

Most of the minor poets, however, followed the romantic and aesthetic path, and this was true of the "Cheshire Cheese" group with whom Yeats was first associated. This group included Lionel Johnson and Ernest Dowson, with Wilde and Francis Thompson on the fringes, and their technique of relentless beautifying appears in much of Yeats' early work, notably "The Secret Rose" and the first version of *Oisin.* He is following the same models also in those poems of escape, like *The Land of Heart's Desire,* which are aesthetic anti-Victorian melodramas with beauty as hero and duty as villain. And in his transformation of a tough, humorous, and extravagant Irish mythology into nostalgic romance and worn-out Court of Love situations, as in *Deirdre,* we can see the poet to whom William Morris said: "You write my sort of poetry." Many features of the aesthetic attitude, too, remained with Yeats all his life. He never lost a sense of the beautiful which was closely allied to a sense of propriety. He never became reconciled to the realistic explorers of art, never understood what Dégas and Ibsen were driving at, and even in his *Last Poems,* when his practice is increasingly contradicting his theory, he is still talking about art in terms of conventional idealized forms, in which the intellectual symmetry of Pythagoras or St. Thomas grows into the organic symmetry of Phidias and Michelangelo.

And yet the deliberate pull of Yeats' genius away from the Cheshire Cheese is unmistakable. Everyone who has studied the early poems has barked his shins over the later revisions of them, and pondered the curiously tasteless blunders which Yeats occasionally makes in these revisions. Cheshire Cheese poetry, like romantic poetry in general, only more so, depends on an evocative and intuitive approach to the significance of poetic imagery; hence it depends, not on things, but on qualifications of things, not on a pattern of images, but on a background of attributes. The emphasis in such poetry therefore falls on carefully composed epithets and radioactive adjectives. Now when Yeats, in "The Sorrow of Love," changes "curd-pale moon" to "brilliant moon," the change from the noisy to the quiet epithet throws a much greater weight on the noun, and indicates that "moon" has acquired a systematic and grammatical meaning in Yeats' poetry. Other changes are motivated by a desire to tighten up the syntax, which in a euphuistic poetry of epithets tends to become flaccid, because the connective tissues of sentences emphasize continuity of meaning rather than radiating suggestiveness. The reasons for Yeats' wanting to rewrite his early poems instead of merely writing them off are not clear, but one guess may be hazarded. Yeats is one of the growing poets: his technique, his ideas, his attitude to life, are in a constant state of revolution and metamorphosis. He belongs with Goethe and Beethoven, not with the artists who simply unfold, like Blake and Mozart. This phenomenon of metamorphic growth, which must surely have reached its limit in Picasso, seems to be comparatively new in the arts, and so a somewhat unwelcome characteristic to Yeats himself, who preferred the more traditional unfolding rhythm. Perhaps it too is a by-product of the breakdown of criticism. Dante unfolds into the *Divine Comedy* because the grammar of its symbolism is present in the culture of his time; Goethe grows into the second part of *Faust* because he has to rediscover the conventions of symbolism for himself. Yeats, then, may have been compelled to "grow" by a personal search for symbols, and if so, his revisions may signify a desire to force the developing body of his work into a single unfolding unit.

II

Yeats looked for a language of symbols in two obvious places: in the traditional mythology of Ireland, including both its heroic saga and its popular folk-lore, and in the occultism of his own day which had a doctrine in theosophy and a discipline in spiritualism. The association between the occult and the native Irish is of long standing, and Yeats' determination to have Blavatsky, Swedenborg, and F. W. H. Myers rubbing shoulders with Fionn and Cuchulain is not due to a merely personal crochet. He looked in this mixture for a mythological pattern which, though not that of traditional Christianity, would be reconcilable with it, in the sense of being another illustration of the same total imaginative apprehension of reality. We are not surprised, then, to find Yeats forming counter-parts to Christian ideas out of his own myths. His first important play was *The Countess Cathleen,* produced amid vociferous boos at the turn of the century. The story concerns a character who is really a female and Irish Jesus, redeeming the world by selling her soul to the devil and then cheating the devil by the purity of her nature, very much as in the pre-Anselm theory of the Atonement. As Yeats calmly remarks in a note, the story illustrates "one of the supreme parables of the world," and it is perhaps not astonishing that some of his more orthodox contemporaries, however foolishly they may have expressed their objections, felt that all was not well. The dying king of the theatre has often proved a formidable rival of the dying god of the Church, and the audience may have real-ized more clearly than Yeats himself that something anti-Christian was taking shape, the traditional cult of Dionysus and Oedipus revived to overthrow that of Christ. We shall return to this in a moment.

The cult of the legend is apt to lead to archaism, to sentimen-talizing a certain period in the past. If we believe with Swinburne that the world has grown gray with the breath of Christ, we are making a historical Fall out of Christianity and a historical Golden Age out of the Classical era. Consequently we shall tend to think of the creative imagination as concerned with reviving the faded splendours of classical culture, which will lead to a good deal of faking and antiquing when we come to deal directly with that culture. The same is true of the romantic medievalism of Morris and Chesterton, where the Fall is placed in the Renaissance or Reformation, as it is by Ruskin, who actually calls the Renaissance a Fall in *The Stones of Venice.* The late romantic milieu of the early Yeats was full of historical myths of this kind and Yeats in-herited a view of history which stems from a writer whom he consistently despised—Carlyle. The age of heroic action and imagi-native splendour, according to this dialectic, died with the age of faith, and since then self-consciousness, Puritanism, rationalism, mercantilism, and all the spectral ghosts of abstraction have de-stroyed the individual and the supernatural at once, and left a thin, bloodless, envious, sedentary, sceptical, materialistic, *bourgeois* sissy as the typical man of our own age. In his early essay on Spenser, for instance, Yeats is so preoccupied with this myth that he hardly succeeds in getting anything intelligent said about Spenser; and he never outgrew it. Ireland thus comes to mean for him among other things a region sheltered from the worst fury of abstraction and metropolitan materialism, where culture still has roots, where communal art-forms like the drama are still possible, and where the brave man and the beautiful woman still command respect.

When Spengler's *Decline of the West* appeared after the First World War it owed its popularity to the fact that it gave both complete expression to a myth which had been widely accepted for a century and an intelligible account of that myth. Cultures were, Spengler said, organisms, subject to the organic rhythms of growth, maturation, and decay, and our present metropolitan civilization is a "Western" culture in the same stage of decline that classical culture was in at the time of the Punic Wars. From 1917 on, Yeats was absorbed by his *Vision*, a complicated occult system based on a twenty-eight-phase lunar cycle and a system of double cones, which was dictated to him by spirits who worked through his wife's gift for automatic writing, and Spengler's was evidently one of the books these spirits read, or possibly wrote. Spengler does not postulate a *general* cyclic movement in history, but his tables of cultures use the names of the four seasons, and if our time is the "winter" of Western culture a returning spring is at any rate suggested. The *Vision* has an interesting passage on the influence of Frobenius on Spengler which suggests, I think correctly, that a general cyclic theory was actually in Spengler's mind. In any case the general cycle is in Vico, one of Spengler's predecessors, who had also a more direct influence on Yeats through Croce, as he had on Joyce.

The *Vision* presents an astrological theory of history, according to which history moves alternately through "antithetical" and "primary" cycles, the former being subjective, aristocratic, violent, and antinomian, the latter objective, democratic, self-sacrificing, and theistic. Each cycle embraces two millennia. The Classical period from 2000 B.C. to the Christian era was an "antithetical" cycle, and our own Christian cycle is a "primary" one. A cycle is at its height halfway through, at the fifteenth phase, when it is also nearest the opposite pole. Thus the Christian era was at its most antithetical in a Byzantine period, in Yeats a quasi-historical fairyland reminding us of Lawrence's Etruscan myth. When Byzantium fell its culture took root in the West, producing the antithetical Renaissance civilization which had always made so strong an appeal to Yeats. Castiglione's *Courtier*, the great textbook of antithetical discipline, was one of his favourite books, and he felt that his pantheon of Irish heroes, Burke being an obvious member, had a deep spiritual affinity with the proud and aristocratic ideals of the age of chivalry, of the noble horseman who casts a cold eye on the squalor of life and death alike, and leaves his servants to do his "living" for him, to quote the famous tag from *Axël* that Yeats kept repeating all his life.

We are now in the last century of the Christian era, at the very nadir of primary abstraction, and are approaching the return of an antithetical age. Like Nietzsche, Yeats prophesies the time when Christianity will give place to an opposing culture of proud beauty and invincible violence, the reign of the Antichrist now slouching toward Bethlehem to be born, of the centaur whose humanity is inseparable from the brute, of Shelley's Demogorgon who awakens from the earth as the "mummy wheat" of the preceding classical culture begins to sprout again. The dove and the virgin are to go and Leda and the swan are to come back, in the form of the watchful and ironic heron of the Irish marshes and his fanatical priestess. The new birth is to be however a welter of blood and pain, full of the screams of the new birds of prey who replace the dove of peace, like the leaderless falcon turning in the widening gyre, and full of the hound voices of furies in pursuit of blood. Like Spengler, though for slightly different reasons, Yeats sees in the fascist cult of brutal violence something profoundly characteristic of our own time and of the immediate future.

He had to talk himself into this, for he saw fascism first as it really is, when Ireland was occupied by the Black and Tans. Later, when Wyndham Lewis was publicizing Hitler and Pound Mussolini, and Eliot was issuing encyclicals to the faithful informing them that the people who think are now reading Charles Maurras, Yeats had a passing dalliance with the Irish Blue Shirts. But there are other features of this new civilization more genuinely attractive to him. As in Lawrence, the Christ of the new era is to be a sexual rather than a virginal god, and in many of Yeats' last poems the sex act, again as in Lawrence, practically becomes the basis of a new fertility ritual. Yeats' preference of the heroic virtues to the Christian ones comes out, too, in his plays *Calvary* and *Resurrection*, where the historical Jesus appears as a rather stupefied and bemused figure, turning the wheel of time towards the surrender of human powers to a dehumanized God.

Yet his celebrations of a new birth are enforced, to use a technical term from the *Vision*, and all through his work runs the melancholy of the *Götterdämmerung*. It is a bitter Kilkenny cat-fight that Yeats makes out of history, the hero and the god, the young man and the old man, destroying one another as the gyres of history grind together on a common axis. Oedipus kills his father and Cuchulain his son, and the hero of *Purgatory* kills both as a sacrifice to his mother, his feelings for whom are a remarkably repulsive mixture of incest and necrophily. In *On Baile's Strand*, Cuchulain after killing his son wanders mad into a world of chaos, like Lear on the heath. But unlike Lear he does not recover his humanity, and only a fool and a blind man are on the stage when the curtain falls. The fool is the last phase of the lunar cycle in the *Vision*, and the blind man I take to represent the dark moonless night that follows it, the Phase One that ends and begins the cycle.

In searching for a new language of symbols, then, Yeats was to a great extent simply fulfilling the romantic tradition from which he had started, his final position being simply a more systematic expression of the romanticism of Nietzsche and Lawrence. Even his Byzantium, the spiritual source of the fifteenth-century culture that was the model of the pre-Raphaelites, betrays its romantic origin. His conception of the great man also falls well within the romantic orbit. One of the fundamental conceptions of early romantic mythology is that the revolutionary political situation of its time is a recreation of the rebellion of Prometheus, the Titanic ally of man, against an abstract tyranny represented by a sky-god. The sky-god is a metropolitan imperialist as his opponent is an earth-bound anarchist; hence the eruption of Promethean heroes in romantic poetry, the Kossuths and Kosciuskos and Bolivars and Garibaldis who fight for the freedom of all humanity in a decentralized or nationalist form. This national aspect of the romantic Messiah myth is especially congenial to countries like Ireland, or like Mexico as Lawrence saw it, where national and radical ideas are closely linked.

In Yeats the sky-god worshipper belongs to a rabble, a pack of curs snarling at the heels of an aloof and aristocratic hero representing the antithetical values of Irish culture, Parnell, for example, or Wilde, or Synge (though Synge is actually a primary type), or perhaps himself. In an aloof and aristocratic civilization such heroes would be leaders, but in a primary one like our own the noble animal is pulled down by the cur, and his heroism fulfils itself, like the setting sun, in the waning glamour of the lost cause. In the rewritten ending of *The King's Threshold* the heroic poet dies having maintained his defiance both of the tyrant king and of the leprous sky-god, Blake's Jehovah, whom he incarnates, but with no other resolution of the conflict than his own death. And in Yeats' last play, *The Death of Cuchulain*, the ignoble and helpless collapse of his favourite hero will give some idea of the imaginative nihilism that the poet's mind finally reached. In Yeats as in most great romantics the cult of the hero turns out to be a cult of the death of the hero, an Eroica symphony with a funeral march at its heart.

III

The language of early romantic symbolism is a Kantian language, by which I do not mean that it is founded on Kant, but that it implies a popularized metaphysic with predominantly Kantian features. The romantic poet splits reality into a world of experience and a world of perception, the former world, Kant's noumenon, being interpreted by poetry and the latter or phenomenal world being the only object of rational knowledge. The gap between rational and poetic knowledge accounts for the importance of suggestion and evocation in romantic art, and for the distrust of didactic qualities. For the poet as well as the reasoner, however, nature is the vehicle of interpretation, hence nature to the poet is, as in Baudelaire's "*Correspondances*," a shrine of mysterious oracles; and in the darkness of the noumenal world, where there must yet be direct contact with nature, we depend less on the expanded pupils of vision than on the twitching whiskers of feeling.

But as romantic art develops, popularized Kant becomes popularized Schopenhauer, and as the phenomenal world is the object of consciousness, the noumenal world tends to become associated with the sub-conscious, a world of will underlying the world of idea. Such a world of will, being sub-moral and sub-intellectual, may from the point of view of consciousness be described as evil and brutal, hence romantic art becomes infused with all the symbols of the "romantic agony": sadism, Satanism, pessimism, the cults of the beauty of pain, the religion of blasphemy, the curse of genius, and, above all, the malignant grinning female, the Medusa, the Sphinx, La Gioconda, La Belle Dame sans Merci, or whatever her name may be, who presides over so many romantic love-affairs, and has affected Yeats' relations with the beautiful Maud Gonne. The world as will is, of course, an essential part of the order of nature, hence it is really a hyperphysical world, and in no sense a spiritual one.

The romantic conception of the hyperphysical world appears in Freud's psychological myth of a sub-conscious libido and a censoring consciousness. Freud himself has noted the resemblance of his metaphysic to Schopenhauer's, though not the significance of that resemblance. The influence of Freud on Yeats was indirect, but there was more of it than Yeats realized, some of it coming again through Lawrence. It is reflected in his choice of Oedipus as the symbol of the antithetical Christ about to be reborn. More immediate were the Darwinian developments of the same idea: a glance at Hardy is enough to show how easily Darwin and Schopenhauer fit together. The evolutionary dialectic destroyed the separateness of created forms, and reduced all life to a single interlocking family: even, one may say, and Samuel Butler did say, a single super-organism, a known God who is also the world of will and life-force. Thus in this conception of a hyperphysical world the old seventeenth-century doctrine of the *anima mundi* is reabsorbed into literary symbolism, though of course with a very different context, and ideas of race memory and telepathy appear as by-products of it.

In Irish mythology there is a world of gods, the Tuatha Dé Danaan, who were driven underground by man long ago and now inhabit a world antipodal to our own, whose "Beltane" (May 1) is our "Samhain" (November 1); a world of fairies or Sidhe living in the Tir-na-n-Og, the country of eternal youth, where personality has much more of that aloof and aristocratic spirit that marks the antithetical, the classical and Nietzschean, idea of the mingling of the divine and human, as opposed to the primary or Christian view of it. This myth of gods buried under the tyranny of consciousness, nature, and reason, in Joyce the Finnegan concealed under the blanket of HCE, corresponds to the Greek myth of the Titans, of whom Prometheus was one, and neatly fits the metaphysical myth we have been tracing. A remark of Blavatsky's that our world has another attached to it at the North Pole, forming a dumbbell-shaped cosmos, is quoted in *The Trembling of the Veil*. And as, according to all romantic presuppositions, the source of the mythopoeic faculty is the sub-conscious, Yeats endeavours, he tells us in *Per Amica Silentia Lunae*, to sink his mind below consciousness into the stream of the *anima mundi*, in order to become a medium of a creative power which has its basis in the organically traditional, the genus or race, rather than the individual, and which will bring the ancestral gods and myths of that race out of a stream of racial memory.

In a rather silly play, *The Hour-Glass*, an exponent of sceptical materialism is told by an angel that he has to accept this antipodal fairy-world or else. He is given an hour to produce a believer in it, and an hour-glass, from which the play takes its name, appears on the stage. This hour-glass, the simplest possible emblem of time, is, though Yeats apparently has tried not to notice the fact, the fundamental symbol of his own *Vision*, the double gyre with time passing from one cone to the other, and reversing its position when the progress is complete. In this play, however, it represents the relation of the fairy world to our own. This relation obviously cannot be historical, like the classical-Christian double gyre; yet the fairies to some extent share a common time and space with us, for they live, like the spirits in Dante's Purgatory, on the other side of our own world, however we interpret the word "side."

We can understand where this world is if we think of spiritualism, which, in spite of its name, investigates on scientific principles a world not of spirits but of nature, a world where the conceptions of time, space, substance, and form appear still to operate, and which seems to be an essential part of the *anima mundi*. Thus the hour-glass really represents the gyre of organic life which goes from birth to death, and then, invisible to the organic world but still within nature, from death to rebirth. The idea of rebirth is essential if the conception is to retain its hour-glass figure. In the *Vision* two double gyres, the four faculties, make up the Spenglerian movement of visible time or history, and two others at right angles to them, the four principles, make up this other cycle of life, death, and rebirth. Yeats gives a detailed account of the half-dozen stages that the dead man goes through on his way to rebirth. One of them consists in reliving, sometimes for centuries, the passionate moments of one's life, as Swift lives through the loves of Stella and Vanessa in *The Words upon the Window Pane.* The chief function of this world however is expiatory or purgatorial, reminding us again of Dante's Purgatory, on top of which is the Garden of Eden from whence all seeds of life fall back into our world, though of course in Dante this cyclic movement does not affect human souls.

The idea of reincarnation came to Yeats from oriental sources through theosophy. A much better account than he gives of the progress from death to rebirth is in *The Tibetan Book of the Dead,* as it is called in the English translation, where the world inhabited is called Bardo. In the Japanese No plays, too, which so deeply affected Yeats' dramatic technique, the Bardo-world is the normal setting. The contrast between the gentleness of the Japanese plays and the ferocity of Yeats is curious. In one of them, *Nishikigi,* two dead lovers are reunited by a priest; in Yeats' *Dreaming of the*

Bones two Irish lovers must be forever separated because of their treachery to Ireland. *The Hour-Glass* is said to have frightened a man into attending mass for some weeks, and in *The Dreaming of the Bones* the evangelist again appears with a knuckle-duster, evidently prepared to adapt the old threats to a new priestcraft. In another No play, *Hagoromo*, a fairy, in order to get back a headdress a priest has stolen from her, teaches him the dance of the phases of the moon. She is a harmless and pretty creature, a Sally Rand who has lost her fan, and it is hardly likely that her lessons had anything of the Procrustean pedantry of Yeats' garrulous and opinionated spooks. In a third, *Kamusaka*, a dead brigand is reconciled to the young man who kills him; in Yeats' *Purgatory* (an ironic title if ever there was one, though it is true that a similar irony is found in *Hamlet*), the double murder already mentioned is combined with the idea of an ancestral curse operating with irresistible power in both this life and the next.

Of course Yeats had read too much mysticism not to postulate a final deliverance from these gyres, a "thirteenth cone" or sphere of the pure present where time and space are transcended. But in spite of this theoretical escape, the *Vision* is a depressing book. Perhaps Yeats is right in believing that he had developed special faculties for communicating with some unknown but objective type of intelligence. But if his "spiritual instructors" have an objective existence, all one can say is that Yeats reminds us of those unfortunate wretches who turn themselves into walking crystal sets by getting manganese dust on their silver fillings, and are thus exposed to a cataract of ethereal drivel that most of us can, up to a point, shut out. Everything that is interesting and valuable in the *Vision* is directly connected with its subjective aspect. For one thing, it suggests what seems to me on other grounds highly probable: that a good deal of our thinking is elaborated from subconscious diagrams. This comes out not only in the geometrical figures we use, "a point of view," "a sphere of influence," "a line of action," and so on, but also in the spatial implications of the most ordinary particles: "beside," "between," "on the other hand," and the like. The *Vision* begins by dividing all human types among twenty-eight phases, and even this, for all its arbitrary straitjacketing, might have become the sub-conscious foundation of an art-form like the one represented in Chaucer's company of twenty-nine pilgrims, who evidently seem to be something of a perfect circle of planetary and humorous temperament. It is a pity that the qualities which enabled Chaucer to transform his perfect circle into great art were qualities that Yeats felt he ought to distrust—characterization and comedy.

I have laid such stress on the *Vision* because it does give an account, for better or worse, of the symbolic structure which underlies Yeats' poetry from at least 1917 onward. And from what we have said about the romantic nature of that poetry, it is clear that the *Vision* is among other things one of the grammars of romantic symbolism. It presents a physical or phenomenal world apprehended by the consciousness and a hyperphysical world apprehended by the sub-conscious, and in so doing it preserves the original romantic cult of nature which led to identifying spiritual and hyperphysical reality. It does not get, except in theory, to any order above that of nature or to any mode of consciousness in which the gap between subject and object is bridged. The poles of the *Vision*, Phases One and Fifteen, are a purely objective condition of self-abnegation and a purely subjective one of complete beauty respectively, both of which are superhuman incarnations. And as the fundamental process in nature as we ordinarily perceive it is the cycle, the *Vision* reflects a romantic pessimism founded on a conception of cyclic fatality, such as we find in Lawrence, in Spengler, in Nietzsche, who also tried to formulate a doctrine of recurrence, and in many others.

It remains finally to compare Yeats' symbolism with that of some earlier poet who knew a greater tradition than the romantic one, a comparison which may involve some rather technical points of symbolic grammar.

IV

Of pre-romantic English poets, the two who had the most formative influence on Yeats were also the two greatest linguists of symbolism in English literature—Blake and Spenser. Yeats and his friend Ellis undertook an edition of Blake in 1889, which appeared in three volumes in 1893. They approached Blake however from the wrong side of Blavatsky: that is, they had already acquired a smattering of occultism, and they expected to find in Blake an occult system or secret doctrine instead of a poetic language. But what Blake needed most in 1889 was a clean, complete, and accurate text, and neither of his editors knew much about editing, nor could they read Blake's handwriting with consistent accuracy. Again, Blake, though a very systematic thinker, sharply warns his reader against what he calls "mathematic form," and this includes all the Euclidean paraphernalia of diagrams, figures, tables of symbols and the like, which inevitably appear when symbolism is treated as a dead language. The result is an over-schematized commentary full of false symmetries, which, itself more difficult to understand than Blake, is still further confused by centrifugal expositions of Boehme and Swedenborg. As Yeats very truly remarks in the course of this work: "The student of occultism . . . should particularly notice Blake's association of black with darkness." But Yeats tells us in his essay on Spenser that Spenser's symbols kept welling up again in his mind long after he had forgotten having met them in Spenser, and it is not possible that the Blake whom he had studied so exhaustively can have failed to influence him in the same way.

Complex as Blake's symbolism is, it is at least uncluttered by all the chain-of-being apparatus of eons, emanations, world-souls, and demiurges which Yeats inherited from the occult tradition. In Blake the world as mental reality, which is inside the human mind, and the world as physical appearance, which is outside it, present a contrast in which the latter is a shadow or reflection of the former, and thus a sort of parody or inversion of it. In the physical world man is an isolated individual centre of perception; in the spiritual world he is identical with a universal circumference of perception, a titanic man whom Blake calls Albion. In the physical world man is aware of an antithesis of divine Creator and human creature; in the spiritual world both of these disappear into the unity of God and Man which is Jesus. In the physical world man seems to be in the centre of a chain of being halfway between matter and God; in the spiritual world Man has pulled this chain into his own body, as Zeus threatens to do in the Iliad. The real form of the mineral world is that of a city; that of the vegetable world a tree of life; that of the animal world a single body; and that of the human world the real presence of the God-Man Jesus: and all these forms are one form.

Hence in Blake's symbolism we find a series of antitheses expressing the contrast of the two worlds. There is a tree of life and a tree of mystery, a city of God and a city of destruction, and so on. This antithetical pattern is found in Yeats too. The two trees appear in the poem of that name, and hints of the two cities in the Byzantium poems, though in the famous "Sailing to Byzantium" it is actually Shelley who takes the lead as Yeats stands in the tomb of Galla Placidia in Ravenna, a cavern of the type that Spengler calls the "prime symbol" of Byzantine culture, and sees in the dome of many-coloured glass above him a reflection of something very like the New Testament city of living stones.

In order to pass from the physical world to the spiritual world in Blake, man's mind has to blow up and turn inside out: in more sober language, man has to use his imagination and train himself, with the help of works of art, to reverse the natural perspective. Blake's symbol for this turning inside out is the vortex, an image rather similar to Yeats' gyre, though the difference is more significant than the resemblance. In Yeats the spiritual life in this world is, again like Dante's Purgatory, a gigantic cone, a mountain or tower encircled by a winding stair spiralling upward through one life after another until it reaches an apex. The source of the idea is not Dante, but a childhood memory of smoke rising from the whirling spools of a "pern mill" so that it looked as though it were coming out of a burning mountain. This cone image supplies the titles of two of Yeats' later books, *The Tower* and *The Winding Stair*.

But if we turn to the early work we find that the chief symbol there is not that of Dante's Purgatory, but that of his Paradise, the multifoliate rose, the flaming tree of life or transfigured cross which is the permanent spiritual form of eternity, the spiral which has lost its progressive or temporal shape. Evidently, then, the thought of passing from the apex of the purgatorial cone into eternity predominated in Yeats' mind up to about 1917, after which the idea of rebirth from the apex, which, as we have seen, is also hinted at in Dante, begins to displace it, though never completely.

Dante puts the Garden of Eden at the apex of his Purgatory, and both Blake and Spenser also have a lower Paradise in their symbolism, associated with the moon and with the Bardo-world of the dead and unborn, which is yet a hyperphysical world and a part of the cyclic order of nature. Blake calls it Beulah and Spenser the Gardens of Adonis. As both poets are Protestants, neither gives it a purgatorial function, but in both it is a place of rebirth to some extent. Blake's Beulah, the more sharply realized conception, has two gates, a lower gate of rebirth and an upper gate of escape, and in Blake's symbolism the crisis or vortex of vision comes at the upper gate; Spenser's *Faerie Queene* ends with a similar crisis at the corresponding place, the sphere of the moon, in the *Cantos of Mutabilitie*.

Yeats' *Vision* is, from Blake's point of view, a vision of the physical world, which Blake calls Generation, and of a hyperphysical world or Beulah with the upper limit sealed off. His account of this cyclical world, as such, has much in common with Blake. Blake too has a historical cycle in which the young man and the old man, whom he calls Orc and Urizen, kill each other off, and a still larger cycle of death and rebirth which he presents in *The Mental Traveller*. Yeats' claim that his *Vision* explains *The Mental Traveller*, or more accurately expounds the same aspect of symbolism, is correct enough. The two poets also make a very similar use of the moon and a lunar cycle of twenty-eight phases. Blake's lower and upper gates correspond to Yeats' Phases One and Fifteen, the phase of total surrender and the phase of complete beauty, both poets being indebted to Homer's cave of the nymphs, and Porphyry's commentary on it, for the conception.

Now the thing that seals off the upper limit of Yeats' *Vision*, again from Blake's point of view, is the uncreative mental condition in which Yeats attained his vision. He stands at his own Phase One, in a state of passivity so abject that he cannot even write his own book, and sees his aloof and aristocratic ideal above him, impossibly remote and lost in the turning stars. An active mind would, on the contrary, be the circumference of such a vision, which would then be lifted up into the spiritual or mental world and so become a created or dramatic form, as Chaucer's circle of pilgrims does. The upper limit of the present *Vision*, Phase Fifteen, the perfect antithetical self, would in that case become the lower limit, the aspect in which the vision appears to the physical world. We should then have what Yeats calls the creative mind and the mask, the mental or imaginative reality of the vision itself and the external form in which it appears to others. And just as Blake, when he spoke of his poems as dictated, was talking about a state of the most active concentration, so Yeats never entrusted anything except the *Vision* to his spirits; everywhere else he is the active circumference and not the passive centre of what he is doing. We should expect, therefore, to find all the rest of his work turning on this conception of creative mind and mask, the opposition of mental reality and physical appearance, the latter, the mask, having all of that proud and aristocratic aloofness which Yeats so valued in the world of appearance.

This is certainly what we get in the essay *Per Amica Silentia Lunae*, the bottle out of which the smoky genie of the *Vision* emerged. There, Yeats sees the artist, as an ordinary or natural man in the physical world, using his creative genius to visualize a mode of existence as different as possible from the one forced on him by his own shortcomings. Thus Morris, a blundering and tactless man, creates an imaginative world of precise and exquisite taste, and the ferociously irascible Landor expresses himself in an art of languid gentleness. The artist searches for a mask, originally to conceal his natural self, but ultimately to reveal his imaginative self, the body of his art. The conception comes of course from drama, perhaps partly from Synge's subtle analysis of such a personal mask in *The Playboy of the Western World*, and it underlies Yeats' own dramatic theory. In his ideal play the audience is select, the actors masked, and the theme traditional and symbolic, so that the outward form of the drama preserves, like the Japanese play from which it is derived, the mask of the heroic and aristocratic virtues. But in this theory of drama the poet must find a common ground with his audience in conventional themes and symbols which emerge from traditions embedded in racial and sub-conscious memories. The true initiates in the audience, when they pierce the mask, find themselves within a mental form which is at once the dramatist's mind and the *anima mundi* of their common sub-consciousness. It is clear, then, that the mask does not relate only to the poet's own life, to his quarrel with himself as Yeats says: if the mask is to reveal anything effective, it must also be to some extent the mask of the age. Hence the great poets of every generation will be those who can identify a personal mask with a historical one.

Thus romanticism, on Yeats' theory, would arise as a mask or countervision, an imaginative protest, against the industrial revolution, and end by being a form in which the culture of the industrial revolution expresses itself. Similarly with the general conspectus of Yeats' thought: modern Italian philosophy with the stress laid on its fascist elements, the Japanese *samurai* code, Spengler's theory of history, Nietzsche's cult of the heroic superman, Irish nationalism, the personal influence of Ezra Pound, and the attempt to reach through the viscera deeper truths than reason knows. This also forms a mask or opposed vision for what to Yeats and the others seemed the essential shortcomings of our age: a cult of mediocre vulgarity and a lack of nobility and heroism. The Yeatsian drama is a curious example of this imaginative opposition. We remember its characteristics: an intimate impersonality, directly addressed to a small audience by the dramatist, full of traditional symbolism, stripped to the barest essentials of costume, scenery, and lighting, tragic or at least melancholy in tone, reflecting aristocratic ideals, and with all individuality of character subordinated to a unity of theme. This dramatic form is, point for point, the exact opposite of the chief dramatic form of our age, the movie, with its vast unselected audience and its comic or sentimental realistic spectacle-form which has no dramatist and in which the private lives of the actors are on the whole more interesting than the play they are in.

But there is one point that Yeats never gets clear in his mind, except in one play called *The Unicorn from the Stars*, and for that very reason we must get it clear. Once a poet finds his mask, and it becomes the outward form of his *creative* life, it loses all real connection with his natural life. Art is not autotherapy: Morris did not cure his tactlessness by writing romances about people with plenty of tact. The poet, by presenting us with a vision of nobility and heroism, detaches that vision from our ordinary lives. He thus works in a direction exactly opposite to that of the political leader who insists on trying to attach it, and so perverts its nature, as fascism perverted the Nietzschean gospel of heroic virtue into the most monstrous negation of it that the world has ever seen. Siegfried may be a genuine enough heroic ideal in Wagner; but whenever anyone attempts to act like Siegfried, he instantly becomes an Alberich. The artist, of course, is always, like Narcissus, apt to become enamoured with the reflecting illusion of his own mask. Yeats himself did not possess every kind of high intelligence, and some affectations resulting from a pedantic streak in his make-up led him into a certain amount of social and political dithering. But for all that we should not be too quick to plaster a fascist label on Yeats' myth merely because a conspiracy of thugs happened to debase that myth instead of some other one. We come back here to our original point that poetic symbolism is language and not truth, a means of expression and not a body of doctrine, not something to look at but something to look and speak through, a dramatic mask. "The poet," said Sir Philip Sidney, "never affirmeth": when he does affirm he not only ceases to be a poet, but is as likely to be wrong as anyone else.

Yeats began his career with a set of romantic values and an intuition, recorded on the first page of his *Collected Poems*, that "words alone are certain good." As he went on, his romantic values consolidated into a tragic mask, through which we hear voices full of terror, cruelty, and a dreadful beauty, voices of the malignant ghosts of the dead repeating their passionate crimes. No one can deny that a tragic and terrible mask is the obvious reflection of our age; nor is it an easy mask to wear, since it is not for those who take refuge either in moral outrage or in facile bravado. But as it begins to settle on the creator of lovely and fragile Victorian poetry a new exuberance comes into the voice. In Yeats' early poems we find neither youth nor age, but an after-dinner dream of both; in the *Last Poems* the lusts of youth break out beside the "old man's eagle mind" flying far above the conflicts of illusion. For while illusion enslaves, vision emancipates, and even the thought of death in a dying world seems a buoyant thought, a defiant upstream leap of the elderly salmon returning to the place of seed.

In the early play *The King's Threshold* a poet goes on a hunger strike at a king's court because he is excluded from the high table where the bishops and councillors sit. But the issue is not fairly presented: the poet does not want mere equality with others; he wants to be recognized as himself the true king, the creator of social values whose praise of gold inspires others to strut about under gold crowns. Like Milton's Samson, or the Jesus of whom Samson was a prototype, he is a tragic hero to his followers and the buffoon of a Philistine carnival; yet the tragedy ends in triumph and the carnival in confusion. In one version the king admits that he has usurped the poet's title and surrenders; in another the poet starves; but in both versions what the poet says is:

> And I would have all know that when all falls
> In ruin, poetry calls out in joy,
> Being the scattering hand, the bursting pod,
> The victim's joy among the holy flame,
> God's laughter at the shattering of the world.

❧ The Realistic Oriole:
A Study of Wallace Stevens

WALLACE STEVENS WAS A POET FOR WHOM THE THEORY AND THE practice of poetry were inseparable.[1] His poetic vision is informed by a metaphysic; his metaphysic is informed by a theory of knowledge; his theory of knowledge is informed by a poetic vision. He says of one of his long meditative poems that it displays the theory of poetry as the life of poetry (486), and in the introduction to his critical essays that by the theory of poetry he means "poetry itself, the naked poem" (*N.A.* viii). He thus stands in contrast to the dualistic approach of Eliot, who so often speaks of poetry as though it were an emotional and sensational soul looking for a "correlative" skeleton of thought to be provided by a philosopher, a Cartesian ghost trying to find a machine that will fit. No poet of any status—certainly not Eliot himself—has ever "taken over" someone else's structure of thought, and the dualistic fallacy can only beget more fallacies. Stevens is of particular interest and value to the critical theorist because he sees so clearly that the only ideas the poet can deal with are those directly involved with, and implied by, his own writing: that, in short, "Poetry is the subject of the poem" (176).

It has been established in criticism ever since Aristotle that histories are direct verbal imitations of action, and that anything in literature with a story in it is a secondary imitation of an action. This means, not that the story is at two removes from reality, but that its actions are representative and typical rather than specific. For some reason it has not been nearly so well understood that discursive writing is not thinking, but a direct verbal imitation of

[1] All references to Stevens' poetry are accompanied by the page number in *The Collected Poems of Wallace Stevens*, 1954, and all references to his critical essays by the page number in *The Necessary Angel*, 1951, preceded by the letters *N.A.* I am sorry if this procedure makes the article typographically less attractive, but the proper place for such references, the margin, has disappeared from modern layout.

238

thought; that any poem with an idea in it is a secondary imitation of thought, and hence deals with representative or typical thought: that is, with forms of thought rather than specific propositions. Poetry is concerned with the ambiguities, the unconscious diagrams, the metaphors and the images out of which actual ideas grow. Poet and painter alike operate in "the flux Between the thing as idea and the idea as thing" (295). Stevens is an admirable poet in whom to study the processes of poetic thought at work, and such processes are part of what he means by the phrase "supreme fiction" which enters the title of his longest poem. The poet, he says, "gives to life the supreme fictions without which we are unable to conceive of it" (N.A. 31), and fictions imitate ideas as well as events.

Any discussion of poetry has to begin with the field or area that it works in, the field described by Aristotle as nature. Stevens calls it "reality," by which he means, not simply the external physical world, but "things as they are," the existential process that includes ordinary human life on the level of absorption in routine activity. Human intelligence can resist routine by arresting it in an act of consciousness, but the normal tendency of routine is to work against consciousness. The revolution of consciousness against routine is the starting-point of all mental activity, and the centre of mental activity is imagination, the power of transforming "reality" into awareness of reality. Man can have no freedom except what begins in his own awareness of his condition. Naturally historical periods differ greatly in the amount of pressure put on free consciousness by the compulsions of ordinary life. In our own day this pressure has reached an almost intolerable degree that threatens to destroy freedom altogether and reduce human life to a level of totally preoccupied compulsion, like the life of an animal. One symptom of this is the popular demand that the artist should express in his work a sense of social obligation. The artist's primary obedience however is not to reality but to the "violence from within" (N.A. 36) of the imagination that resists and arrests it. The minimum basis of the imagination, so to speak, is ironic realism, the act of simply becoming aware of the surrounding pressures of "things as they are." This develops the sense of alienation which is the immediate result of the imposing of consciousness on reality:

From this the poem springs: that we live in a place
That is not our own and, much more, not ourselves. (383)

The "act of the mind" (240) in which imagination begins, then, is an arresting of a flow of perceptions without and of impressions within. In that arrest there is born the principle of form or order: the inner violence of the imagination is a "rage for order" (130). It produces the "jar in Tennessee" (76), the object which not only is form in itself, but creates form out of all its surroundings. Stevens follows Coleridge in distinguishing the transforming of experience by the imagination from the re-arranging of it by the "fancy," and ranks the former higher (ignoring, if he knew it, T. E. Hulme's clever pseudo-critical reversal of the two). The imagination contains reason and emotion, but the imagination keeps form concrete and particular, whereas emotion and reason are more apt to seek the vague and the general respectively.

There are two forms of mental activity that Stevens regards as unpoetic. One is the breaking down of a world of discrete objects into an amorphous and invisible substratum, a search for a "pediment of appearance" (361), a slate-colored world of substance (15, 96) which destroys all form and particularity, symbolized by the bodiless serpent introduced in "The Auroras of Autumn" (411), "form gulping after formlessness." This error is typically an error of reason. The other error is the breaking down of the individual mind in an attempt to make it a medium for some kind of universal or pantheistic mind. This is typically an error of emotion, and one that Stevens in his essays calls "romantic," which is a little confusing when his own poetry is so centrally in the Romantic tradition. What he means by it is the preference of the invisible to the visible which impels a poet to develop a false rhetoric intended to be the voice, not of himself, but of some invisible super-bard within him (N.A. 61). In "Jumbo" (269), Stevens points out that such false rhetoric comes, not from the annihilation of the ego, but from the ego itself, from "Narcissus, prince Of the secondary men." Such an attitude produces the "nigger mystic" (195, 265), a phrase which naturally has nothing to do with Negroes, but refers to the kind of intellectual absolute that has been compared to a night in which all cows are black, a world clearly no improvement on "reality," which is also one color (N.A. 26).

A third mode of mental activity, which is poetic but not Stevens' kind of poetry, is the attempt to suggest or evoke universals of mind or substance, to work at the threshold of consciousness and produce what Stevens calls "marginal" poetry and associates with Valéry (N.A. 115). Whatever its merit, such poetry for him is in contrast with "central" poetry based on the concrete and particular act of mental experience. Stevens speaks of the imagination as moving from the hieratic to the credible (*N.A.* 58), and marginal poetry, like the structures of reason and the surrenderings of emotion, seeks a "hierophant Omega" (469) or ultimate mystery. There is a strong tendency, a kind of intellectual death-wish, to conceive of order in terms of finality, as something that keeps receding from experience until experience stops, when it becomes the mirage of an "after-life" on which all hierophants, whether poets or priests, depend. But for the imagination "Reality is the beginning not the end" (469), "The imperfect is our paradise" (194), and the only order worth having is the "violent order" produced by the explosion of imaginative energy, which is also a "great disorder" (215).

This central view of poetry is for Stevens based on the straight Aristotelian principle that if art is not quite nature, at least it grows naturally out of nature. He dislikes the term "imitation," but only because he thinks it means the naive copying of an external world: in its proper Aristotelian sense of creating a form of which nature is the content, Stevens' poetry is as imitative as Pope's. Art then is not so much nature methodized as nature realized, a unity of being and knowing, existence and consciousness, achieved out of the flow of time and the fixity of space. In content it is reality and we are "Participants of its being" (463); in form it is an art which "speaks the feeling" for "things as they are" (424). All through Stevens' poetry we find the symbol of the alphabet or syllable, the imaginative key to reality which, by bringing reality into consciousness, heightens the sense of both, "A nature that is created in what it says" (490).

However, the imagination does bring something to reality which is not there in the first place, hence the imagination contains an element of the "unreal" which the imaginative form incorporates. This unreal is connected with the fact that conscious experience is liberated experience. The unreal, "The fabulous and its intrinsic verse" (31), is the sense of exhilaration and splendor in art, the "radiant and productive" atmosphere which it both creates and breathes, the sense of the virile and the heroic implied by the term "creative" itself, "the way of thinking by which we project the idea of God into the idea of man" (*N.A.* 150). All art has this essential elegance or nobility, including ironic realism, but the nobility is an attribute of art, not its goal: one attains it by not trying for it, as though it were definable or extrinsic. Although art is in one sense an escape from reality (i.e., in the sense in which it is an escape *of* reality), and although art is a heightening of consciousness, it is not enough for art simply to give one a vision of a better world. Art is practical, not speculative; imaginative, not fantastic; it transforms experience, and does not merely interrupt it. The unreal in imaginative perception is most simply described as the sense that if something is not there it at least ought to be there. But this feeling in art is anything but wistful: it has created the tone of all the civilizations of history. Thus the "central" poet, by working outwards from a beginning instead of onwards toward an end, helps to achieve the only genuine kind of progress. As Stevens says, in a passage which explains the ambivalence of the term "mystic" in his work: "The adherents of the central are also mystics to begin with. But all their desire and all their ambition is to press away from mysticism toward that ultimate good sense which we term civilization" (*N.A.* 116).

Such ultimate good sense depends on preserving a balance between objective reality and the subjective unreal element in the imagination. Exaggerating the latter gives us the false heroics that produce the aggressive symbols of warfare and the cult of "men suited to public ferns" (276). Exaggerating the former gives us the weariness of mind that bores the "fretful concubine" (211) in her splendid surroundings. Within art itself there has been a corresponding alternation of emphasis. In some ages, or with some poets, the emphasis is on the imaginative heightening of reality by visions of a Yeatsian "noble rider"

> On his gold horse striding, like a conjured beast,
> Miraculous in its panache and swish. (426)

At other times the emphasis is ironic, thrown on the minimum role of the imagination as the simple and subjective observer of reality, not withdrawn from it, but detached enough to feel that the power of transforming it has passed by. These two emphases, the green and the red as Stevens calls them (340), appear in Stevens' own poetry as the summer vision and the autumn vision respectively.

The summer vision of life is the *gaya scienza* (248), the "Lebensweisheitspielerei" (504), in which things are perceived in their essential radiance, when "the world is larger" (514). This summer vision extends all over the *Harmonium* poems, with their glowing still lifes and gorgeous landscapes of Florida and the Caribbean coasts. Its dominating image is the sun, "that brave man" (138), the hero of nature who lives in heaven but transforms the earth from his mountain-top (65), "the strong man vaguely seen" (204). As

"we are men of sun" (137), our creative life is his, hence the feeling
of alienation from nature in which consciousness begins is really
inspired by exactly the opposite feeling. "I am what is around me"
(86), the poet says; the jar in Tennessee expresses the form in Ten-
nessee as well as in itself, and one feels increasingly that "The
soul . . . is composed Of the external world" (51) in the sense
that in the imagination we have "The inhuman making choice of a
human self" (*N.A.* 89), a subhuman world coming to a point of
imaginative light in a focus of individuality and consciousness.
Such a point of imaginative light is a human counterpart of the
sun. The poet absorbs the reality he contemplates "as the Angevine
Absorbs Anjou" (224), just as the sun's light, by giving itself and
taking nothing, absorbs the world in itself. The echo to the great
trumpet-call of "Let there be light" is "All things in the sun are
sun" (104).

There are two aspects of the summer vision, which might be
called, in Marvellian language, the visions of the golden lamp and
of the green night. The latter is the more contemplative vision of
the student in the tradition of Milton's penseroso poet, Shelley's
Athanase, and Yeats's old man in the tower. In this vision the sun
is replaced by the moon (33 ff.), or, more frequently, the evening
star (25), the human counterpart of which is the student's candle
(51, 523). Its personified form, corresponding to the sun, is often
female, an "archaic" (223) or "green queen" (339), the "desired"
(505) one who eventually becomes an "interior paramour" (524)
or Jungian anima (cf. 321), the motionless spinning Penelope (520)
to whom every voyager returns, the eternal Eve (271) or naked
bride (395) of the relaxed imagination. Here we are, of course, in
danger of the death-wish vision, of reading a blank book. Some of
the irony of this is in "Phosphor Reading by his Own Light" (267),
as well as in "The Reader" (146). The bride of such a narcist
vision is the sinister "Madame La Fleurie" (507). But in its genuine
form such contemplation is the source of major imagination
(387-8), and hence Stevens, like Yeats, has his tower-mountain of
vision or "Palaz of Hoon" (65; cf. 121), where sun and poet come
into alignment:

> It is the natural tower of all the world,
> The point of survey, green's green apogee,
> But a tower more precious than the view beyond,
> A point of survey squatting like a throne,
> Axis of everything. (373)

From this point of survey we are lifted above the "cat," symbol of life absorbed in being without consciousness, and the "rabbit" who is "king of the ghosts" and is absorbed in consciousness without being (209, 223).

The autumnal vision begins in the poet's own situation. To perceive "reality" as dingy or unattractive is itself an imaginative act ("The Plain Sense of Things," 502), but an ironic act, an irony deepened by the fact that other modes of perception are equally possible, the oriole being as realistic as the crow (154), and there can be no question of accepting only one as true. It is a curious tendency in human nature to believe in disillusionment: that is, to think we are nearest the truth when we have established as much falsehood as possible. This is the vision of "Mrs. Alfred Uruguay" (248), who approaches her mountain of contemplation the wrong way round, starting at the bottom instead of the top. (Her name is apparently based on an association with "Montevideo.") The root of the reductive tendency, at least in poetry, is perhaps the transience of the emotional mood which is the framework of the lyric. In *Harmonium* the various elaborations of vision are seen as projected from a residual ego, a comedian (27 ff.) or clown (Peter Quince is the leader of a group of clowns), who by himself has only the vision of the *"esprit bâtard"* (102), the juggler in motley who is also a magician and whose efforts are "conjurations." When we add the clown's conjurations to the clown we get "man the abstraction, the comic sun" (156): the term "abstraction" will meet us again.

This *esprit bâtard* or dimmed vision of greater maturity, *un monocle d'un oncle,* so to speak, comes into the foreground after the "Credences of Summer" (372) and the "Things of August" (489) have passed by. In September the web of the imagination's pupa is woven (208); in November the moon lights up only the death of the god (107); at the onset of winter the auroras of a vanished heroism flicker over the sky, while in the foreground stand the scarecrows or hollow men of the present (293, 513).

To this vision belong the bitter "Man on the Dump" (201), the ironic "Esthetique du Mal" (313), with its urbane treatment of the religio-literary clichés, such as "The death of Satan was a tragedy For the imagination," which are the stock in trade of lesser poets, and the difficult and painfully written war poems. It is more typical of Stevens, of course, to emphasize the reality which is present in the imaginative heightening of misery, the drudge's dream of "The Ordinary Women" (10) which none the less reminds us that

"Imagination is the will of things" (84). The true form of the autumnal vision is not the irony which robs man of his dignity, but the tragedy which confers it ("In a Bad Time," 426).

At the end of autumn come the terrors of winter, the sense of a world disintegrating into chaos which we feel socially when we see the annihilation wars of our time, and individually when we face the fact of death in others or for ourselves. We have spoken of Stevens' dislike of projecting the religious imagination into a world remote in space and time. The woman in "Sunday Morning" (66) stays home from church and meditates on religion surrounded by the brilliant oranges and greens of the summer vision, and in "A High-Toned Old Christian Woman" (59) it is suggested that the poet, seeking an increase rather than a diminishing of life, gets closer to a genuinely religious sense than morality with its taboos and denials. For Stevens all real religion is concerned with a renewal of earth rather than with a surrender to heaven. He even says "the great poems of heaven and hell have been written and the great poem of the earth remains to be written" (N.A. 142). It is part of his own ambition to compose hymns "Happy rather than holy but happy-high" (185) which will "take the place Of empty heavens" (167), and he looks forward to a world in which "all men are priests" (254). As this last phrase shows, he has no interest in turning to some cellophane-wrapped version of neo-paganism. He sees, like Yeats, that the poet is a "Connoisseur of Chaos" (215) aware that "Poetry is a Destructive Force" (192), and Stevens' imagery, for all its luxuriance and good humor, is full of menace. From the "firecat" of the opening page of the Collected Poems, through the screaming peacocks of "Domination of Black" (8), the buzzard of "The Jack-Rabbit" (50; cf. 318), the butcher of "A Weak Mind in the Mountains" (212), the bodiless serpent of "The Auroras of Autumn" (411) and the bloody lion of "Puella Parvula" (456), we are aware that a simple song of carpe diem is not enough.

In the later poems there is a growing preoccupation with death, as, not the end of life or an introduction to something unconnected with life, but as itself a part of life and giving to life itself an extra dimension. This view is very close to Rilke, especially the Rilke of the Orpheus sonnets, which are, like Stevens' poetry in general, "a constant sacrament of praise" (92). "What a ghastly situation it would be," Stevens remarks, "if the world of the dead was actually different from the world of the living" (N.A. 76), and in several poems, especially the remarkable "Owl in the Sarcophagus" (431), there are references to carrying on the memories or "souvenirs" of the past into a world which is not so much future as timeless, a world of recognition or "rendezvous" (524), and which lies in the opposite direction from the world of dreams:

> There is a monotonous babbling in our dreams
> That makes them our dependent heirs, the heirs
> Of dreamers buried in our sleep, and not
> The oncoming fantasies of better birth. (39)

In the poems of the winter vision the solar hero and the green queen become increasingly identified with the father and mother of a Freudian imago (439). The father and mother in turn expand into a continuous life throughout time of which we form our unitary realizations. The father, "the bearded peer" (494), extends back to the primordial sea (501), the mother to the original maternity of nature, the "Lady Lowzen" of "Oak Leaves are Hands" (272). In "The Owl in the Sarcophagus" these figures are personified as sleep and memory. The ambivalence of the female figure is expressed by the contrast between the "regina of the clouds" in "Le Monocle de mon Oncle" (13) and the "Sister and mother and diviner love" of "To the One of Fictive Music" (87). The poet determined to show that "being Includes death and the imagination" (444) must go through the same world as the "nigger mystic," for a "nigger cemetery" (150) lies in front of him too, just as the sunrise of the early play, *Three Travellers Watch a Sunrise*, is heralded by a hanged man. The search for death through life which is a part of such recreation leads to a final confronting of the self and the rock (*N.A.* viii), the identification of consciousness and reality in which the living soul is identified with its tombstone which is equally its body (528). In this final triumph of vision over death the death-symbols are turned into symbols of life. The author of the Apocalypse prophesies to his "back-ache" (which is partly the *Weltschmerz* of the past) that the venom of the bodiless serpent will be one with its wisdom (437). The "black river" of death, Swatara (428), becomes "The River of Rivers in Connecticut" (533), a river *this* side of the Styx which "flows nowhere, like a sea" because it is in a world in which there is no more sea.

If we listen carefully to the voice of "the auroral creature musing in the mind" (263), the auroras of autumn will become, not the after-images of remembrance, but the *Morgenrot* of a new recognition. As the cycle turns through death to a new life, we meet images of spring, the central one being some modification of

Venus rising from the sea: the "paltry nude" of the poem of that name (5); "Infanta Marina" (7); Susanna lying in "A wave, interminably flowing" (92); "Celle qui fût Heaulmiette" (438) reborn from the mother and father of the winter vision, the mother having the "vague severed arms" of the maternal Venus of Milo. This reborn girl is the Jungian anima or interior paramour spoken of before, the "Golden Woman in a Silver Mirror" (460). She is also associated with the bird of Venus, "The Dove in the Belly" (366; cf. 357 and "Song of Fixed Accord," 519). It is also a bird's cry, but one outside the poet, which heralds "A new knowledge of reality" in the last line of the *Collected Poems*. The spring vision often has its origin in the commonplace, or in the kind of innocent gaudiness that marks exuberant life. Of the spring images in "Celle qui fût Heaulmiette" the author remarks affectionately, "Another American vulgarity"; the "paltry nude" is a gilded ship's prow, and the "emperor of ice-cream" presides over funeral obsequies in a shabby household (64). "It is the invasion of humanity That counts," remarks a character in *Three Travellers Watch a Sunrise*. "Only the rich remember the past," the poet says (225) and even in "Final Soliloquy of the Interior Paramour" (524) there is still a parenthetical association of new vision with a poverty which has nothing to lose.

In "Peter Quince at the Clavier" beauty is called "The fitful tracing of a portal." Portal to what? The word itself seems to mean something to Stevens (*N.A.* 60, 155), and in the obviously very personal conclusion of "The Rock" it is replaced by "gate" (528). Perhaps Stevens, like Blake, has so far only given us the end of a golden string, and after traversing the circle of natural images we have still to seek the centre.

The normal unit of poetic expression is the metaphor, and Stevens was well aware of the importance of metaphor, as is evident from the many poems which use the word in title or text. His conception of metaphor is regrettably unclear, though clearer in the poetry than in the essays. He speaks of the creative process as beginning in the perception of "resemblance," adding that metamorphosis might be a better word (*N.A.* 72). By resemblance he does not mean naive or associative resemblance, of the type that calls a flower a bleeding heart, but the repetitions of color and pattern in nature which become the elements of formal design in art. He goes on to develop this conception of resemblance into a conception of "analogy" which, beginning in straight allegory, ends in the perception that "poetry becomes and is a transcendent analogue composed of the particulars of reality" (*N.A.* 130). But nowhere in his essays does he suggest that metaphor is anything more than likeness or parallelism. "There is always an analogy between nature and the imagination, and possibly poetry is merely the strange rhetoric of that parallel" (*N.A.* 118).

Clearly, if poetry is "merely" this, the use of metaphor could only accentuate what Stevens' poetry tries to annihilate, the sense of a contrast or great gulf fixed between subject and object, consciousness and existence. And in fact we often find metaphor used pejoratively in the poems as a form of avoiding direct contact with reality. The motive for metaphor, we are told, is the shrinking from immediate experience (288). Stevens appears to mean by such metaphor, however, simile or comparison, "the intricate evasions of as" (486; cf. "Add This to Rhetoric," 198). And metaphor is actually nothing of the kind. In its literal grammatical form metaphor is a statement of identity: this is that, A is B. And Stevens has a very strong sense of the crucial importance of poetic identification, "where as and is are one" (476), as it is only there that one finds "The poem of pure reality, untouched By trope or deviation" (471). Occasionally it occurs to him that metaphor might be used in a less pejorative sense. He speaks of "The metaphor that murders metaphor" (*N.A.* 84), implying that a better kind of metaphor can get murdered, and "Metaphor as Degeneration" (444) ends in a query how metaphor can really be degeneration when it is part of the process of seeing death as a part of life.

When metaphor says that one thing "is" another thing, or that a man, a woman and a blackbird are one (93), things are being identified *with* other things. In logical identity there is only identification *as*. If I say that the Queen of England "is" Elizabeth II, I have not identified one person with another, but one person as herself. Poetry also has this type of identification, for in poetic metaphor things are identified with each other, yet each is identified as itself, and retains that identity. When a man, a woman and a blackbird are said to be one, each remains what it is, and the identification heightens the distinctive form of each. Such a metaphor is necessarily illogical (or anti-logical, as in "A violent disorder is an order") and hence poetic metaphors are opposed to likeness or similarity. A perception that a man, a woman and a blackbird were in some respects alike would be logical, but would not make much of a poem. Unfortunately in prose speech we often use the word identical to mean very similar, as in the phrase "identical twins," and this use makes it difficult to express the idea of poetic identity in a prose essay. But if twins were really identical they would be the same person, and hence could be different in form, like a man and the same man as a boy of seven. A world of total simile, where everything was like everything else, would be a world of total monotony; a world of total metaphor, where everything is identified as itself and with everything else, would be a world where subject and object, reality and mental organization of reality, are one. Such a world of total metaphor is the formal cause of poetry. Stevens makes it clear that the poet seeks the particular and discrete image: many of the poems in *Parts of a World*, such as "On the Road Home" (203), express what the title of the book expresses, the uniqueness of every act of vision. Yet it is through the particular and discrete that we reach the unity of the imagination, which respects individuality, in contrast to the logical unity of the generalizing reason, which destroys it. The false unity of the dominating mind is what Stevens condemns in "The Bagatelles the Madrigals" (213), and in the third part of "The Pure Good of Theory" (331-2), where we find again a pejorative use of the term metaphor.

When a thing is identified as itself, it becomes an individual of a class or total form: when we identify a brown and green mass as a tree we provide a class name for it. This is the relating of species to genera which Aristotle spoke of as one of the central aspects of metaphor. The distinctively poetic use of such metaphor is the identifying of an individual with its class, where a tree becomes Wordsworth's "tree of many one," or a man becomes mankind. Poets ordinarily do not, like some philosophers, replace individual objects with their total forms; they do not, like allegorists, represent total forms by individuals. They see individual and class as metaphorically identical: in other words they work with *myths*, many of whom are human figures in whom the individual has been identified with its universal or total form.

Such myths, "archaic forms, giants Of sense, evoking one thing in many men" (494) play a large role in Stevens' imagery. For some reason he speaks of the myth as "abstract." "The Ultimate Poem is Abstract" (429; cf. 270, 223 and elsewhere), and the first requirement of the "supreme fiction" is that it must be abstract (380), though as far as dictionary meanings are concerned one would expect rather to hear that it must be concrete. By abstract Stevens apparently means artificial in its proper sense, something constructed rather than generalized. In such a passage as this we can see the myth forming out of "repetitions" as the individual soldier becomes the unknown soldier, and the unknown soldier the Adonis or continuously martyred god:

> How red the rose that is the soldier's wound,
> The wounds of many soldiers, the wounds of all
> The soldiers that have fallen, red in blood,
> The soldier of time grown deathless in great size. (318)

Just as there is false metaphor, so there is false myth. There is in particular the perverted myth of the average or "root-man" (262), described more expressively as "the total man of glubbal glub" (301). Whenever we have the root-man we have, by compensation, "The super-man friseured, possessing and possessed" (262), which is the perversion of the idea of *Übermenschlichkeit* (98) into the Carlylean great man or military hero. Wars are in their imaginative aspect a "gigantomachia" (289) of competing aggressive myths. The war-myth or hero of death is the great enemy of the imagination: he cannot be directly fought except by another war-myth; he can only be contained in a greater and more genuine form of the same myth (280, section xv). The genuine form of the war-hero is the "major man" (334; 387-8) who, in "The Owl in the Sarcophagus," is personified as peace (434), the direct opposite of the war-hero, and the third of the figures in "the mythology of modern death" which, along with sleep and memory, conquer death for life.

We thus arrive at the conception of a universal or "central man" (250), who may be identified with any man, such as a fisherman listening to wood-doves:

> The fisherman might be the single man
> In whose breast, the dove, alighting, would grow still. (357)

This passage, which combines the myth of the central man with the anima myth of the "dove in the belly" (366), is from a poem with the painfully exact title, "Thinking of a Relation between the Images of Metaphors." The central man is often symbolized by glass or transparency, as in "Asides on the Oboe" (250) and in "Prologues to What is Possible" (515). If there is a central man, there is also a central mind (298) of which the poet feels peculiarly a part. Similarly there is a "central poem" (441) identical with the world, and finally a "general being or human universe" (378), of which all imaginative work forms part:

FABLES OF IDENTITY

> That's it. The lover writes, the believer hears,
> The poet mumbles and the painter sees,
> Each one, his fated eccentricity,
> As a part, but part, but tenacious particle,
> Of the skeleton of the ether, the total
> Of letters, prophecies, perceptions, clods
> Of color, the giant of nothingness, each one
> And the giant ever changing, living in change. (443)

In "Sketch of the Ultimate Politician" (335) we get a glimpse of this human universe as an infinite City of Man.

To sum up: the imaginative act breaks down the separation between subject and object, the perceiver shut up in "the enclosures of hypothesis" (516) like an embryo in a "naked egg" (173) or glass shell (297), and a perceived world similarly imprisoned in the remoteness of its "irreducible X" (N.A. 83), which is also an egg (490). Separation is then replaced by the direct, primitive identification which Stevens ought to have called metaphor and which, not having a word for it, he calls "description" (339) in one of his definitive poems, a term to which he elsewhere adds "apotheosis" (378) and "transformation" (514; cf. N.A. 49), which come nearer to what he really means. The maxim that art should conceal art is based on the sense that in the greatest art we have no sense of manipulating, posing or dominating over nature, but rather of emancipating it. "One confides in what has no Concealed creator" (296), the poet says, and again:

> There might be, too, a change immenser than
> A poet's metaphors in which being would
>
> Come true, a point in the fire of music where
> Dazzle yields to a clarity and we observe,
>
> And observing is completing and we are content,
> In a world that shrinks to an immediate whole,
>
> That we do not need to understand, complete
> Without secret arrangements of it in the mind. (341)

The theoretical postulate of Stevens' poetry is a world of total metaphor, where the poet's vision may be identified with anything it visualizes. For such poetry the most accurate word is apocalyptic, a poetry of "revelation" (344) in which all objects and experiences are united with a total mind. Such poetry gives us:

> . . . the book of reconciliation,
> Book of a concept only possible

In description, canon central in itself,
The thesis of the plentifullest John. (345)

Apocalypse, however, is one of the two great narrative myths that expand "reality," with its categories of time and space, into an infinite and eternal world. A myth of a total man recovering a total world is hardly possible without a corresponding myth of a Fall, or some account of what is wrong with our present perspective. Stevens' version of the Fall is similar to that of the "Orphic poet" at the end of Emerson's *Nature:*

> Why, then, inquire
> Who has divided the world, what entrepreneur?
> No man. The self, the chrysalis of all men
>
> Became divided in the leisure of blue day
> And more, in branchings after day. One part
> Held fast tenaciously in common earth
>
> And one from central earth to central sky
> And in moonlit extensions of them in the mind
> Searched out such majesty as it could find. (468-9)

Such poetry sounds religious, and in fact does have the infinite perspective of religion, for the limits of the imagination are the conceivable, not the real, and it extends over death as well as life. In the imagination the categories of "reality," space and time, are reversed into form and creation respectively, for art is "Description without Place" (339) standing at the centre of "ideal time" (*N.A.* 88), and its poetry is "even older than the ancient world" (*N.A.* 145). Religion seems to have a monopoly of talking about infinite and eternal worlds, and poetry that uses such conceptions seems to be inspired by a specifically religious interest. But the more we study poetry, the more we realize that the dogmatic limiting of the poet's imagination to human and subhuman nature that we find, for instance, in Hardy and Housman, is not normal to poetry but a technical *tour de force*. It is the normal language of poetic imagination itself that is heard when Yeats says that man has invented death; when Eliot reaches the still point of the turning world; when Rilke speaks of the poet's perspective as that of an angel containing all time and space, blind and looking into himself; when Stevens find his home in "The place of meta-men and para-things" (448). Such language may or may not go with a religious commitment: in itself it is simply poetry speaking as poetry must when it gets to a certain pitch of metaphorical concentration.

Stevens says that his motive is neither "to console Nor sanctify, but plainly to propound" (389).

In *Harmonium*, published in the Scott Fitzgerald decade, Stevens moves in a highly sensuous atmosphere of fine pictures, good food, exquisite taste and luxury cruises. In the later poems, though the writing is as studiously oblique as ever, the sensuousness has largely disappeared, and the reader accustomed only to *Harmonium* may feel that Stevens' inspiration has failed him, or that he is attracted by themes outside his capacity, or that the impact of war and other ironies of the autumnal vision has shut him up in an uncommunicative didacticism. Such a view of Stevens is of course superficial, but the critical issue it raises is a genuine one.

In the criticism of drama there is a phase in which the term "theatrical" becomes pejorative, when one tries to distinguish genuine dramatic imagination from the conventional clichés of dramatic rhetoric. Of course eventually this pejorative use has to disappear, because Shakespeare and Aeschylus are quite as theatrical as Cecil de Mille. Similarly, one also goes through a stage, though a shorter one, in which the term "poetic" may acquire a slightly pejorative cast, as when one may decide, several hundred pages deep in Swinburne, that Swinburne can sometimes be a poetic bore. Eventually one realizes that the "poetic" quality comes from allusiveness, the incorporating into the texture of echoes, cadences, names and thoughts derived from the author's previous literary experience. Swinburne is poetic in a poor sense when he is being a parasite on the literary tradition; Eliot is poetic in a better sense when, in his own phrase, he steals rather than imitates. The "poetic" normally expresses itself as what one might loosely call word-magic or incantation, charm in its original sense of spell, as it reinforces the "act of the mind" in poetry with the dream-like reverberations, echoes and enlarged significances of the memory and the unconscious. We suggested at the beginning that Eliot lacks what Stevens has, the sense of an autonomous poetic theory as an inseparable part of poetic practice. On the other hand Eliot has pre-eminently the sense of a creative tradition, and this sense is partly what makes his poetry so uniquely penetrating, so easy to memorize unconsciously.

In Stevens there is a good deal of incantation and imitative harmony; but the deliberately "magical" poems, such as "The Idea of Order at Key West," "To the One of Fictive Music," and the later "Song of Fixed Accord" have the special function of expressing a stasis or harmony between imagination and reality, and hence have something of a conscious rhetorical exercise about them. In "The Idea of Order at Key West" the sense of carefully controlled artifice enters the theme as well. In other poems where the texture is dryer and harder, the schemata on which "word-magic" depends are reduced to a minimum. The rhymes, for instance, when they occur, are usually sharp barking assonances, parody-rhymes (e.g., "The Swedish cart to be part of the heart," 369), and the metres, like the curious blank *terza rima* used so often, are almost parody-metres. A quality that is not far from being anti-"poetic" seems to emerge.

Just as the "poetic" is derived mainly from the reverberations of tradition, so it is clear that the anti-"poetic" quality in Stevens is the result of his determination to make it new, in Pound's phrase, to achieve in each poem a unique expression and force his reader to make a correspondingly unique act of apprehension. This is a part of what he means by "abstract" as a quality of the "supreme fiction." It was Whitman who urged American writers to lay less emphasis on tradition, thereby starting another tradition of his own, and it is significant that Whitman is one of the very few traditional poets Stevens refers to, though he has little in common with him technically. It is partly his sense of a poem as belonging to experiment rather than tradition, separated from the stream of time with its conventional echoes, that gives Stevens' poetry its marked affinity with pictures, an affinity shown also in the curiously formalized symmetry of the longer poems. "Notes Towards a Supreme Fiction," for instance, has three parts of ten sections each, each section with seven tercets, and similarly rectangular distributions of material are found in other poems.

When we meet a poet who has so much rhetorical skill, and yet lays so much emphasis on novelty and freshness of approach, the skill acquires a quality of courage: a courage that is without compromise in a world full of cheap rhetoric, yet uses none of the ready-made mixes of rhetoric in a world full of compromise. Stevens was one of the most courageous poets of our time, and his conception of the poem as "the heroic effort to live expressed As victory" (446) was unyielding from the beginning. Courage implies persistence, and persistence in a distinctive strain often develops its complementary opposite as well, as with Blake's fool who by persisting in his folly became wise. It was persistence that transformed the tropical lushness of *Harmonium* into the austere clairvoyance of *The Rock*, the luxurious demon into the necessary angel, and so rounded out a vision of major scope and intensity. As a result Stevens became, unlike many others who may have started off with equal abilities, not one of our expendable rhetoricians, but one of our small handful of essential poets.

❧ Quest and Cycle in *Finnegans Wake*

Finnegans Wake BELONGS TO THE EPIC TRADITION, AND EPIC WRITERS have always been unusually conscious of tradition. Joyce's immediate predecessors in his type of epic were the mythological poets of the Romantic period, and among these Blake is clearly the most important for the study of Joyce. Blake's work is middle-class, nineteenth-century, moral, romantic, sentimental and fervently rhetorical, and these were the cultural qualities that Joyce, to the dismay of many of his critics, most deeply loved and appreciated. I propose first to set out the major parallels between Blake's myth of Albion and Joyce's myth of Finnegan.

Blake's myth is derived chiefly from the Bible, and the Bible for Blake was a kind of definitive myth extending from the beginning to the end of time (creation to apocalypse) and from the centre to the circumference of space (individual to universal man). The chief principle of Blake's symbolism is the concrete universal, the identity of the individual and the class, which he expresses in the metaphor of distance: "When distant they appear as One Man, but as you approach they appear Multitudes of Nations." The two poles of Blake's myth are man awake, or Jesus, and man asleep, or Albion. Man awake is God; man asleep is historical and biological man. The Bible is revelation, a message from Jesus to Albion, but an imaginative or poetic revelation, for Jesus employed parables, not syllogisms. Churches, being social, are founded on rational and legal versions of revelation, and hence are subordinate in authority to the agents of the creative Word itself, the prophets and prophetic artists. What the latter communicate is a completely catholic Christianity or "everlasting gospel," in which "all religions are one."

In Joyce there is also the doctrine of the priority of the imaginative over the doctrinal Word. In the *Portrait* the artist and the priest, who are both aspects of Stephen, struggle for the possession of this Word, and the artist wins out. In Joyce's personal life his break with the Catholic Church meant, not that he wanted to believe in something else, but that he wanted to transfer the mythical structure of the Church from faith and doctrine to creative imagination, thereby exchanging dogmatic Catholicism for imaginative catholicity. The usual cliché that art is no substitute for religion does not begin to apply to either Blake or Joyce. Blake thought of his Prophecies, especially *The Four Zoas,* which is subtitled "A Dream of Nine Nights," as addressed by the artist to the ear of the sleeping Albion, and the same point is expressed in Joyce's symbol of the earwig. In Joyce too the concrete universal, the identity of individual and total man, is the organizing principle of the symbolism.

Albion has the same connexions with England and London that Finnegan has with Ireland and Dublin. Both are what Blake calls "giant forms," embracing both the subjective and the objective worlds, the landscape of England and Ireland respectively being formed out of their bodies. In Blake, the fact that Albion is asleep means that he has "fallen" asleep, and his fall was into the dream world of external nature. This world moves in circles, or perhaps rather ellipses, revolving around two foci that Blake calls Orc and Urizen. Orc is youth, energy, rebelliousness and sexual vitality; Urizen is age, prudence, law and worldly wisdom. Orc is the dying god or John Barleycorn who is killed at the height of his powers; Urizen is the Olympian sky-god or "President of the Immortals." In his later works Blake tends to employ the single term "Luvah" for the whole Orc-Urizen cycle.

Luvah in Joyce is HCE, who in his earlier phases is the immanent dying god of the cyclical fertility of nature, and is said to be submerged under Lough Neagh in north Ireland, just as the sleeping Albion in Blake is the true Atlantis, submerged under the Atlantic Ocean. In Blake the sleeping Albion *is* Luvah, just as the fully awakened Albion would be identified with Jesus. The analogy suggests the solution of a vexing problem in Joyce. As in *Alice Through the Looking Glass,* to which it owes so much, the final question left with the reader of *Finnegans Wake* is "Which dreamed it?" If the dreamer is HCE, the place of Finnegan, who is also the husband of ALP, seems difficult to account for, and the simplest answer is that the dreamer is Finnegan, the communal human unconscious of Dublin, who while he is asleep is identical with HCE, and to a lesser extent with the other speaking characters. In the course of the book HCE gradually sinks under a mounting body of forgetfulness, rumor and calumny until he becomes Urizenic, associated with the Scandinavian, Roman and English invaders who have imposed structures of external authority on Ireland. In Blake the opposition of Orc and Urizen is accompanied by certain paired symbols, such as the spear and the shield, which correspond to the tree and stone in Joyce.

In both Blake and Joyce the cyclical movement of nature extends to human history. Joyce derives from Vico, probably with some help from Spengler, a conception of a historical cycle in four stages, an age of myth, an age of metaphysics, an age of positivism, and a final age of dissolution bringing us back to the beginning again. Blake's cycle has four parallel stages, symbolized by the birth of Orc, a moment of terror corresponding to Joyce's "thunderclap"; the imprisoning of Orc, corresponding to the shift in power from the Word to the Church recorded in *The Mookse and the Gripes;* Urizen "exploring his dens," which is eighteenth-century positivism and corresponds to British imperialism in Joyce; and a final age of chaos. In Blake there is the possibility of choosing, in the final stage, between an apocalypse or awakening of Man and a return to another cycle: Blake stresses the apocalyptic alternative and Joyce the cyclical one. In Blake the ninth night of *The Four Zoas* and the fourth part of *Jerusalem* are given over to the apocalypse; at the end of the eighth night of *The Four Zoas* and the third part of *Jerusalem* we have a vision of pure cycle, the end of the age of Luther, or Blake's own time, going back to the beginning of history "in eternal circle." This corresponds to the end of Joyce's sixteenth chapter, just before the Recorso or last chapter begins: "Tiers, tiers and tiers. Rounds." The last page of *Finnegans Wake* describes the sinking of ALP into her "old feary father," as the Liffey river finally reaches the sea. As *Finnegans Wake* goes around in a circle, this event immediately precedes the fall of Finnegan on the first page, and corresponds exactly to the first event of *The Four Zoas,* the sinking of Enitharmon into the sea-god Tharmas, an event immediately followed by the fall of Albion.

Human history according to Blake occupies seven great ages, which are subdivided into a series of twenty-eight "Churches," or historical versions of the creative Word. In each age an imaginative polarity shapes up between the artist and the priest, the prophet and the worldly wise man. In *The Marriage of Heaven and Hell* Blake calls the artist-prophets "Devils" and their opponents "Angels"—both, he says, are essential to human life, for "without Contrarieties is no Progression," but it is also inevitable that each group should regard the other as demonic. In Joyce too there are seven periods of HCE's sleep, symbolized by the seven colors of the spectrum and by female figures who represent a dim but constant infidelity to HCE. A similar role is played by the twenty-eight "Maggies," who in the literal allegory are the schoolmates of HCE's daughter Isabel. Constantly throughout history, too, there is a "collideorscape," or conflict of what Blake would call "mental fight" and worldly prudence in which one contender is Shem, the outcast artist-prophet, and the other Shaun, the worldly priest. From the reader's point of view Shaun is merely a derivative and distorted version of Shem, but from the world's point of view the struggle of the brothers is a "mime of Mick and Nick," a contest of Michael and Satan in which Shaun is Michael and Shem the conquered power of darkness, and it is to this latter point of view that the "Maggies" adhere. Blake's poem *Milton* is also based on a conflict of Michael and Satan, in which Michael represents the artist and Satan worldly wisdom, and here too Satan is the hero to the female characters who in Blake's myth correspond to the "Maggies."

In Blake the struggle between good and evil conceals a genuine dialectic of eternal life and eternal death, the separation of which is achieved only in the apocalypse. Satan in Blake is the death-principle, including not only physical death but all the workings of the death-impulse in human life, the discouraging or prohibiting of free activity which Blake calls the "accusation of sin," and which he associates with the three accusers of Socrates and the three comforters of Job. In Joyce the dream of HCE is unable to escape from a neurotic circling around some accusation of guilt which seems to emanate from a mysterious "cad," who is associated with the serpent in Paradise and with three male figures, generally soldiers, sometimes the sons of Noah or the human race in general. These in turn melt into the lampooners of HCE, and are closely associated with twelve "Morphios," the patrons of HCE's pub, whose function it is to encourage and continue the sleeping state. Similarly in Blake the sleep of Albion is encouraged and prolonged by twelve "sons of Albion" who, like their counterparts in Joyce, are associated both with the zodiac and with jury trials.

In Blake what man, in any context, creates is his "emanation," and exists in a feminine relation to him. God the Creator is male, and everything he creates is at once his wife and daughter. Just as "companies of nations" appear as one man at a distance, so a multitude of created things appears as "a City, yet a Woman," called Jerusalem in Blake. In the fall Albion abandoned his creative power for the contemplation of his creation, which then separated from him and became external to him, the teasing, tantalizing female nature which Blake calls Vala. In Joyce there are several Vala figures, apart from the "Maggies" already mentioned. The original fall of HCE is connected somehow with two elusive but not quite hidden girls, whom Joyce, for etymological reasons, calls "minxes," and whose many names seem to revolve around "Rose" and "Lily"— the symbolism of red and white has affinities with the fact that Vala in Blake is called indifferently a virgin and a harlot, the two aspects in which Vala is named Tirzah and Rahab respectively. Then there is the mirror or leap-year girl, the twenty-ninth Maggie and the narcist reflexion of Isabel, who is associated with Isoult, as Blake associates Vala with the convention of Courtly Love, and also with Swift's Stella and Vanessa: one is reminded of the way that Tirzah and Rahab are associated with Milton's wives and daughters in Blake's poem on Milton.

These are the major parallels between the two myths: the parallel sometimes suggested between Blake's four Zoas and Joyce's four old men is not a genuine one. The Zoas in Blake are his major figures Los, Orc, Urizen and Tharmas, and are fully individualized: the four old men in Joyce are always a chorus, and seem unintegrated to the rest of the symbolism. These four men are inorganic tradition, or, more accurately, the conscious memory: they are linked to the four evangelists, the four historians of Ireland, and to the psychoanalytic technique of trying to clear the mind of guilt by awakening the memory. In Joyce, as in Blake, the memory and the creative imagination are distinct or even opposed principles. The nearest equivalent in Blake to the four old men would be the four chief sons of Los in their "abstract" form.

We pass now to the major point of contrast between the two. The hero of Blake's Prophecies, who is at once artist, prophet, blacksmith and the spirit of time, is called Los. The "emanation" of Los is Enitharmon, who represents space, and is consequently the presiding spirit of the false daylight world of common sense. In the fallen world her natural affinities are with Urizen or worldly reason, and Los has the task of subduing her to himself. In Joyce a similar connexion of time with imagination and of space with rationalism appears in the relation of Shem and Shaun. In both Blake and Joyce, of course, this creative time, which is something like Bergson's *durée,* is quite distinct from clock time, which is an element in the fall. In Blake clock time is represented by the Spectre of Urthona. another principle that Los has to subdue; in

Joyce it appears in the "cad's" original demand for the time which produced a stuttering or repetitive response from HCE. But there is no Los figure in *Finnegans Wake;* the spirit of time and the source of Shem's creative power is the female figure of ALP, Blake's Enitharmon.

The *Portrait of the Artist* ends with Stephen's appeal to the "old father, old artificer." This father, the spiritual or imaginative Dedalus who built the labyrinth and then flew out of it, is a figure very close to Blake's Los, the prophetic blacksmith who builds the Mundane Shell. An association is implied between Stephen and Icarus, and in some respects *Ulysses* is a version of the fall of Icarus. Stephen, an intellectual of the type usually described as in the clouds or up in the air, comes back to Dublin and in his contact with Bloom meets a new kind of father, neither his spiritual nor his physical father but Everyman, the man of earth and common humanity, who is yet isolated enough from his society to be individual too, an Israel as well as an Adam. Stephen approaches this communion with a certain amount of shuddering and distaste, but the descent to the earth is clearly necessary for him. Traditionally, however, the earth is Mother Earth, and what we are left with is a female monologue of a being at once maternal, marital and meretricious, who enfolds a vast number of lovers, including Bloom and possibly Stephen, and yet is narcist too, in a state of self-absorption which absorbs the lover. Marion Bloom is a Penelope who embraces all her suitors as well as her husband, and whose sexual versatility seems much the same thing as the weaving of her never-finished web—the web being also one of Blake's symbols for female sexuality. The drowsy spinning of the earth, absorbed in its own cyclical movement, constantly affirming but never forming, is what Marion sinks into, taking the whole book with her. Blake, if he had read *Ulysses,* would probably have recoiled in horror from its celebration of the triumph of what he calls the "female will," the persistence of the sleep of externality.

In most epic fictions there are two main elements: the quest of the hero and the shape of the hero's world. The quest is dialectic: when the dragon dies or the enemy falls there is an upward movement from bondage to liberty, from the powers of darkness to renewed life. The hero's world however is the order of nature, which moves in what Joyce calls "vicious cicles." The relation of the dialectic quest to the cycle of nature depends on the dimensions of the hero. At one extreme we have the divine quest, or myth of the hero as god, where all the symbols of the turning year are swallowed up in the quest. The myth of Christ subordinates all the cyclical symbolism of Christmas and Easter to the separation of death and hell from the resurrection. At the opposite extreme is the ironic vision, where the quest is seen inside an inevitably and perpetually recurring cycle, where everything that is done, however heroic, has sooner or later to be done over again. In between we have, first, the romantic quest, or myth of the hero in a marvellous or miraculous world, where the laws of nature are slightly suspended in the hero's favor. At its most concentrated the romantic quest takes the form of a sacramental ascent out of the order of nature, as it does in Dante and the Grail romances. Next comes the heroic quest proper, the theme of the traditional Classical epic, where the action begins *in medias res,* and then works forward to the end and back to the beginning of a cyclical total action. In the *Odyssey,* for example, the total action moves from Ithaca back to Ithaca; in the *Aeneid* from Troy to New Troy, and in *Paradise Lost,* where Christ is the hero, from the presence of God back to his presence again. In each epic the finishing point is the starting point renewed and transformed by the hero's quest.

In the mythological poems of Blake's day, such as *Prometheus Unbound, Faust,* or Blake's own *Jerusalem,* the epic action is normally an intellectual quest, and the mythical events are symbols of psychological ones. Hence there is a strong tendency to revert, in a more subjective way, to the sacramental quest of romance. Here again the quest takes precedence over the cycle: in Shelley, man is redeemed, and nature follows obediently with an enormous springtime rebirth. Yet in the minor poems of this period there are more ironic patterns. Blake's *Mental Traveller,* for example, presents a cycle in which two characters, one male and one female, act on one another in what Yeats would call a double gyre, the man growing old as the woman grows young and vice versa. There are four main phases of the relationship: a mother-son phase, a husband-wife phase, a father-daughter phase and a fourth phase that Blake calls spectre and emanation, terms corresponding roughly to Shelley's alastor and epipsyche. None of these relations is quite true: the "mother" is a nurse, the "wife" is merely "bound down" for the male's delight, the "daughter" is a changeling and the "emanation" does not emanate, but remains elusive and external. The male figure represents humanity, and therefore includes women; the female figure is external nature, which humanity partially subdues in a series of cyclical movements known as cultures or civilizations. The controlling symbolism, as the four phases and the continual failure of contact suggest, is lunar.

Most of the epics and epic actions of the twentieth century are ironic, and it is *The Mental Traveller*, not *Prometheus Unbound* or *Jerusalem*, that is nearest in form to them. In Proust, as in Blake and Joyce, creative time is the hero, but it is subordinate to clock time, and the only paradise it can reach is a lost paradise. In Yeats we find again a lunar symbolism and a double gyre, the cycle of Leda and the swan giving place to the cycle of the dove and the virgin and then returning, a vision which Yeats was quite correct in associating with *The Mental Traveller*. In Eliot's *Waste Land* there is a fire sermon and a thunder sermon, both with apocalyptic contexts, but again the natural cycle of the river flowing out to sea and returning through death by water in the spring rains is the containing form of the poem. The latest recruit to the ironic vision is Robert Graves, in whom, as in Blake and in Yeats, the presiding genius of the natural cycle is an ambivalent female figure, a white goddess associated with the moon, partly a virgin and partly a harlot.

In Blake, then, the central figure is male because the containing form of Blake's epic is apocalyptic and dialectic, giving priority to a spiritual and imaginative quest which ends by breaking clear of the natural cycle altogether. In Joyce the central figure is female because the containing form is ironic and cyclical. ALP, like Blake's Vala, grows younger as HCE grows older; she is introduced as a grandmother but by the end of *Haveth Childers Everywhere* she has become filial. Yet we notice two things about ALP: she has very little of the religious quality of the Beatrice and Virgin Mary figures who loom so large in Eliot, yet she has even less of the malignant grinning female, the femme fatale of the Romantic agony and of Yeats and Graves in our day. She is an endlessly faithful and solicitous wife and mother, patiently collecting, like Isis, the fragments of her disorderly husband, patiently waiting, like Solveig, for him to finish his wanderings and come back to her. She runs through her natural cycle and achieves no quest herself, but she is clearly the kind of being who makes a quest possible.

Who then is the hero who achieves the quest? It is not Shem, for here as in *Ulysses* the artist is part of the cycle, and Joyce's view of him is detached and ironic. It is not HCE, nor Shaun, nor even Finnegan, who never does wake up even if HCE does. Eventually it dawns on us that it is the *reader* who achieves the quest, the reader who, to the extent that he masters the book of

Doublends Jined, is in a position to look down on its rotation, and see its total form as something more than rotation. The dreamer, after establishing contact with the vast empire of unconscious knowledge, wakes up forgetting his dream, like Nebuchadnezzar, leaving it to "the ideal reader suffering from an ideal insomnia," as Joyce calls him, to reforge the broken links between myth and consciousness. In Blake the quest contains the cycle and in Joyce the cycle contains the quest, but there is the same challenge to the reader, and the same rewards for him, in Joyce's "mamafesta" that there is in Blake's "allegory addressed to the intellectual powers."

❧ Notes

p. 8. "stock exchange." Shocking as the admission may be, I was not aware when I wrote this that the same figure had appeared in Mr. Eliot's own essay "What Is Minor Poetry?"

p. 33. "Educators." See "An Articulated English Program: A Hypothesis to Test," *PMLA* (September 1959), pp. 13–19. My chief reservation to the argument of this article is that it seems strange not to require from doctoral students (p. 16) some knowledge of the degrees by which they did ascend—that is, some scholarly understanding of the connexions between mythology and literature.

p. 65. "*Prometheus Unbound.*" See Harold Bloom, *Shelley's Mythmaking*, 1959, a study not available to me when writing this essay. Earl Wassermann, *The Subtler Language,* 1959, is also largely devoted to the study of what is here called topocosm, in both neo-Classical and Romantic poets.

p. 72. "axioms and assumptions." What follows draws a good deal on the parallel argument of A. S. P. Woodhouse, "Nature and Grace in *The Faerie Queene,*" *ELH* (September 1949).

p. 114. "Professor Harold S. Wilson." See "Nature and Art in *Winter's Tale* 4.4.86ff," *SAB* (July 1943), pp. 114–20.

p. 130. "Professor Crane." See "On Writing the History of English Criticism, 1650–1800," *UTQ* (July 1953), pp. 376–91.

p. 133. "Professor Maclean." See "From Action to Image," in R. S. Crane, ed., *Critics and Criticism,* 1952, pp. 408–60.

p. 167. When this essay appeared in *Major British Writers* (1959) it was accompanied by "Reading Suggestions" recording some of my obvious debts to Byron scholars, notably Leslie A. Marchand, *Byron: A Biography,* 1957. Similarly with the essay on Emily Dickinson which follows, and which of course could not possibly have been written without the editorial and biographical work of Thomas H. Johnson in particular.

p. 222. "long standing." Cf. Rosalind's reference to Pythagoras and Irish rats in *As You Like It,* 3.2.165, and Samuel Butler's description of Ralph, the squire of Hudibras, as

> *A deep occult Philosopher,*
> *As learn'd as the wild Irish are.*

NOTE: These papers have been reprinted from a variety of books and periodicals, each with its own conventions of spelling and punctuation, not one of which corresponds exactly to my own usage. I have not imposed rigorous consistency on them, as the variations can hardly interfere with the reader's comfort.

CPSIA information can be obtained at www.ICGtesting.com
Printed in the USA
BVOW04s1501280914

368611BV00001B/35/P